# The Intellect and the Exodus
Authentic *Emuna* for a Complex Age

Jeremy Kagan

# THE
# INTELLECT
# AND THE
# EXODUS

**AUTHENTIC EMUNA
FOR A COMPLEX AGE**

Maggid Books

*The Intellect and the Exodus*
Authentic Emuna for a Complex Age

First Edition, 2018

Maggid Books
An imprint of Koren Publishers Jerusalem Ltd.

POB 8531, New Milford, CT 06776-8531, USA
& POB 4044, Jerusalem 9104001, Israel
www.maggidbooks.com

Copyright © Jeremy Kagan

The publication of this book was made possible through the generous support of *Torah Education in Israel*.

All rights reserved. No part of this publication may be reproduced, stored in a retrieval system or transmitted in any form or by any means, electronic, mechanical, photocopying, or otherwise, without the prior permission of the publisher, except in the case of brief quotations embedded in critical articles or reviews.

ISBN 978-1-59264-513-8, *hardcover*

A CIP catalogue record for this title is available from the British Library

Printed and bound in the United States

*In memory of*

## *HaGaon Rav Moshe Shapiro, zt"l*

*who brought a unique and much needed light to our world. Rav Moshe added his penetrating insight, dedication, and intellectual honesty to the wisdom of the Sages passed to him by the greats of the previous generation. In so doing, he revealed Torah's depth in a language that spoke directly to the heart of our shallow and orphaned generation, giving us the ability to honestly and genuinely connect with it and bringing meaning and significance to our lives. May his influence live on through his countless students – many of them teachers and leaders in their own right – and the students that they are inspiring and will inspire in the future.*

*May the ideas in this* sefer *serve as an instrument through which Hashem brings Klal Yisrael closer to Him. May He bless all of Klal Yisrael, keep us safe, grant us success, and provide us with an abundance of good.*

**Charles Fleischner**

ڿ

לע״נ
ברכה בת חיים יצחק הכהן

**In memory of Barbara Kagan**
*who through thirty-eight years of dedicated teaching inspired young people to live as she did, a meaningful life of caring for others*

ڿ

*It is our great privilege to have a share in this momentous work by our dear friend and teacher Rav Jeremy Kagan. May we merit more works like this from him!*

**R. Ely and Rebecca Allen**

לע"נ
אהרן בן יששכר
שלמה ברוך בן יצחק אלימלך
חי'ה בת צבי הלוי

Dedicated by their children
**Michael and Suri Kest**

₰

לזכרון עולם ולעילוי נשמת
אלימלך בן דוד ע"ה
מסר נפשו על תורה ומצוות

ורעיתו הנכבדה
מרת שושנה בת יעקב ע"ה
פיה פתחה בחכמה

ולעילוי נשמת מרת דינה רבקה בת צבי ארי"ה ע"ה
רוח הבריות נוחה הימנה

# Contents

**Acknowledgments** .................................................. xiii

### PART 1: GATEWAY TO THE EXODUS

**Introduction** ........................................................ 3
1. The Mitzva of *Emuna* ........................................... 11
2. Challenges to Faith ............................................. 35
3. Recovering Communication ....................................... 45
4. Oral Torah in a Changed Environment ............................ 57
5. Assault on the Miraculous ...................................... 63
6. Breaking Through the Bubble .................................... 79
7. Rome and Christianity .......................................... 91
8. Materialism and the Shallow Self .............................. 103
9. The Path to the Creator ....................................... 117
10. Summing Up and Moving On ..................................... 141

**PART 2: THE CHARACTER OF FAITH**

**Introduction** .................................................... 149
11. Foundations of Faith........................................ 155
12. The Process of Creation..................................... 171
13. The Ten Stages of Creation ................................. 179
14. The First Plagues ........................................... 195
15. The Middle Plagues......................................... 219
16. The Final Plagues .......................................... 247
17. Externally and Internally Based *Emuna*...................... 267

Appendix: The Passing of an Honest Man ....................... 289

# *Acknowledgments*

This book is the fruit of many people's labor, either directly or indirectly. I hope that the reader will discover a refreshing depth in what is written here. Though I write in order to give that gift, I cannot take credit for it. I have had the opportunity to learn from teachers who have access to Torah and understanding that goes far beyond anything that I can hope to reach and what depth I have gained has come through them. It is my hope that readers will hear in my words at least an echo of what they have and had to give.

Rav Moshe Shapiro is certainly my primary influence; anyone familiar with his Torah will recognize that. I merited the opportunity to hear shiur from him over the course of decades. I wrote a short eulogy to him in an appendix to this volume which is titled, "The passing of an honest man." So as not to repeat myself I refer the reader to that. It is my honor to have a dedication in the book to his name.

Rav Aharon Feldman was the *rosh yeshiva* at Ohr Somayach during my formative first experience with Torah. He personified for me what a person can make of himself through Torah if he genuinely cares. His ability to make the most esoteric of concepts personally relevant and meaningful has influenced my approach to Torah ever since. He continues to be an inspiration to me.

## Acknowledgments

I was once giving a *parasha shiur* in a local shul one Friday night and a *talmid ḥakham* that happened to daven there came up to me afterwards and said, "You learned with Rav Uziel Milevsky, didn't you!" Rav Milevsky, *zt"l*, had been my first Talmud rebbi in Ohr Somayach some thirty years earlier. I had the honor of learning with him for about eight months, but the impact of that short time has lasted a lifetime. He had a realism about him that was for me very important. In addition to his genius, he was matchless at teaching his students how to think. When I was tested to enter a mainstream yeshiva after Ohr Somayach, after a few minutes the rebbi looked up at me and said, "Somewhere along the line someone taught you how to learn."

I first met Rav Zevulun Schwartzman when he sat down next to me on a bus traveling from Beer Sheva to Jerusalem. I was mesmerized and sought out an opportunity to learn with him. Unfortunately for me, he soon left for the States. Thankfully for me, he eventually returned to Jerusalem. He was extremely generous with his time when I was writing my previous book, *The Choice to Be*. And when it became necessary while I was writing this book to clarify the mitzva of *emuna* I turned to Rav Schwartzman who, once again, was very generous with his time. The first chapter was hammered out over the course of about a year peppered by visits to his office. Both the specifics of what I learned and what I gained from the opportunity to learn with him significantly influenced me and the book.

I also want to thank Rav Akiva Tatz who was kind enough to look over an early draft of this book. His inspiration during my early years in yeshiva as a *chevruta*, friend, and role model were invaluable.

I also want to extend my continuing thanks to Rav Dovid Refson who has provided me with the teaching opportunity through which many of the ideas expressed here were developed. His continuous support for our school Midreshet Tehillah has been magnanimous, while he has accepted that its rewards come primarily in the form of deferred payments.

I would be remiss if I did not also thank Professor Karsten Harries. My first brush with true genius left an indelible mark on my thinking and what I learned from him continues to play a major role in my thinking.

# Acknowledgments

I also wish to thank Esther Cameron, my long-suffering editor. Her eagle eye for what was missing was invaluable in getting me to open the file once again and fill in the holes that were letting the meaning drain out of the text. This thanks extends to the larger Koren staff, especially Ashirah Yosefah and Ita Olesker, who have been very patient with me, and Tani Bayer, who designed the cover.

Though I was an intellectual before I met my wife, all wisdom I have about life has been gained under her tutelage. This, together with the superhuman patience that writing this book required of her makes this book as much hers as mine. In the words of Rebbi Akiva, "*Sheli shelkhem shela*, mine and yours are hers."

I will never know the sacrifices that my ancestors made that have allowed me to enter the tents of Torah, live the life I live, and have this book come through my "pen." I cannot possibly thank them enough for that. I wish to thank my mother and late father *a"h* for all that they have done for me and through whom I am connected to this chain. I am honored that my Uncle Arnold and Aunt Golda chose to make a dedication to my late aunt Barbara in this book. We are all together part of this same chain.

I would also like to thank those people who made dedications in the book. I can put in the work to write this, but without support it would not see the light of day. More than the calf wants to drink… I am certainly the greatest beneficiary of the project. So, thank you.

*Harbe sheluḥim leMakom*, God has many messengers. All these people that I have mentioned and so many more that cannot be named that are part of my life come from one Source as does life, capability, opportunity, and everything else. I take this opportunity to express my thanks for all that has been given to me.

# Part 1

*Gateway to the Exodus*

## Introduction

I have spent much of my life seeking authenticity in Torah. I am not talking about emotional connections to the mitzvot, the commandments. I mean a sense that Torah is true. Had it been my perspective on the world from the birth of my consciousness, its vision would be the filter through which I always experienced my self and, therefore, would naturally seem real. But because I did not grow up religious, that wasn't the case for me.

Rather, I first encountered Torah on a serious level when I was in college. I was introduced to its depth by an Orthodox roommate and my interest was awakened. But, as would be true for anyone discovering Torah at that stage in life, I was acutely aware that its central text, the Ḥumash, described a world that bore little resemblance to the one we live in today. After all, we do not see seas splitting and anyone claiming prophecy is headed for a lengthy hospital stay. Torah was intriguing, but it did not seem real.

As a child of Western culture I was trained to give priority to physical reality. Therefore, I could not just dismiss this, as might a person raised from his youth to respect the truth of Torah. So even though the understanding I gained from Torah about myself and my world was profound and compelling, I could not embrace Torah without dealing with the issue of its reality.

As it turns out, it is not just latecomers to Torah who are bothered by this. The great Torah Sages were as alive to the world as they were to Torah, so the fact that the two do not mesh smoothly was not lost on them. I explored their views on this topic in my previous books *The Jewish Self* and *The Choice to Be*.[1] Those explorations led me to appreciate that the dissonance between our present experience and Torah's description of the past is actually the key to understanding Torah's vision of history. Torah identifies the primary significance of history with the constant evolution of the nature of human awareness over time – a view we will be reexamining in this book. Torah's depiction of the past is strange to us; yet rather than undermining Torah's legitimacy, this strangeness provides us with essential perspective on the way we experience reality today.

Coming to this understanding did more than address a formidable block on my integration with Torah. It also extended certain ideas I had been working on previously in college[2] and thus brought a greater continuity to my intellectual journey. Moreover, it opened a new level of depth to my perception of reality. While little questions lend themselves to little answers, the big ones – the kind that call a whole system into question – can only be resolved by reaching a new level of understanding of the entire structure.

My attachment to Torah has grown in part from the times I have experienced these major shifts in understanding. At a certain point I stopped looking at contradictions as problems and, instead, saw them as opportunities. They mark thresholds of understanding which invite us to find the door. I guess that was when Torah changed for me from an idea to reality – at least a level of reality. Reality is never wrong. Our understanding of it might be – contradictions arise signaling that we must dig deeper. But reality itself cannot be wrong. It just *is*, waiting to be understood.

---

1. Jerusalem: Feldheim, 1998 and 2011 respectively.
2. See appendix.

*Introduction*

## LIVING IN THE PRESENT

The Torah vision of history that emerged from this investigation is strikingly modern, or at least lends itself to a formulation that resonates strongly with modern views. It closely parallels, at least structurally, the academic understanding of the unfolding of human consciousness over historical time that has been building in philosophical, anthropological, and psychological circles since the time of Kant.

I do not mean by that to say, "Yeah, we always knew that anyway." Rather, I am suggesting that when we engage the Torah in the context of honest awareness of our present experience while remaining open to the questions that it raises, the understanding we develop is relevant to who we are today.

Not coincidentally, it is also relevant to the rest of mankind. The development of humanity, at least in the context of civilization, is universal; we are all in it together. While Torah gives us our unique slant on the issues, the issues are shared across the board. So an open engagement of Torah allows us who study it to locate ourselves in and communicate with the larger intellectual world if we so choose.

Moreover, through this honest and genuine inquiry we fulfill our obligation to constantly make Torah new[3] – that is, to revitalize our understanding of it. The idea is not that we should come to a different understanding so much as to understand what we have always known, but in a new way – a way that genuinely speaks to who we truly are in the generation in which we live. By pressing the self that we are against the Torah and asking the questions that bother us, we develop an understanding of Torah that reflects our concerns, highlighting the aspects of Torah most relevant to our place in history. It is this process that gives exile meaning, as we are forced to explore Torah from all the different vantages afforded by the halting evolution of human culture and experience.

## THE CHALLENGE OF *EMUNA*

This book will explore a different distance between Torah and our awareness of reality – at the very least, my awareness of reality. God is

---

3. Rashi, Deut. 11:13.

central to all Torah understanding, yet I am not filled with a sense for the immediacy of God – *emuna* (faith) did not come naturally to me. This didn't concern me, for as I grew in Torah I remained conscious that I was the product of conflicting worldviews, with my Western roots leaving little space or need for God's existence. So my expectations for intuitive conviction were low. But I certainly *wanted* to integrate my *emuna* with my self.

As I worked on the question of how to accomplish this, I found myself returning to the question of why *emuna* is so challenging to the Western mind – why we are so deeply committed to a secular outlook. After all, you cannot solve a problem unless you know what is causing it. This brought me back to the topic of my previous books – the development of human awareness over historical time. I eventually accepted that my project would not be complete without reviewing this material. Initially, I thought I could get away with a synopsis of my previous writing. But as I revisited the issues in the context of my present focus, they came alive for me in a new way.

I was already in the midst of a revived interest in history, but in a different manner than I had approached it previously. In my earlier books I traced the developing nature of human awareness through the successive peoples that have dominated civilization by relating to those peoples and their cultures as abstract entities – I identified the dominant trait of their cultures and little more. But I found myself wanting to extend my knowledge of these peoples to their *actual* history – to understand how they carried and expressed these various forms of awareness and what it was like to be them and live among them. After all, on our journey through time we have not been alone. We are part of mankind. Other peoples experienced their cultures while we were experiencing ours. Their experience affected us just as ours affected them.

Moreover, since the destruction of the First Temple we have found ourselves in exile, living among these peoples and building our national life as part of a much broader cultural entity. The focus of our development has been directed by this environment and by the challenges it raises. Trying to understand ourselves and our history without understanding that of the nations of the world would be like trying to fathom the motions of a swimmer without recognizing that he is in water.

My newfound desire for details pushed me to explore academic sources. This has altered my understanding of these cultures in important ways. And this in turn has forced a more nuanced reading of Torah sources. Though I formulate my views within a midrashic and aggadic framework, the academic perspective now informs my understanding of the particulars of these cultures. This has produced a clearer understanding of the basis of human awareness in the era in which Torah emerged and how that fostered a spiritual perception of reality. It also clarified the process by which abstract reason's growing dominance of consciousness constricted spiritual awareness, eventually leading to the secular mindset characteristic of Western civilization today.

Though the more general understanding found in my earlier books was sufficient for their core project of explaining the Sages' vision of the structure, direction, and purpose of history, this book aims for more precision. Its goal of understanding the challenges that the historical process brings to our *emuna*, how we meet those challenges, and how the nature of our *emuna* has changed as a result, requires that we engage more of the details. This material comprises chapters 2 through 8 of this book.

### EMUNA IN THE CREATOR

The examination of *emuna* that eventually grew into this book began when I was exploring the process by which Abraham came to recognize the existence of the Creator.[4] Because Abraham achieved conviction about this through his own efforts before he received prophecy, I thought he might act as a guide to how I could bring more personal conviction to my own relationship with God. Moreover, since Abraham discovered God specifically in His role as *Creator*, I felt that studying Abraham's journey would accentuate this aspect of God in my own faith. This spoke to my desire for increased integration of my *emuna*.

We tend to isolate our relationship with God in our heads, disconnecting Him from our primary experience, which is material reality. This

---

4. Midrashim are our only source for the details of the life of Abraham. I will explain the approach toward midrashim followed in this book when we begin working with them directly, as some of the reasons behind it are best understood in that context.

is because God is not physical. True, He expresses Himself in physical reality. But out of concern for idolatry, we expend extreme effort to guard against associating God with anything physical – we keep our ideas about Him very abstract. This, however, gives God an almost ghostly, unreal quality, leaving us with an *emuna* that seems artificial. *Emuna* in God specifically as Creator, however, develops from direct engagement with physical reality. I felt that reinforcing my awareness of God in this role would give my relationship with Him a concrete anchor while avoiding associating physicality directly with God Himself.

As I was working through this material, I realized that when the commentaries define our Torah obligation of *emuna*, they also speak of God as Creator.[5] In other words, though we relate to God in numerous capacities that are central to our vision of Him – such as Giver of Torah, Judge, and Savior – our mitzva of *emuna* is to recognize Him specifically in His capacity as Creator.

It occurred to me, then, that by studying Abraham's path I could both enhance the sense of reality in my *emuna* (a personal priority) and also strengthen my fulfillment of the Torah obligation of *emuna* (a priority for all of us). I began developing the material on Abraham's path with this larger project in mind. It forms chapter 9 of this book.

But I also realized that I could not properly help people strengthen their observance of the mitzva of *emuna* without a clear understanding of the mitzva. This required an additional research effort. To give a broad treatment, I focused on the approach of Rambam as representative of the philosophical school and of Ramban as representative of the more mystical school. The results of this investigation are brought in the first chapter.

**THE IMPORTANCE OF THE EXODUS**

An important consequence of this research was an appreciation of the centrality of the Exodus to achieving the mitzva of *emuna*. This forced the addition of another layer to the book. I have been working for many years on understanding the plagues of the Exodus and how we are

---

5. Rambam, *Mishneh Torah, Sefer HaMadda, Hilkhot Yesodei HaTorah* 1:6; Ramban, *Ḥiddushei Ramban*, Ex. 20:2.

supposed to develop *emuna* from their study. The interpretation which speaks most deeply to me sees each plague directed at a specific facet of character. As each plague purifies a trait, the aspect of reality "seen" by that trait is revealed for what it is: a consequence of God's act of creation.

An act of creation is accomplished through a series of stages – ones that are internal, ones that are emotional, and actions. Each stage is realized through a specific trait of character. The Exodus structured our personality along the lines of those character traits of creation so that we experienced ourselves as creators. Creators see the world through the lens of creation. This sensitized us to the acts of creation reflected in the world around us and, therefore, to the Creator.

This approach to the Exodus brings the concept of integrated *emuna* to an entirely new level. *Emuna* becomes something that is embedded in our personality and emanates directly from our experience of reality, rather than an isolated concept that fits uncomfortably within the complex of our general understanding of the world.

The Exodus thus speaks directly to the desire for integration that launched the book in the first place, closing the circle. I come to a conclusion that was anything but intuitive at the beginning of the project, which is that the path to genuine, integrated *emuna* is not only through personal meditation but also through assimilation of this event from our distant past. This material forms the second half of the book.

Before we begin, a note on translations. All translations herein, unless otherwise stated, take as their starting point the Soncino Press translations. I have, however, liberally altered them both to modernize the language and, in numerous cases, to focus on a meaning of the text different from that found in the Soncino, one that is more appropriate to the context in which I am citing the source.

The structure of the book is as follows: First we will examine the mitzva of *emuna* and what is required to fulfill the obligation (chapter 1). Then we will explore the development of human consciousness in the context of civilization to appreciate the difficulties we face in trying to achieve *emuna*. This will include a discussion of the mechanisms the Sages have instituted to overcome these difficulties (chapters 2–8). Based on this exploration I will suggest that, beyond our traditional halakhic obligations, each individual needs to independently pursue personal conviction about the existence of the Creator. We will then turn to Abraham for guidance on how to do that, analyzing the path by which he came to his *emuna* (chapter 9).

For reasons that we will discuss, the *emuna* that can be achieved in this way is both incomplete in its conviction and limited in scope. So in the second half of the book we will turn to the Exodus. We will learn how the plagues can guide us to full *emuna* by structuring our personality and perception in such a way that our recognition of the Creator becomes integral to our experience of self and our vision of reality.

For all its power, however, we cannot make this vision a part of ourselves without some internal awareness to testify to its truth and anchor it in the self. We therefore conclude with an analysis of how the Jews developed exactly this in their journey from Egypt to Mount Sinai, where *emuna* became the eternal foundation of Jewish identity.

*Chapter 1*

# The Mitzva of *Emuna*

When the Jewish people stood at Mount Sinai, they experienced a revelation of unprecedented clarity that immediately became the foundation of our national relationship with God.[1] That relationship had begun earlier with our salvation from Egypt, an event that already obligated us to God's service and even included several specific commandments. That Exodus experience was so critical that when God revealed Himself at Sinai He identified Himself as the One responsible for it: "I am the Lord your God that took you out of Egypt…."[2] Still, at Sinai the process of revelation that began in Egypt came to its completion and was of such depth that it formed the essential core of the Jewish people, shaping not only that generation but also their descendants.[3] While the Exodus is vital, it is through Sinai that we connect to the Exodus.[4]

"I am the Lord your God…" was actually the opening line of the Sinai revelation. It commands us to have *emuna* (faith) in God's

---

1. See Rashi, Deut. 4:35; Ramban, Deut. 4:9.
2. Ex. 20:2.
3. Ex. 19:9; *Tanḥuma, Pekudei* 3.
4. We will discuss this further in the final chapter of the book.

existence.[5] Since Sinai is the basis of our relationship with God and *emuna* was the first command we heard there, it is conceptually the beginning and the root of all our obligations. All mitzvot extend from this command and serve to actualize it.[6]

This makes sense, since the commands of the Torah are all elements in a relationship with God. The prerequisite and foundation of any genuine relationship is the true recognition of the other – a statement that is not as trivial as it sounds. In our relationship with God we call this *emuna*.

Our goal in this book is to learn how to achieve this mitzva. That is not a simple task, for while *emuna* is the most fundamental of the mitzvot, in our age it is also among the most challenging. There are many reasons for this, which we will discuss in the coming pages as we try to figure out how to overcome them. First, however, we need to understand the mitzva. To do that we begin by analyzing the verse from which the mitzva is derived.

**THE BASIS OF *EMUNA***

The verse we mentioned as obligating us in *emuna* is, in full: "I am the Lord your God that took you out from the land of Egypt, from the house of bondage."[7] At first glance this is a surprising source from which to derive our obligation of *emuna* as it focuses on God in His capacity as redeemer of Israel. Though obviously the Exodus is central to our discovery of and unique national relationship with God, this should not determine the identity or defining characteristic of the God we are obligated to recognize. Surely the significance of His role as redeemer pales in comparison to that of His being the basis of existence. We expect the mitzva to be directed at God as the Creator.

In fact, as we mentioned in the introduction, this is the case. The major commentaries understand that the mitzva of *emuna* is directed

---

5. Rambam, *Hilkhot Yesodei HaTorah* 1:6; *Ḥiddushei Ramban*, Ex. 20:2.
6. *Zohar* II 82b. See Rav Moshe Chaim Efrayim, *Degel Maḥaneh Efraim, Parashat Tzav V'Ata*.
7. Ex. 20:2.

at the Creator. What, then, do they do with the part of the verse that references the Exodus?

If the verse is obligating us to believe specifically in the Creator, then the phrase "that took us out of Egypt" is not defining whom we are to believe in. Presumably, then, it is identifying the event through which the Jews came to recognize the Creator. But by including the process by which the first generation of Jews came to their *emuna* as an integral part of the eternal command, the verse obligates us to come to our *emuna* through that same process as that first generation.

According to this reading, the verse requires us to build our *emuna* on the Jewish people's historical experience of the miracles of the Exodus. Such a reading would exclude personal investigation from building *emuna* – at least in pursuit of the mitzva – severely narrowing our options as we search for ways to strengthen its fulfillment. This concern is parried by Rambam's understanding of the verse.[8]

## EMUNA ACCORDING TO RAMBAM

Surprisingly, Rambam makes no mention of the Exodus at all in his description of the mitzva of *emuna*.[9]

To understand this omission we first have to realize that when discussing Rambam's view of this mitzva, the term *emuna*, which translates as "faith," is misleading. He actually speaks of an obligation *"leida* that there is a First Reality Who brings into being all that exists."[10] *Leida* means "to know."[11] Rambam's position is that what most commentators

---

8. The treatment of Rambam's and Ramban's approach to the mitzva of *emuna* that follows was developed with the kind assistance of Rav Zevulun Schwartzman, who generously gave of his time to answer my many questions and direct me. Though I take sole responsibility for my words, I think they accurately reflect what I heard from him on this topic.
9. *Hilkhot Yesodei HaTorah* 1:1–6. When Rambam cites the verse that obligates us to have *emuna,* he leaves out the part referencing the Exodus, quoting only the first half of the verse: *Ani Hashem Elokekha,* "I am the Lord your God."
10. *Hilkhot Yesodei HaTorah* 1:1.
11. In the classic translation from the Arabic original of *Sefer HaMitzvot* and *Moreh Nevukhim,* Rambam tells us we are commanded to *naamin,* "believe," in the existence of God. However, the term translated from the Arabic as *"naamin"* is in dispute. Rav Kapach in his translation of *Moreh Nevukhim* states that in these places the appropriate

## Part 1: Gateway to the Exodus

understand to be a mitzva of *belief* is actually an obligation to come to *rational certainty* of the Creator's existence.[12]

Rambam's view of this mitzva has its roots in the specific nature of our experience at Sinai. Though eight of the Ten Commandments were relayed to us by Moses, the Jews heard the first two, including "I am the Lord your God," directly from God.[13] At the moment He spoke to us we did not *believe* that God existed, we *knew* it![14] We were not *ordered* to recognize God; rather, hearing the statement brought us to absolute clarity about His existence! For this reason there is no actual command in the verse. Rather, it is a statement of fact: "I am the Lord your God."

Yet Rambam, like most other commentators, derives a mitzva from the verse.[15] What, then, is our mitzva in this regard?

Having had this experience of clarity at Sinai, the collective "we," the Jewish people, know that God exists. We are forever obligated to recognize that truth, not because we are commanded to do so by God – we are not – but rather because an overarching necessity to "accept the truth because it is true" is woven into the structure of existence.[16] This makes clear why Rambam insists that our obligation is to "know" that God exists, rather than to "believe" it. And if we as individuals don't know this truth of God's existence, we must come to know it – because it is true. And if we know it but our knowledge is unsure, we have to strengthen it.

---

translation is "*ladaat*," "to know" (Rav Yosef Kapach, *Moreh Nevukhim* [Jerusalem: Mosad HaRav Kook, 1977], p. 5, note 7). The only source where the Hebrew is directly from Rambam is in *Mishneh Torah* (see previous note). There, as we said, he uses the language of *leida*, "to know," rather than *l'haamin*, "to believe."

12. This is not an exclusively intellectual process; we will learn later that Rambam considers perfection of character to be a prerequisite to clarity of thought and integration of understanding with the self (Rav Zevulun Schwartzman).
13. Makkot 23b. See introduction to part 2, note 4.
14. *Moreh Nevukhim* III:22.
15. *Hilkhot Yesodei HaTorah* 1:6.
16. Ibid. The phrase "accept the truth because it is true" is Rav Schwartzman's and echoes the Rambam's statement that we must do the mitzvot not out of a desire for reward but, rather, to "do the truth because it is true." See *Hilkhot Teshuva* 10:2; see also *Mishneh Torah, Sefer Zemanim, Hilkhot Kiddush HaḤodesh* 17:24.

## The Mitzva of Emuna

Though we must accept every truth, this does not mean that recognizing every truth is a mitzva. I do not have a Torah obligation to acknowledge the existence of the Swiss Alps. But the truth of God's existence was revealed to us by God. Thus without commanding it, He is the One that caused there to be the obligation to recognize His existence. The force of necessity behind the obligation is, at least for man, *a priori*. But God, through His revelation, is the One who caused this knowledge to enter this category of *a priori* necessity, elevating the acknowledgment of this truth to a mitzva. In fact, it is *the* mitzva.

The distinction between being obligated and being commanded in the mitzva of recognizing God is an important one, as it answers several critical difficulties. First, how can God command us to believe in His existence? He is talking to us – obviously He exists! Answer: He is not commanding. He is revealing His existence through the statement, "I exist"; the obligation is a consequence of the revelation. This also explains how we derive a mitzva from a statement. Rambam's approach circumvents another problem as well. This "command" is prior to the full establishment of the king-to-subject relationship between God and the Jewish people.[17] Yet a command only obligates when the commander has a prior basis of authority. According to Rambam this is not an issue because the *necessity* to recognize the truth being revealed is not from God's command; it is *a priori* to us from the creation.

When Rambam obligates us to "know," he does not mean some inexplicable feeling. The ongoing mitzva is to bring ourselves to a certainty in God's existence that echoes the clarity we experienced at Sinai. Since *reason is man's only vehicle to genuine certainty,* and the existence of God is susceptible to logical proof, we are obligated to use our rational intellect to achieve conviction that God exists.

In line with Rambam's philosophical approach to Torah in general, the highest level of *"emuna"* – for Rambam, knowledge – comes through philosophical inquiry. This is because the strength of the logic employed, along with the pure submission to intellect that individuals trained in genuine philosophical thought achieve, compels the most forceful and legitimate certainty about God. But obviously this most

---

17. See Maharal, *Tiferet Yisrael*, chapter 37.

## Part 1: Gateway to the Exodus

basic of mitzvot is not the exclusive preserve of philosophers. Every individual has a rational capacity. According to Rambam the obligation is to harness that capability to achieve personal certainty in the existence of the Creator, each person on his own level.[18]

### THE MEANING OF "CREATOR"

We have said that our obligation of *emuna* is directed at God in His capacity as Creator. That Rambam requires us to achieve a certainty in our *emuna* that can only be achieved through rational proof, forces us to be more discerning in our understanding of this. For not all aspects of our understanding of God are susceptible to proof.

Rambam agrees with the Greek philosophers that though it can be demonstrated logically that there is an Entity standing outside of physical existence that is its basis, it cannot be proven that reality has a specific beginning – that is to say, that it came into being through a distinct act of creation that began time. An alternative is possible – that while supported by God, physical reality has always existed with no beginning to time. This position, which we call *kadmut*, was the position of Aristotle. So Rambam, who requires us to achieve *emuna* through rational proof, can only have in mind *emuna* in God with respect to His role in underpinning existence, not in creating it.[19]

Once we are sensitive to this distinction, we can see that this is exactly what Rambam states in describing the mitzva: "The foundation of all foundations and the pillar of wisdom is that there is a first Existence that is bringing into being all that is…";[20] Rambam makes no mention of a past act of creation.

---

18. There are levels and levels of achievement to this mitzva. Less-developed or less-capable individuals may be satisfied with "proofs" that are weak. Whatever argument someone uses to strengthen this certainty of the existence of God, so long as it is processed through his rational faculty, produces some level of meaningful conviction. If he reaches some level of logical certainty of God's existence, he "knows" that there is a God and fulfills the mitzva (Rav Schwartzman).
19. See *Moreh Nevukhim* II:13, 25. Rav Zevulun Schwartzman made the significance of this point in Rambam clear to me
20. *Hilkhot Yesodei HaTorah* 1:1.

## The Mitzva of Emuna

Rambam's description of the mitzva captures the precise meaning of the verse commanding us in *emuna*. Though we translate the first of the commandments at Sinai as "I am the 'the Lord'…," the actual text is "I am 'יהוה'…." This four-letter name of God is a composite of the verb "to be" in past tense (היה), present tense (הוה), and future tense (יהיה).[21] It conveys that God *is* being. If God is being, then nothing can exist except as a manifestation of God – and God is reality's basis and support. The command "I am יהוה…" then commands us to believe in God as the basis of existence without reference to God having created it in a unique act.

Torah tells us through revelation that the world was created. Based on that, Rambam accepts that God created reality. But this fact of the past is far less significant than that God is the ongoing basis of existence now, always was, and always will be. This was what was revealed at Sinai, is logically provable, is directly relevant to our present awareness, and is the focus of our mitzva of *emuna* according to Rambam.

It is still reasonable – and simplifies our discussion considerably – to describe our mitzva of *emuna* as directed at the Creator even according to Rambam. Once we recognize that God *is* being, even having created reality He could not give it existence independent of Him – for *He* is being. Attributing to God an act of creation, then, requires that He remain the basis of that creation – Creator implies Basis.[22]

That we conflate these two aspects of God in our minds is reflected in common usage. We sometimes refer to God as the Creator in the specific sense of the One who initiated existence through a specific act of creation. But generally our primary intent is to convey the idea that God underlays existence. We use the term Creator because we take for granted that the first concept implies the second, while we intend the second because that is the far more fundamental and pressing realization.[23]

---

21. Rabbenu Yaakov ben Asher, *Tur Oraḥ Ḥayim* 5.
22. *Tehillim* 136:7. See Rabbi Hayim of Volozhin, *Nefesh HaḤayim* 1:2.
23. In the ancient world the concept of Creator did not imply a need for continuous support. However Abraham's discovery of the utter transcendence of the Creator – what we have identified with the name יהוה – was synonymous with an appreciation of physical reality's dependence on the Creator for ongoing existence. See chapter 9.

*Part 1: Gateway to the Exodus*

For example, when I said earlier that we would find it surprising if our mitzva of *emuna* was directed at the One who redeemed us from Egypt rather than at the Creator, the surprise was a consequence of this more fundamental characteristic that God is the basis of existence.[24] The conflation also goes in the opposite direction. When I read Torah sources that specify God as the basis of existence, I used to unthinkingly identify that with the Creator. That is why for years I understood the Rambam to be requiring *emuna* in the Creator. If we are precise, however, the two concepts are distinct, and Rambam is clear that our mitzva is directed at the Being who underlies existence, not its Creator.

**SUMMING UP RAMBAM**

Rambam sees rational inquiry as the *only* road to *emuna*. Historical experience, even an event as powerful as the Exodus, cannot bring the certainty achievable through logical proof. The Exodus revealed the Jewish people's unique relationship with God.[25] It can substantiate and strengthen *emuna* for someone who has already gained rational clarity about God's existence. It provides a basis for relationship with God for those who do not have the space for developing rational clarity about His existence or as a stop-gap until they develop it.[26] But the Exodus does not establish rational certainty about the existence of God;[27] therefore it cannot provide a basis for fulfilling the mitzva of *emuna*.

---

24. This is also the case with my stated attempt to reinforce through this book my relationship with God in His capacity of Creator. The intent there was to link my *emuna* to my awareness of physical reality in order to make it more real. God as the ongoing basis of existence makes that connection much more sharply than His role in the past act of Creation. Then also, the term Creator was really shorthand for "the basis or Upholder of existence." So my personal goal of "grounding" my *emuna* is only sharpened by this distinction.
25. *Mishneh Torah, Sefer Zemanim, Hilkhot Ḥametz uMatza* 7:4.
26. See *Moreh Nevukhim* I:34
27. As we will explain, Rambam reasons that since violations of nature can be pre-programmed into the natural system, miracles are not an absolute proof of God's existence. They strongly indicate it; they may provide a level of probability that we would normally accept for establishing our view of things. But miracles cannot bring certainty, which is Rambam's standard for *emuna*. This can only come through logical argument or the kind of enlightenment we had on Mount Sinai.

## The Mitzva of Emuna

Why, then, according to Rambam, is the Exodus mentioned in the verse commanding *emuna*? It is in order to link the Being we recognized at Sinai with the events of the Exodus, which, as we said, establish the unique relationship of the Jewish people with God.[28] In other words, we do not need the Exodus to establish our *emuna*. Rather, we need our *emuna* to enlighten us about what actually happened during the Exodus.[29]

By separating the Exodus experience from our obligation of *emuna*, Rambam allows the option of personal investigation as a means of pursuit of the mitzva of *emuna*. But it is important to bear in mind that because Rambam sees the experience at Sinai as the source and paradigm for *emuna*, he requires a level of certainty in our faith that narrows the possible avenues of investigation to *logical* proofs.

### EMUNA ACCORDING TO RAMBAN

Not everyone follows the approach of Rambam. Ramban is representative of the mystical tradition of Torah. He differs with Rambam in two obvious respects. First, Ramban accepts the more traditional view that our mitzva of *emuna* is directed toward the Creator in the classic sense – the One who created existence through a unique act.[30] And second, he accepts the simple interpretation of the verse commanding *emuna* – that it mentions the Exodus because the Exodus must be the basis of our *emuna* even today.[31]

Ramban's approach to *emuna* is that we develop it through the experience of miracles – at least, through miracles that demonstrate a

---

28. See *Sefer HaMitzvot*, mitzva 2, and *Hilkhot Ḥametz uMatza*, 7:1 and 7:4, that God's kingship over us comes through the Exodus. Though Rambam separates the mitzvot of kingship and *emuna*, he still needs to link the object of our *emuna* with the King established through the Exodus. Maharal in *Tiferet Yisrael*, chapter 37, explains how the language of the verse (Ex. 20:2) links it to the unique relationship that the Jewish people have with God's kingship.
29. Since Rambam does not hold Ramban's position that miracles in and of themselves prove a Creator or are even necessarily the consequence of a transcendent Being, we need the verse to ensure that the events of the Exodus are connected to the Creator revealed on Mount Sinai.
30. Ramban, Ex. 20:2.
31. Ibid.

systemic overriding of the order of nature.[32] Violations of natural law show that those laws do not define existence. Rather, they function in and are superseded by a larger context that is the source of their functioning. In other words, the laws of nature have a Creator.

This view is very different from that of Rambam. He does not accept miracles as *proof* of a higher power because there is always the possibility that what appear as breaks in the order of nature may be preprogrammed into nature – that is, they simply reveal a higher order of nature.

This is not an isolated argument; it actually cuts to a fundamental difference between Rambam's and Ramban's understanding of God's relationship with creation. According to Ramban, the occasional openly revealed interventions by God in the workings of physical reality are indicative of the fact that there is no such thing as natural reality. Rather, every moment of reality is the consequence of a distinct *decision* by God to recreate the world in whatever manner we encounter it.[33] In other words, every moment is a miracle – a direct intervention. So for Ramban recognizing God through miracles is recognizing Him through His general relationship with reality.

Rambam, on the other hand, sees the natural order we encounter as a set reality – a set relationship with creation – which God at most alters occasionally. Whether or not Rambam ever allows for a change is in dispute among the commentators.[34] He certainly attributes to the Sages the position that whatever appears to us as a miracle was

---

32. See Ramban, Ex. 13:16. He describes these miracles as "great and renowned." Ramban presumably means by this miracles that contradict the natural order on a systematic level. Logically, any passing violation of nature would not be sufficient (Rav Schwartzman). After all, in those generations magic was practiced, and those violations of the normal order of nature did not lead to *emuna*.

33. See Ramban, Ex. 13:16.

34. In *Shemona Perakim* 8 and *Perush HaMishnayiot Avot* 5:6, Rambam states that miracles are preprogrammed from *maaseh bereshit*, basing himself upon midrashim (e.g., according to Genesis Rabba 5:5, God placed a condition on the sea when it was created that it split for the Jews when they left Egypt). In *Moreh Nevukhim* II:29, however, he attributes this opinion to the Sages while he himself seems to allow for the occasional miracle. *Moreh Nevukhim* is a much later work. See also *Maamar Teḥiyat Hametim*, an even later work.

preprogrammed from the days of creation.[35] This approach is a response to the Greek view that God's perfection requires that He is unchanging and therefore cannot modify anything in His relationship with reality (we will discuss this Greek understanding later in the book).[36] In any case, since there is certainly the possibility that miracles are preprogrammed, they cannot be the basis of our *emuna* according to Rambam.

But if Ramban draws his proof from the occurrence of miracles, why must we relate specifically to the miracles of the Exodus? More powerful miracles obviously catalyze a deeper recognition. During the Exodus we witnessed an extraordinary level of miracle. Perhaps this is the reason why it must remain the basis of our *emuna* in the Creator.

This interpretation is problematic because there was a time when we were given even deeper insight into the complete omnipotence of the Creator – when we received the Torah on Mount Sinai.[37] Yet that was the very occasion when, according to Ramban, God tied our *emuna* back to the Exodus by identifying Himself as the One who redeemed us from Egypt!

In addition to the differences we have already discussed, Ramban's path to *emuna* also adds another dimension to the mitzva beyond that of Rambam. Since miracles are direct interventions in world affairs, they reveal not only that the Creator exists but also that He created with a purpose which He is intent upon and involved in achieving.[38] For Ramban the obligation to recognize this aspect of the Creator's relationship with creation is inseparable from the obligation to recognize His existence. We cannot fully recognize *that* He is without on some level recognizing *who* He is to His creation – how He interacts with it. Once we accept that God created with a goal, we, as His creations, are necessarily implicated in attaining that goal – at least in a general manner. Thus according to Ramban, *emuna* and some degree of obligation to God are inextricably linked.

---

35. Ibid.
36. *Moreh Nevukhim* II:29.
37. Deuteronomy Rabba 2:32.
38. Ramban, Ex. 13:16. Ramban explicitly mentions there that the miracles were directed toward the specific cause of saving those who serve Him.

*Part 1: Gateway to the Exodus*

The miracles of the Exodus bring this aspect of *emuna* to an unprecedented level. The Exodus saved the Jewish people from the absolute bondage of Egyptian slavery, giving us existence as a distinct people. Salvation from bondage brings obligation; salvation from absolute bondage brings absolute obligation.[39] Together with proving the Creator's existence, the Exodus obligated the Jewish people to accept the Creator's direct and full kingship – that we are *defined* by our service to the Creator.[40]

Ramban thus understands the mitzva of *emuna* to have two facets: *emuna* in the existence of God and acceptance of God's kingship. This is reflected in the verse from which we derive the mitzva. It does not merely state, "I am the Lord"; it adds the words "your God" (in the sense of King or Ruler).[41] While God's existence is evident in any major miracle, His complete kingship over the Jewish people is specifically a consequence of the Exodus.

By basing *emuna* on the events of the Exodus, Ramban also answers the questions we raised when discussing Rambam's approach to *emuna:* How do we derive a command from a statement, and how could we be commanded by the Creator in the first of the Ten Commandments when the Creator's authority over us had not yet been accepted?

Ramban's answer is that our salvation from Egypt had already created the king-servant relationship, so God's authority was established before we heard any of the commandments on Sinai. And for that very reason also, the command to believe in and accept the kingship of God came as a statement of fact – it legislated an obligation we had already accepted, a reality that merely needed to be declared. The statement

---

39. Kiddushin 22b. See also *Arukh HaShulḥan* 403:22, that since through the Exodus we were redeemed from slavery we become servants of that redeemer. Rambam agrees with Ramban that the Exodus obligated us in God's kingship. He, however, considers this kingship a distinct mitzva from the mitzva of *emuna*. See note 28.
40. Ramban's gloss to *Sefer HaMitzvot, mitzvat aseh* 1 and *lo taaseh* 5, with his citation of the *Mekhilta*, and Ramban, Ex. 13:16, 20:2. Though Ramban clearly states this, it was Rav Schwartzman who pointed out to me the significance of this for understanding the differences between the positions of Rambam and Ramban on *emuna*. See also Maharal, *Gevurot Hashem*, chapter 60, on the significance of the Passover sacrifice.
41. Ramban, Ex. 20:2.

"I am the Lord your God that took you out of Egypt" implies the authority and obligation that stem from the event recorded in the statement.

But if our *emuna* must be tied to the miracles of the Exodus, does an individual quest to discover God have any relevance to our own achievement of the mitzva? Do we have leeway or alternative paths to fulfill our mitzva of *emuna*? Ramban does not appear to acknowledge any. At first glance this sounds strange: What could be questionable about building faith through proofs, intellectual arguments, and personal investigation?

When we consider Ramban's particular understanding of *emuna*, it does make sense, since Ramban's *emuna* is inseparable from acceptance of servitude to the kingship of God. *Emuna* derived from Rambam's pure rationality is indifferent to this commitment.[42] Though Rambam obviously recognizes that we have this obligation, it is a distinct mitzva from *emuna*.[43] Separating it out has important ramifications. Since *emuna* is the essential basis of all the mitzvot, the qualities specific to it implicate the whole relationship with God. Rambam's form of *emuna* implies that contemplation of God is the highest ideal.[44] Ramban's *emuna* leads directly to service.

Whereas Rambam does not accept Ramban's miracle-based *emuna* for its lack of logical certainty, Ramban does not accept Rambam's rational *emuna* because it is too ethereal and ultimately misses the point.

But is it really the case that Ramban considers intellectual investigation irrelevant? According to Ramban, must *emuna* rest solely on the historical record?

To answer this we need to further clarify why Rambam and Ramban approach *emuna* in the ways that they do. Are there alternatives? Or are the paths of rational reason and miraculous experience the only ways to reach *emuna*?

---

42. Though Aristotle proved the existence of God, he did not understand this to imply any obligations on man. He believed the only effect of worship was the psychological impact on the worshipper. See chapter 5.
43. See Rambam, *Sefer HaMitzvot*, mitzvat aseh 1 and 2.
44. See, for example, Rav Avraham Yitzchak HaKohen Kook, *Ein Ayah* I (Jerusalem: The Institute for Publishing Rav Kook, 2007), 32.

*Part 1: Gateway to the Exodus*

Personally, I can say that neither of these approaches played any role in at least the initial stages of my journey to *emuna*. To better understand what considerations are driving the positions of Rambam and Ramban, it will be helpful to contrast them to the path by which I came to *emuna*.

### A FIRST APPROACH TO FAITH

Because I was first exposed to Torah when I was halfway through college at a liberal university, building *emuna* on the miracles of the Exodus in the manner of Ramban was not an option for me. At the time I felt certain that miracles do not happen. But Rambam's rational approach did not speak to me either. I had studied the philosopher Immanuel Kant, who concludes that the existence of God *cannot* be rationally proven. Though this point is hotly disputed by many theologians,[45] I was not interested in pursuing it because, in any case, logical proofs seemed a very external means to something that I felt needed to be internally grounded.

I was open to exploring Torah because before I was introduced to it I had already become skeptical of Western materialism's claim to being a *complete* vision. We are trained, consciously or unconsciously, to assume that science is well on its way to explaining how everything that exists in our reality came to be, starting from the beginning of time. If this were in fact true it would not contradict the Torah; but it would leave less room for someone like myself, who was not familiar with the Torah, to be interested in investigating it. I, however, was in doubt about science's ability to close the circle.

I came to Yale with a strong background in science. My father was a successful and dedicated scientist, I went to a predominantly math/science high school, I had already completed all my college requirements in both those subjects before arriving at Yale, and I went as a declared math and physics major. But my high school study of college-level biology had left me questioning the ability of natural selection to produce the sophistication of the organic world in which we live. I graduated in the

---

45. The Jesuit philosopher Frederick Copleston debated the validity of this argument with the analytic philosopher Bertrand Russell on the BBC. This debate may be heard online at www.youtube.com/watch?v=hXPdpEJk78E.

mid-'70s and even then we knew more than enough about biochemistry and the structure of the cell to make it seem far-fetched to think that a random process could explain life as we know it. Subsequent study of the math more than confirmed this intuition.[46]

This did not bring on any "crisis of faith" in the Western tradition. I simply took note of the impression. But it did leave me open to the possibility that the system of understanding to which I was committed was not the whole picture.

It was something else, however, that actively drew me to Torah: I saw in it a possible answer to a question that bothered me deeply. It was clear to me that it is not just nice to be nice – being good is somehow essential, necessary, objective. But I didn't find a compelling way to justify or ground that intuition within the Western tradition. Torah provided an approach. According to Torah, reality is the consequence of an uncaused act of creation. This was *ḥesed* (giving, kindness) in the purest sense possible: since the Creator does not need anything from creation, existence is an altruistic gift. The trait of *ḥesed*, therefore, is foundational to existence. We cannot resonate with reality on its deepest levels unless we ourselves also embody this trait.

My only difficulty with this concept was that I had to believe in God for it to make sense.

## EMUNA AND SUBJECTIVE EXPERIENCE

My path to *emuna* began with extrapolating from my internal experience. The only thing which I know in its being – as opposed to how it merely appears – is myself. Though I have a physical aspect as well as a non-physical one, I experience my physical aspect as the vessel of my non-physical consciousness, while I identify with my inner experience along with its history. That is me; it is who I am.[47]

---

46. Robert Shapiro (former professor emeritus in chemistry at NYU), *Origins: A Skeptic's Guide to the Creation of Life on Earth* (New York: Bantam, 1987), 117–31.
47. That is not to say that every form of internal experience reaches the essential self. There are many facets to human personality, some linked to our true self and some based in more superficial aspects of or attachments to our personality. But our internal experience remains our only window on being, even if it is not obvious which aspects represent our true self. How to identify that true self is discussed in the appendix.

*Part 1: Gateway to the Exodus*

This means that all "being" to which I have access is an internal, spiritual entity which merely takes on expression through a physical vessel. Therefore, the most logical starting point for understanding reality is to assume, unless proven otherwise, that the "being" of all things – at least those which appear to be animate like me – even though I can only access them through their physical appearance, must consist of hidden, spiritual cores. We instinctively extrapolate our inner experience of being to the world around us; we are not satisfied to interact with mere appearances.

Moreover, if I perceive existence as an organic entity or whole,[48] it also must have this essence. That essence is a first approximation of God. Though God is much more than the essence of creation, this thought process at least brought me to the point of accepting the possibility of His existence.[49] I found it an adequate basis from which to seriously consider *emuna* and explore its implications.

That *emuna* was strengthened by my conviction that transcendent morality exists – an extension of my sense that "it's not just nice to be nice." This conviction is central to who I am – take it away and the remaining "I" would not be a "me" that I would recognize.[50] My commitment to the existence of morality, therefore, is inseparable from my identity.

This is relevant to my *emuna* because I am unable to understand the validity of moral principles without recognizing God. Attempts with which I am familiar to ground morality in something else, such as a social contract, are ultimately based on self-interest – however sophisticated the subsequent development of the argument. Self-interested morality is not the morality to which I am committed. The sense of morality that is an integral part of my identity is inextricably bound up with objectively

---

48. This is actually the crucial step, the one, as it turns out, that allowed Abraham to eventually discover the transcendent Creator. We presume the unity of existence as a projection of our own experience of unity of self. To the extent that a person is sensitive to that unity of self, to that extent he will perceive existence as a unity. Unity of self is a consequence of our *tzelem Elokim*. So it is really the Godliness in us that is recognizing itself reflected in the world.
49. See Berakhot 10a.
50. This is the way Rav Moshe Shapiro defined the Hebrew concept "*daat.*"

grounded right and wrong, good and bad – not interest or utility (which is why I specified "transcendent" morality).

In other words, if I see a large adult beating a small child I run up to him and scream, "Stop!" He asks me, "Why?" Personally, I must say to him, "Because it is wrong." Part of me would die if I said, "Because it will lead to higher taxes to supply the kid with therapy in the future."[51]

Moreover, our culture's smug rejection of God's existence is a consequence of the overwhelming character of today's experience of physical reality. This, coupled with the ability science has given us to manipulate material with increasing precision and success, leaves us with the conviction that matter is real. In comparison, all non-physical existence, be it spiritual or intellectual, seems unreal. Our rejection of God is part of a larger dismissal of these other dimensions of existence. But if reality is truly confined to material, then *our entire internal life – our ideas, ideals, emotions, and values – has no objective significance, in fact no reality at all.* It is, at best, fantasy. Such an amoral vision was anathema to me.[52] This made me realize that belief in God is implicitly part of my consciousness and identity.

These arguments were enough to start me on my path to *emuna*. We do not, however, find these lines of thought or anything comparable in the classical commentaries on the mitzva of *emuna*. We find only Rambam and Ramban with minor variations on their basic themes. Why are their approaches the only options?

The answer is that my approach is based on extrapolation from subjective experience.[53] Though I valued its personal character, this

---

51. Kant offers a different alternative. When you boil it down, his answer to the attacker is "Because it is illogical." This did not speak to me, for reasons that will be discussed when we speak further of Rambam's *emuna*.
52. In fact, in our current cultural environment our ideals and values don't even attain the status of fantasy. The materialist vision from which our culture so confidently rejects the existence of God, when taken to its logical conclusion, leads to the denial of the *existence* of subjective experience altogether! There are respected and honored academics who adopt this position!
53. Rav Zevulun Schwartzman. This subjective approach is generally the one followed in *sefarim* that come to aide us in strengthening our *emuna*. The point here is that though they support our sense of connectedness to God they do not directly bring us to fulfillment of the actual mitzva of *emuna*, which must be objectively grounded.

*Part 1: Gateway to the Exodus*

could only bring me to recognize something *I* must accept. That is to say, I can realize that I cannot be me if I do not believe a certain thing. But this approach cannot lead to the realization of something that *must be* – a certainty whose compulsion is independent of me and my personal identity, which is what the Torah requires to properly fulfill the mitzva of *emuna*.

This absolute *emuna* cannot be built from subjective experience – at least for people on our spiritual level.[54] Rather, it must be grounded in something objective. So the very thing I mentioned earlier that led me to disregard a rational proof of God – its objectivity – is a requirement of the Torah to achieve *emuna*. I will have something to say about my intuitive preference for a subjective path to *emuna* at the end of this book. The Torah's ultimate standard, however, is objectivity. This leaves only the position of Rambam, that the grounding is in rationality, and the position of Ramban, that the grounding is in our historical experience of miracles.

**COMPLICATIONS WITH RAMBAM AND RAMBAN**

That said, this objective *emuna*, which is the ideal of Torah, is challenging for us. With regard to Rambam's approach, how many people today are capable of the purity of logic that Rambam requires? Furthermore, few of us now genuinely embrace the results of logical arguments as compelling and binding truths. We do not respect intellect or its products to the extent people did in earlier ages; rational proofs often leave us with a nagging sense of doubt unless they confirm what we already thought was true.

---

We will discuss the relevance and status of subjective *emuna* more at the end of the book.

54. There is certainly a subjective experience, meaning a private, internal, unshareable experience that penetrates to objective reality. The midrash asks from where Abraham learned Torah. Rabbi Levy answers, "*Me'atzmo lamad Torah*," from himself he learned Torah, meaning from the depths of his internal experience of self (Genesis Rabba 95:3). But to reach objective reality "subjectively" one must achieve clear vision of *tzelem Elokim*, the Image of God within. The forefathers reached this level, but it is not reachable by us today. At the end of chapter 9, I will give another reason why they were able to achieve certainty through their internal experience.

## The Mitzva of Emuna

This skepticism is particularly strong with regard to ideals. The larger culture of which we are a part regards ideals (which would include *emuna*) as no more than *personal* convictions; if there is any truth to them we are taught to doubt our ability to access it.[55]

There are numerous reasons for this ambivalence toward intellect. Perhaps the most important rests on a concept that we will discuss in more detail later in this book[56] – that the time when human personality was anchored in the intellect has passed. When our personality was identified with our intellect (roughly the period of Greek hegemony), we equated reality with ideas and thought, and by extension logical proof with truth. But though Greek culture continues to exert a powerful influence on Western culture, we are no longer Greeks, in the sense that though ideas are important to us they do not constitute essential reality for us in the way they did for the Greeks.

This disconnect between our sense of self and intellect has direct consequences for our pursuit of *emuna*. I already mentioned my personal reticence about using logic as the basis for belief. It seems to us external and thus artificial. How can we use something that is for us a mere tool of the self to determine something definitive of the self? It is like determining that we love someone by using algebra! With this awareness it became easy to understand an observation made by Rav Yosef ben Chayim Ya'avetz, who was part of the Spanish exile. He noted that while the simple Jews during the Spanish Inquisition gave up their lives to sanctify God's name, the sophisticated Jews, those influenced by Rambam, usually converted. It seems that a commitment created by intellect does not penetrate to the essential self.

I then realized that Rambam himself does not look at intellectual thought as a *tool* of the self – he sees it as the *essential* self. Our intellect is our *tzelem Elokim* (image of God),[57] with God the ultimate "Intellect"

---

55. As a standard for choosing what to do, the paramount value given in today's world to acting in a manner that is "true to one's self" only makes sense if we deny the relevance of any objective standard. As a quality of an act *already chosen by an objective standard*, being "true to one's self" in the sense of being genuine in our acts is valued by Torah also.
56. Chapters 5–7. The process is summarized in the appendix.
57. *Hilkhot Yesodei HaTorah* 4:8.

thinking Abstract Thoughts that are Him.[58] According to Rambam, the more we purify our rational thought and become centered in it, the more we truly exist and become ourselves. In a sense Rambam wants to return us to the Greek period when our selfhood was centered in our intellect.

But we do not naturally experience ourselves in this manner. We see this, for example, after we work our way through an Aristotelian proof of the existence of God. We do not suddenly sense ourselves to be *maaminim* (believers). Rather, we congratulate ourselves on having followed an abstruse argument that is about as natural to us as translating an ancient text in an unfamiliar language using a dictionary.

People who know me consider me someone who is unusually focused on ideas. I know people who are much more intellectual than I am, but I am certainly toward the extreme end of the spectrum. And I find Rambam's vision of the essential self unrecognizable! Contemplating the twenty-six propositions from which God's existence is proven – external agents causing actualization, accidental movement necessarily ending, the impossibility of an infinity of finite magnitudes, etc. – does not make me feel at home with myself.

Genuine *emuna* must be experienced as personally compelling. For it to come through a proof, the necessity of the demonstration must grab us to the core of our being! With purely abstract proofs, this can only happen with those who have transformed themselves into beings centered in and defined by rational thoughts. This is why Rambam talks of the long path to philosophy. It does not come naturally or easily; the capability must be painstakingly developed.

In other words, Rambam's approach to the mitzva of *emuna* cannot be taken in isolation. It only makes sense in the larger context of his vision of reality, humanity, God, and, crucially, the revolution of self he requires us to achieve. To return to an earlier metaphor, perhaps a true mathematician, someone who lives everything and every moment through math, might very well use algebra to determine his love. But this would probably only be possible if the object of his love was also math.

With this point in mind, we can perceive the soaring beauty of Rambam's approach and appreciate the remarkable spiritual level he

---

58. Ibid., 2:10; *Moreh Nevukhim* I:69.

achieved in his personal life. But this also forces us to confront just how far most of us are from following his approach to achieve integrated faith. Though we recognize the greatness of the Rambam's vision, to most of us it is external and forced. Therefore, many question the relevance of Rambam's approach to anyone in our generation outside the *very* select few. In fact, Rambam himself writes in *Moreh Nevukhim* that even in his generation he was writing only for those few who, while fully accepting Torah, were trained in and committed to the centrality of philosophy.[59]

With Rambam's approach to *emuna* beyond most of us, we are left with Ramban's reliance on miracles as the preferred path to faith.[60] But it is not as if building *emuna* on the Exodus is without complications in our time.

## COMPLICATIONS WITH MIRACLES

How are we to base our *emuna* on miracles when we live in a time when they have disappeared from human experience and our surrounding culture views reality as relentlessly natural? How can we develop well-grounded conviction out of our historical tradition of miraculous experience when the very possibility of miracles is under such assault? This is another instance of a question that I am awake to because I did not grow up religious – my *girsa d'yankusa* (early formative learning) was the Western tradition. Perhaps people who were raised in Torah are able to take also this for granted. In *The Choice to Be*, however, I argue that the question should bother almost all of us, because only the select few can succeed in integrating themselves with Torah to the point that they are genuinely impervious to the influences of our surrounding culture.

Our loss of confidence in miracles comes at the end of a long process of increasing alienation from all things spiritual, which is one of the central themes of the historical development of culture. The story begins with the slow decay of spiritual experience in the Near Eastern societies that carried civilization before the rise of the West.[61] The Jews,

---

59. *Petiḥa* to *Moreh Nevukhim*. See also *Moreh Nevukhim* I:34.
60. Rav Schwartzman.
61. Thornkild Jacobsen, *The Treasures of Darkness: A History of Mesopotamian Religion* (New Haven: Yale University Press, 1976), epilogue.

*Part 1: Gateway to the Exodus*

as one of those societies, shared this weakening of spirituality.[62] Then our exile to the Western empires dragged us through their even more pronounced spiritual decline.[63] This has diluted our capacity for *emuna* generally. But the West's focus on physical reality and natural processes has been particularly toxic to belief in miracles which, according to Ramban, is our vehicle for building *emuna*.

We concluded that Rambam's rational approach to *emuna* is out of reach for most of us because of the purity of intellect it requires, so we turned for guidance to Ramban. Are we now concluding that Ramban's miraculous approach is beyond us so that we need to reconsider our abandonment of Rambam?

Ramban's reliance on miracles for achieving *emuna* is certainly a challenging approach. Yet we will see that it is not unachievable. And in any case we need to deal with our difficulties with miracles, because Rambam also requires them.

In the second half of this book we will broaden our examination of *emuna* beyond God's existence to include our recognition that all aspects of reality emanate from God alone – what is called *yiḥud Hashem* (the Unity of God). Although the necessity of God's unity can also, according to Rambam, be proven rationally,[64] for reasons we will discuss later Rambam ties *yiḥud Hashem* to the Jews' unique obligation to God's kingship.[65] And Rambam agrees with Ramban that this relationship came through our miraculous salvation from Egypt.[66]

---

62. See, for example, Makkot 24a and *Seder Olam Rabba*, chapter 30. See also Rabbenu Nisim ben Reuven, *Drashot HaRan*, drash 8. See also Rabbi Tzadok HaKohen, *Maḥshavot Ḥarutz* 72a. Rabbi Tzadok explains that the causality actually starts with the Jews. As their spiritual depth wanes so does that of the nations of the world.
63. See, for example, Eiruvin 53a.
64. *Moreh Nevukhim* II:1.
65. See Rambam, *Sefer HaMitzvot, mitzvat aseh* 2.
66. *Hilkhot Ḥametz uMatza* 7:1, 4. If Rambam does not accept miracles as an adequate basis to build *emuna* in God's existence, how can he say we use it to accept God's kingship? First, as we mentioned, the experience at Sinai set a unique standard of clarity for achieving the mitzva of *emuna* in the existence of God – a standard that does not apply to other mitzvot. And second, as we mentioned, God revealed at Sinai that He was responsible for the Exodus – whether through performing miracles or programming them into creation from the start. The revelation at Sinai and the

*The Mitzva of Emuna*

The mitzva of accepting God's kingship, which Ramban saw as a facet of *emuna*, Rambam sees as synonymous with *yiḥud Hashem*. So Rambam also must eventually engage the miracles of the Exodus to achieve *emuna*, at least this more sweeping form of it. According to everyone, then, we must develop our ability to rely on them.

**WHERE TO FROM HERE?**

Our next step is to chronicle the spiritual decline we are describing. Just knowing that in the past we witnessed open miracles and viewed reality in a manner that allowed them to integrate comfortably into our experience goes a long way toward blunting the uneasiness we feel over the distance between our miraculous narrative and today's experience of reality as relentlessly natural. Understanding that cultural forces have wrought this change transforms our current spiritually barren view of existence from objectively based truth to a historically based perspective.

This will give us some ground to stand on as we push back against our current culture's full repudiation of miracles. We will combine this with an analysis of how the Sages responded to our increasingly difficult spiritual environment, shoring up our capacity to reach *emuna* by developing new capabilities. At that point we can evaluate how effective those measures are today and determine if there are additional responsibilities that we need to accept to strengthen our efforts to achieve *emuna*.

Those interested in an overview of this historical section before plunging into the more detailed treatment of the book can turn to my eulogy for Rav Moshe Shapiro in the appendix. The eulogy describes who this remarkable man was to me – his influence on my understanding is readily apparent to anyone familiar with his thought. To explain the challenges Rav Shapiro faced communicating Torah on the level that he did, I go through a brief explanation of the history covered at more length in this book. The eulogy also makes clear why what I am attempting to do in this book is important. Alternatively, the eulogy can be used as review once you have completed the first half of the book. It is more than a mere synopsis, so reading it at some point is valuable.

---

*emuna* we have in its occurrence provide the basis for building on the miracles of the Exodus for other mitzvot.

## Chapter 2
# Challenges to Faith

We concluded that our path to *emuna* necessarily passes through the miracles of the Exodus. But living in today's world with its relentlessly natural view of reality, we must ask ourselves with what authenticity we accept that these miracles actually took place. Each year at Passover we are meant to revitalize our faith by connecting ever more deeply to the historical events of the Exodus, specifically by recounting the miracles through which the Exodus was accomplished – the ten plagues. We do that with a 45-second listing of those plagues, often recited as a singsong nursery-rhyme by a five-year-old who is rewarded for her efforts with praise and adoration from all present.

This recitation commemorates that God decimated the population of the greatest nation of its era, utterly shattering the worldview of its people, breaking its strength, and destroying its economy. Though Egypt was our enemy, this level of devastation would give anyone pause. The angels were not allowed to sing God's praises for saving the Jews at the splitting of the sea because it was accomplished through so much death.[1] Yet our children sing the plagues! Would we let them sing about

---
1. Megilla 10b.

the firebombing of Dresden or the nuclear attack on Hiroshima? Are we so callous?

We aren't. We simply don't connect to the event as an actuality. We are profoundly removed from the Exodus – that is, from the Exodus being a reality. We can intellectualize it and derive deep, relevant lessons from the plagues. But if we ask ourselves if we believe the Exodus *actually* happened, though we might answer yes, the fact is we do not relate to it as history – certainly not in the same way that we relate to, say, the Second World War. The Exodus may be an actual part of our philosophy, but it is not part of our actual reality.

It is not the nearly three and a half thousand years intervening between us and the Exodus that weakens our sense of its actuality. We are able to assimilate events of ancient history into our worldview. For example, Alexander's conquest of the Persian Empire at the Battle of Gaugamela, though it occurred nearly two and a half thousand years ago, is real to anyone who has studied enough history to be aware that it happened. We connect to it as real because Alexander's victory while fantastic (he probably defeated an army five times the size of his own), was not miraculous. We know Alexander was a military genius; we even know the brilliant tactics he employed. We understand how it happened. The Exodus, on the other hand, *was* miraculous. In fact, the only reason we commemorate it is to reconnect with its miraculous quality.[2]

Today our culture is suffused with the assumption that reality is based on material existence with physical law determining all functioning. According to this, miracles cannot happen. And though we may affirm our belief in miracles, few of us can prevent these unspoken assumptions from undermining the foundations of that belief. On a conscious level we may assume the possibility of miracles, but the structure of our thinking contradicts that assumption. This disconnect compromises any genuine sense for the reality of miracles whether we are conscious of it or not. So while recounting the miraculous history of the Exodus is supposed to revitalize our faith, we need to do a lot of preparatory work before this can happen in an authentic and integrated way.

---

2. Rambam, *Mishneh Torah, Ḥametz uMatza* 7:1; Ramban, Ex. 13:16.

This should not surprise us. The midrash tells us that the generation of the Exodus merited leaving Egypt because of their faith, even though the purpose of the Exodus experience was to establish their faith.[3] We see that even the Jews of Egypt required some prior level of *emuna* for the miracles of the Exodus to be effective in fully developing their *emuna*.

The reason for this is simple enough to understand. When God saved the Jews it was not only to redeem them from the slavery of Pharaoh; it was simultaneously to establish a relationship with them. In a sense the reason for the slavery was to create the opportunity to be saved, and thus to form the relationship.[4] Achieving relationship through salvation was dependent upon our recognizing God's hand in the redemption; we had to recognize the miracles as miracles. This required a prior level of *emuna*.

A recent example of what happens when miracles occur without a prior foundation of faith is the Six-Day War of 1967. In the days leading up to that momentous event, the specter of what was expected to happen was enough to drive the chief of staff, Yitzchak Rabin, to a mental breakdown. Just prior to the conflict, park land in Tel Aviv was being publicly consecrated for a potential 50,000 graves. After six days of battle Israel emerged as the preeminent military power in the Middle East, having suffered remarkably few casualties and minimal damage.

The only turnaround of comparable magnitude in our history was the Purim story. In that case, because we recognized God's involvement, it led to a renewal of our covenant with Him. The opportunity in '67, however, was squandered. Many feel that was because the victory was attributed to Israeli brilliance, skill, and daring, so that instead of national redemption we developed a pridefulness that left us ill-prepared for the Yom Kippur war in 1973.

---

3. *Yalkut Shemoni Shemot* 14:240.
4. The Sages identify various transgressions of our ancestors as the cause of the exile. Maharal (*Gevurot Hashem*, chapter 9) points out that none of these transgressions is of a magnitude that would justify the severity of the exile. He explains that the exile and the salvation from it were experiences we needed to go through in order to prepare us for our relationship with God and our role in history. The transgressions were more a catalyst than a cause of the exile.

The need for prior *emuna* to recognize miracles *of the past* is demonstrated by the modern response to the Hanukka story. In 162 BC the Jewish people, led by the Maccabees, rebelled against the Greek Seleucid kingdom in response to its attempts to Hellenize Israel. The Jews, a ragtag band of amateurs, met the Greeks in open combat and, against staggering odds, routed one of the world's strongest armies. The victory was miraculous, and this was reinforced by the miracle we most associate with the holiday – the Temple Menora burning for eight days on one day's worth of oil.

We associate the miracle of the Menora so strongly with the holiday because that is where the Sages focused our attention. The only mitzva they decreed as a result of the war was that we light candles in remembrance of what happened with the Temple Menora. This was because it was incontrovertibly miraculous. The battles were no less miraculous – we were practically pitting butter knives against the ancient equivalent of tanks – war elephants. But miracles in combat can easily be confused with bravery, especially by those not present at the actual engagement. So the Sages built our commemoration on the Menora to testify to the true source of the victory.

Salvation through miracles was really the point of the event. As we will discuss, the focus of our cultural battle with Greece was over whether or not God intervenes in history to achieve His ends. So it was essential that we recognize the miracle. Yet, despite this, how does the secular Jewish world remember the Maccabees? They commemorate the courage and prowess through which the Maccabees *themselves* achieved this victory. To emphasize the point they established the Maccabee Games, basking in individual physical strength and skill in emulation of the very Greeks we were struggling to defeat! What leads to such a blatant distortion?

Because the secular community understands reality in a manner that precludes miracles, they cannot see miracles. When a battle elephant is felled with a butter knife, it *must* be attributed to exceptional strength because there is no alternative. To recognize miracles one has to believe they can happen – it takes a prior basis of faith.

Likewise, we cannot expect to revitalize our faith through recounting the Exodus unless there is a genuine foundation of faith upon which to base a sense for the reality of the miracles of the Exodus. Presumptions of belief are not enough. We must actively counter the influences of the larger society within which we operate – the influences that develop within us a worldview that unconsciously contradicts the possibility of miracles. Otherwise our conscious narrative of faith is a small raft bobbing precariously on an ocean of disbelief which, though we may not be mindful of it, undercuts the solidity and integration of that faith. But how do we counter those influences? How do we gain the level of *emuna* needed to view miracles as possible in our present and part of our past?

**THE STRUCTURE OF *EMUNA***

Before outlining a path to faith, we need to know on a more detailed level what is complicating its attainment. To do so, we must first understand the structure of faith.

Rav Yosef Albo in *Sefer HaIkarim* identifies three recognitions that are necessary for *emuna* in any relationship with God. They are: (1) the transcendent Creator exists, (2) He knows what is happening in the world and intervenes to further His intent, and (3) He makes His will known to man.[5] After the Exodus, this third component comes exclusively in the form of God's communication with the Jewish people through Torah.[6] Effectively, then, this third component is synonymous with recognizing the special relationship of the Jews with God.[7]

---

5. Rav Yosef Albo, *Sefer HaIkarim* 1:4. There are other lists, the most famous being Rambam's Thirteen *Ikarim* or Essentials of Faith (Rambam actually started the whole genre). But as Rav Albo himself points out, Rambam's Thirteen divide neatly into three categories that correspond to Rav Albo's three essentials. Rambam's list simply includes branch principles as well as root principles. Why Rambam did it this way is beyond the scope of our discussion.
6. Berakhot 7a, combined with Rashi's statement on Deut. 33:17 that "*Shekhina*" is synonymous with prophecy.
7. Torah is God's communication with man. We see from the second blessing we recite over saying the *Shema* that Torah and God's relationship with the Jewish people are one and the same, for we fulfill our obligation to say a blessing over Torah through the words, "Blessed are You, God, Who loves Israel" (*Shulḥan Arukh, Oraḥ Ḥayim* 47:7).

*Part 1: Gateway to the Exodus*

The Exodus validated all three of these beliefs[8] and allowed us to internalize their truth on a deep level, something we will discuss in detail in the second half of this book.[9] They also hang together as a logically coherent whole. (1) By virtue of our existence we are witness to the fact that there is a Creator. This awareness obligates us to His service. (2) Since God created reality, our understanding requires us to presume that He did so with a purpose. Since He created existence, He can alter it. Combining these ideas together we expect the Creator to intervene in history, at least if achieving His purpose necessitates it. (3) We observe that God created us with self-consciousness, intelligence, and free will – we knowingly choose our actions and develop ourselves and the world through those actions. Since the world must come to its goal and we affect the path of the world through our choices, we need to know what to do in order to play our role in bringing the world to its conclusion. Therefore God must communicate our responsibilities to us.[10]

Despite their internal logic, these beliefs sound contrived to the modern ear. Since we view the world as functioning entirely through natural causality, any concept of God that sees Him as an active participant seems unnecessary. If we do consider His existence, because we intuitively respect abstractions as the deepest truths, we assume that God must be part of that realm of abstraction.[11] This means that He has no interest in interacting, or even capacity to interact, with the bland particulars of physical reality and history – and certainly not specifically for our sake. So the idea of a purpose to this world, of God intervening in history, and of His taking interest in a particular people and communicating with them, all sound dissonant to us. The logic of these beliefs no longer speaks to us, and whatever internalization was achieved at the Exodus has ceased to be evident.

---

8. Ramban, Deut. 13:16.
9. See chapter 11.
10. Alternatively, Ramban understands that *emuna* in the Creator and recognizing His kingship are one and the same mitzva. He reasons that it is inconceivable that a Being would create the world unless He intended to rule over it (Rav Schwartzman). This requires that He communicate with man.
11. We will soon see that this outlook is a consequence of the continuing influence of Greek thought.

## THE HISTORY OF DISTANCE

Our present attitude is the consequence of a long historical process. That process is structured by a succession of four kingdoms that ruled civilization, Babylon, Persia, Greece, and Rome.[12] Each brought a culture with distorted views of humanity, God, and the relationship between the two. Through our exiles to these kingdoms we came under the influence of their cultural umbrellas and the cumulative effect has eaten away at the foundations of our faith.

For our purposes the exiles to Babylon and Persia can be considered one continuous experience, as both were idolatrous societies and therefore challenged our *emuna* in roughly similar ways.[13] Though idol worship was practiced by the Greeks, we will see that it played only a superficial role in their national ethos so the challenge their culture presented was new. Therefore, these four kingdoms represent three distinct phases: Babylon/Persia, Greece, and Rome.

These three phases line up with the three foundations of faith we discussed. That is to say, though exile complicates all aspects of our

---

12. The Assyrian exile of the ten tribes, which preceded the Babylonian destruction and exile, is viewed by the Sages as falling into its own category and is not relevant to our discussion. See Rabbi Tzadok HaKohen, *Resisei Laila*, *ot* 35 as interpreted by Rav Moshe Shapiro (lecture given on the Thursday of *Parashat Vayeḥi*, 5748). Rabbi Tzadok teaches that Assyria severed the connection of its exiles to their respective native lands (Berakhot 28a). This undermined national identity and, with it, connection to the structure of meaning and purpose associated with that identity; all that was left to the exiles was to focus on physical survival or physical advancement. Assyria distracted the Jews from the pursuit of meaningful goals *(emuna)*, rather than introducing alternatives. The four kingdoms that concern us, on the other hand, each introduced a distorted and competing vision of ideals and meaning, which brought a different kind of complication to our pursuit of *emuna*. Understanding these distortions and the challenges they create is the focus of this book.
13. Both the Babylonian and Persian exiles resulted from the idolatry that destroyed the First Temple, and the rule of one followed immediately upon the rule of the other without any significant change in the nature of our situation. For the differences between the two exiles, see *The Choice to Be*. There, in section 3, the empires are analyzed in terms of the various facets of character that animated each of them, how these differing character traits determined the succession of the empires, and the purpose behind this historical process. In this book our analysis of the empires comes in the context of an exploration of *emuna* and is focused specifically on how they challenged our *emuna* and how the Sages addressed these challenges.

*emuna*, the corruption unique to each exile primarily affected a specific pillar of faith. As each kingdom rose to power, another foundation of our *emuna* stopped being intuitive.

The third of those foundations is that God communicates His will to man, which we said is funneled through His communication with the Jews. Under Babylon and Persia the lack of any overt act by God to save the Jews made it appear that our special relationship with God was finished. This, coupled with the end of revealed prophecy, seemed to put an end to God's communication with man and the third pillar of *emuna*.

Though the Greeks recognized the existence of God, they conceived of Him as an abstract, rational Being. In the Greek view, God lacked any cognizance of or connection to the shifting details of reality. This intensified the pressure on our belief in our unique relationship with God – the Greek understanding made the very idea an impossibility. Of more significance and specific to Greece their understanding of God also precluded the possibility of Him intervening in history through miracles, shaking the second pillar – that God directly intervenes in the workings of the world.

Rome completes the process of undercutting the foundations of our *emuna*. Rome's materialism in all of its forms undermines the first pillar of *emuna* – that the *transcendent* Creator exists. Once Rome became Christian, Roman materialism led the Romans to distort the understanding of God through their concept of the Trinity, which saw God taking on physical form and subject to the limitations of physical existence.[14] The corruption inherent in this conception was fully revealed when it morphed into the purely materialist view of reality we have today, denying the very existence of any transcendent realm and with it, God.

Rome also intensified the pressure on Jewish uniqueness with a frontal attack on the concept of the chosenness of the Jewish people;

---

14. The Catholic Church committed itself to this position at the Council of Nicaea in 321 under the direction of Constantine, the emperor who made the Roman Empire Christian. They specifically intended that God should suffer death to ensure God's empathy for man's trials. See Peter Brown, *The Rise of Western Christendom: Triumph and Diversity, A.D. 200–1000*, 2nd ed. (Malden, Oxford, Melbourne, Berlin: Wiley-Blackwell, 2003), 116–20.

once Rome became Christian, the Christians claimed to have replaced the Jews as God's nation.[15]

Modern Jewish history encompasses the period of time during which we confront these cultures. Facing down the challenge that each presents to our *emuna*, we are forced to learn how to perceive that which was once obvious – to take responsibility for each facet of our faith in reaction to the encroaching darkness. The Sages have had to adjust and fortify the way we approach our relationship with the Creator in order to achieve this. Without their innovations the Jewish people would long ago have lost their *emuna* and, with that, disappeared as a distinct people. We need to trace this path more precisely so that we can better understand the challenges against which we struggle and the resources we have at our disposal to face them.

---

15. Ramḥal, *Daat Tevunot* 36. This is called replacement theology, or supercessionism. See, for example, Matthew 21:43. This has been the position of the Catholic Church since the time of the early Church Fathers, though it was somewhat softened by the Nostra Aetate ("Declaration on the Relation of the Church with Non-Christian Religions") promulgated by Paul VI in 1965.

*Chapter 3*

# Recovering Communication

The long road of Jewish exile and the hiding of God's revelation which it entailed began with the exile to Babylon and Persia. The particular challenge to *emuna* that this exile presented is evident in the book of Esther, which records the salvation of the Jews from Haman during the Persian portion of the exile. As we read through it we find an absence in the text unprecedented in the rest of the Written Torah: the name of God is never mentioned. This is singularly peculiar when we remember that the Written Torah is the record of the unfolding relationship between the Jewish people and God.

Names are labels for relationships. A person is called different names by the different individuals who relate to him. Taking myself as an example, there are some who call me *Abba* (Dad), there are some who call me Rabbi Kagan, there are some who call me Jeremy. The specific relationship I have with each of these people is evident in the name by which he or she calls me. My children call me *Abba*, my students call me Rabbi Kagan, my mother and friends call me Jeremy.

The absence of all names of God from the book of Esther, then, implies the seeming absence of any relationship with God. This is because God had no *obvious* involvement in the events recorded there. Despite the existential threat faced by the Jewish people, no clearly revealed miracle – the *classic* expression of God's participation – brought them salvation.

This first exile was destabilizing for the Jews. We knew that we had turned away from God through idolatry; we knew that we would be punished. We had been warned by the prophets and already had a long history of experience with divine justice. So the fact of punishment in and of itself was not surprising. Prophets going all the way back to Moses had even told us that the punishment would be exile.[1] Still, the *reality* of exile from the land was new and overwhelming. Our land was the home we shared with God; it was the vessel of our relationship. What did the loss of that home say about the status of our relationship?[2] The extended lack of intervention by God to pull us out of exile further sharpened the question.

## A RELATIONSHIP IN CRISIS

The Talmud deduces from verses in Isaiah that because of the new reality, the Jews thought that God had abandoned us permanently. Effectively, He had divorced us:

> Ten men came and sat down before the prophet. He said to them, "Return and repent." They answered, "If a master sells his slave, or a husband divorces his wife, has one a claim upon the other?"[3]

The prophet vehemently repudiated this understanding.

> Thus says the Lord, "Your mother whom I have put away, where is her bill of divorce? To which of my creditors have I sold you? Behold, it is because of your sins that you have sold yourselves, and because of your transgressions your mother is put away." This agrees with Reish Lakish, who said: "Why is it written in Scripture both that David is 'My servant' and that Nebuchadnezzar

---

1. See Lev. 26:44; Deut. 30:3.
2. See Nedarim 85a (*al ma avda ha'aretz*), as explained by Maharal in his introduction to *Tiferet Yisrael*, for the connection between exile and our relationship with God.
3. Sanhedrin 105a.

is 'My servant'? Because it was known to God that Israel would attempt to justify [renouncing Torah] because God had turned them out. Therefore the Holy One, blessed be He, preempted them by calling Nebuchadnezzar His servant. For when a servant acquires property, to whom does the servant belong and to whom does the property he acquires belong?[4]

God made clear that the special bond between Himself and the Jewish people was not broken. In fact, He even stated that it never will be broken:

> That which has come into your mind will not be. You say, "We will be as the idolaters, as the families of the nations, serving wood and stone." As I live, says the Lord God, with a mighty hand, with an outstretched arm, and with fury poured forth will I rule over you.[5]

But what are we to do in a situation in which we no longer perceive God's relationship with us? How is the connection alive? For that matter, in what sense is "fury poured forth" a relationship? The Talmud answers these questions elsewhere:

> R. Eliezer said, "If Israel repents they will be redeemed and if they do not they will not be redeemed." R. Yehoshua responded, "If they do not repent they will not be redeemed? [That cannot be.] Rather the Holy One will place upon them a king whose decrees are as severe as those of Haman so that Israel will repent and return."[6]

When God is distant, pain and threat are the result. The greatness of the Jewish people, at least on a national level, is that when pressed

---

4. Ibid.
5. Ibid.
6. Sanhedrin 97b. In Y. Taanit 1:1 the answer is cited as R. Eliezer's rebuttal to R. Yehoshua's objection.

hard enough we eventually recover our knowledge that God is our King and repent of having turned away.[7]

This then brings redemption, as the human soul is the medium through which God connects to physical reality. Our internal distance from God undermines His expression in physical reality, leading to our suffering. This suffering forces the nation as a whole to repent, re-actualizing our connection to God. This rejoins God to the world, renewing His active involvement in physical reality and bringing our salvation. In other words, creation has a kind of equilibrium mechanism built in that restores us to our proper relationship with God.

It is, however, reasonable to ask what kind of relationship this is. Whenever we move away from God, we are reminded of our need for Him and forced to return? This sounds more like captivity than relationship! How are we to understand this?

**THE CONCEPT OF COVENANT**

There are two major portions in the Torah that describe the disasters that will befall the Jewish people if they turn away from God.[8] In both cases, the disasters are invoked as the penalty for violating a covenant.[9]

Covenants form deep unions. Yet the Hebrew verb for making a covenant is *karat,* which means "cut." Why is the verb for making a connection "cut"? It can be understood as a reference to the ancient practice of symbolizing a covenant by cutting animals in half and walking between the pieces.[10] But that realization just shifts the question to "why this practice?"

The word for covenant in Hebrew is *brit*. It is related to the word *briah* (creation).[11] This conveys the idea that a covenant is not merely a contractual agreement. Rather, it is the creation of a new entity

---

7. See Deut. 30:1–3. See also Rav Eliahu Dessler, *Mikhtav MeEliahu* vol. 1, 14th ed. (Jerusalem: The Committee for the Publication of the Writings of Rabbi E. L. Dessler, 1978), 233, and Maharal, *Or Ḥadash,* in *Ner Mitzva/Or Ḥadash* (Bnei Brak: Yahadut), 221.
8. *Parashat Beḥukotai* in Leviticus and *Parashat Ki Tavo* in Deuteronomy.
9. Deut. 28:69.
10. See Gen. 15:9–18. References to the practice are also found in non-Jewish sources. See F. M. Cornford, *From Religion to Philosophy* (Mineola, NY: Dover Publications, 2004), 24.
11. Ramban, Gen. 6:18.

composed of the two parties. This can only happen if each loses his identity as an individual unit – meaning they each come to be defined by, and only exist through, the new union. After a covenant has been made, two individuals that were originally wholes unto themselves become incomplete halves outside the union. Forming a covenant is therefore understood to be a cutting, because both parties effectively cut themselves and become individually incomplete in order to fully join in the larger whole.[12]

Because we made a covenant with God we have no existence outside of our relationship with Him – hence the destruction that follows our turning away from God. It is less a punishment than the reality of what we are without the relationship. It does not show God's domination so much as measure the depth to which the relationship is constitutive of who we are.[13] When we move away from God, we are actually losing ourselves. Effectively, it is a slow-acting suicide. Through our suffering we realize this in time to turn back and regain our selves and our existence.

## AN EVOLVING RELATIONSHIP

When we return to God, however, we do not recover the relationship *as it was*. The relationship must be different because we have become different. What led to the rupture was our acting on a desire for more independence, motivated by pridefulness or selfishness. When we eventually repent, we repent of that original intent. But we cannot undo the fact that we have changed through our choices; when we acted on our desire for independence we became more independent. Therefore the relationship that is appropriate to us from this point on is not the one we had before.

We are like a child who, upon becoming a teenager, turns away from his parents. When he matures and realizes their true value he returns to them. But the family does not revert to the style of relationship of his childhood, which was characterized by dependence; the

---

12. I understood this interpretation from a lecture of Rav Moshe Shapiro. It also makes sense of the practice of walking between the split halves of animals to mark the covenant.
13. As heard from Rav Moshe Shapiro.

## Part 1: Gateway to the Exodus

teenager is not forced to suckle.[14] What was the height of intimacy in infancy becomes perverse once independent individuality develops.

The equivalent of dependence in a relationship with God is one in which He reveals Himself, for then His revelation carries the relationship.[15] In a relationship of independence God is hidden so that we have to take responsibility for finding Him. After turning away from God – declaring our independence – we do not return to a revealed relationship with Him, where we are compelled to recognize God through His obvious revelation. Rather, because the independence that motivated our original break still defines our personality and identity even after repentance the renewed relationship with God is hidden, requiring us to create relationship with Him through our own initiative. God saves us, but with miracles that are only recognizable by those who search. This was the case with the events recorded in the book of Esther (the "Megilla").

### LEARNING THE SKILLS OF A NEW RESPONSIBILITY

The Purim experience developed in us the skills to perceive God's involvement when it is not visible. We preserve and disseminate those skills to future generations through the Megilla because this change in the nature of our relationship – that God is no longer obviously revealed – is the new normal.[16]

In *The Choice to Be* I compared the book of Esther to a "magic eye" photo. This is an ordinary-looking picture with two black dots in the margin. You look at the dots and cross your eyes in just the right way so that the dots appear to converge. Then you return your gaze to the picture and suddenly a completely different image jumps out. The magic eye photo has a second image superimposed, but coded in at a depth below the surface. When looking at a two dimensional picture we naturally focus on its surface. But if we train ourselves to look behind it, we can see the hidden image. That is what we do by merging the dots – we cross our eyes, effectively focusing behind the page.

---

14. Numbers Rabba 19:12.
15. See Rashi, Num. 20:12.
16. See the Vilna Gaon's metaphor in his commentary on Esther 1:2.

Similarly, the book of Esther trains us to look below the surface of natural events to detect an otherwise-hidden pattern that clearly reveals the guidance and oversight that determine them. The book of Esther covers a slice of history that unfolds over a nine-year period. All the "news" of that time would fill a library. The Megilla sifts out thirty minutes of relevant facts. When we focus exclusively on them, the baffling juxtaposition of events in time and space that was required to bring about the salvation becomes evident, and the unseen guidance at work is made obvious.

God's participation in the Persian miracle was not blatantly obvious the way it was when He split the sea during the Exodus. But it can be seen clearly by those who accept the responsibility and look skillfully. The Megilla teaches us how to look.

## IDENTIFYING THE SPECIFIC CHALLENGE TO OUR *EMUNA*

We have so far viewed this first exile as a kind of identity crisis, in which the Jews questioned their continued status as a people before God. But beyond our national identity, this experience also had significant implications for our *emuna*.

We said in the name of Ramban that revealed miracles both establish our *emuna* in the existence of the Creator and also teach us of His constant involvement in history – that there is no such thing as nature; there are only revealed miracles and hidden miracles.[17] From where, then, does our *emuna* come in the post-exile world where we no longer experience revealed miracles?

Had miracles come to an end, we would have had a very serious problem. This, however, was not the case; they merely went underground, and the Megilla gave us the tools to find them there. But for us this still represented a significant reversal. Prior to exile our experience of obvious miracles had revealed the existence of God and given us faith that what appeared to be the workings of nature were really a process of hidden miracles. Now we have to directly detect the hidden miracles behind our naturally functioning world and learn from them of the existence of God.

---

17. Ramban, Ex. 13:16.

*Part 1: Gateway to the Exodus*

Ultimately, we require the miracles of the Exodus to build complete *emuna*. But recognition of these hidden miracles also provides a basis for belief that revealed miracles are possible, allowing us to relate to the events of the Exodus and, through them, build a deeper *emuna*.[18]

It should be noted that the above paragraphs refer to the way we use the Megilla to bolster our faith today. At the time of the events of the exile in Persia, however, this particular support for our *emuna* was not yet necessary. It would become necessary only after Greece had brought its purely rational worldview to civilization, calling into question the possibility of miracles.

While we were still in Persia, despite all the difficulties created by our exile, we remained within a Near Eastern cultural milieu where man was defined by worship, as we shall see in a subsequent chapter. Though that worship was idolatrous, at least everyone was aware that there was a source to reality, so the idea of belief was not under serious pressure. And because we understood our situation to be a consequence of divine judgment, we still directed that belief at God.[19] Similarly, the surrounding culture did not pose any challenge to our belief in God's *ability* to perform miracles; Mesopotamian culture was acutely aware of the power of the gods and we still had our historical tradition of miracles with no reason to question its veracity.

From the verses in Isaiah quoted at the beginning of this chapter, we see that though the Jews assumed God no longer wanted a relationship with them there was no question about either the existence of God or of our past relationship with Him. We merely assumed God did not want to perform miracles *for us* anymore because He was no longer interested in a relationship. When the book of Esther was written its purpose

---

18. This is reflected in the yearly cycle of holidays. Purim, while it ends the year, also serves as a base from which to celebrate Passover and begin the year anew. On Purim we read the Megilla to sharpen our awareness that God operates in nature despite the absence of revealed miracles in our day. This renews our faith in His involvement in our lives sufficiently for us to appreciate the *genuine possibility* of His performing revealed miracles. On Passover night we can then recount the events of the Exodus and build from them toward a deeper *emuna* that is real to us.
19. The Talmud (Yoma 69b) notes that during this exile we never ceased describing God as "*gadol*" – great.

was to show that God still intervened in the world *on our behalf* – that our unique relationship continued.

This had implications for our *emuna*. As we discussed earlier there are three components to complete *emuna*: belief in the existence of the Creator, belief that He miraculously intervenes in affairs, *and belief that He communicates with man, revealing our responsibilities*. We explained in the previous chapter that God's communication comes specifically through His relationship with the Jews. But our unique relationship with God was the very thing put in question by the exile. Without relationship there could not be communication, so this third component of our faith was under threat.[20] This weakened our overall *emuna*, since *emuna* only makes sense and, therefore, can only be at full strength when all three of its components support one another as an integrated whole.[21]

## ABANDONMENT AND THE LOSS OF TORAH

When I say that without relationship there cannot be communication, I do not mean this just in the sense that God has no one with whom to talk. Torah, the content of the communication, is the guide to relationship with Him. Through Torah God reveals how He wants His partner in creation to act. If there is no partner, not only is there no one to talk to, there is also nothing to talk about; *there cannot be Torah*.

Even this formulation does not reach the core of the matter. We said earlier that our covenant with God is the reason for the destructiveness that follows our turning away from Him. We are who we are only through this covenant. This covenant we spoke of was actually a covenant *of Torah*.[22] Torah is the medium of our connection to God.[23]

---

20. As cited in note 2 of this chapter, Maharal explains Nedarim 85a (*al ma avda ha'aretz*) as a source for the connection between exile and the breakdown of our relationship with God. That relationship comes through Torah, and therefore exile comes about as a consequence of the breakdown of our appreciation of Torah.
21. As noted in chapter 2, since man's actions alter the direction of Creation, we can only fully appreciate that our world was created if we understand that its Creator has expectations of us that He communicates.
22. Rambam, *Mishneh Torah, Sefer Ahava, Hilkhot Berakhot* 2:3.
23. Maharal, *Netzaḥ Yisrael,* chapter 2, commenting on Y. Shekalim (we have the text in Y. Taanit 4:6).

## Part 1: Gateway to the Exodus

We see mirrored in it who we are as partners with God, which, because of the covenant, is the only "who" we can be. Through it we actualize that self, but on a deeper level than our consciousness can reach. In a sense Torah is more us than we are.[24]

This explains the otherwise-enigmatic halakha that we can fulfill our obligation to bless the Torah by the words "Blessed are You, Hashem, *the lover of His people Israel!*"[25] For this reason also we entered the covenant of Torah through the statement, "We will do (whatever the Torah tells us to do) and we will (strive to) understand it."[26] This means we accept the obligation to obey the commands even before we know what they are or why they are. We are capable of such a leap both because of our trust in God and because of our understanding that Torah is actually representative of our deepest self.

Therefore our sense in exile of a loss of relationship with God necessarily implied an end to Torah and with it an end to God's communication with man. We saw earlier that the Jews attempted to justify jettisoning the Torah by claiming there was no longer a special connection with God. The Talmud records them saying, "No relationship, no obligation." By this they meant "No relationship, no relevance to Torah," no purpose to communication.[27]

---

24. Man is an upside-down tree, with his roots in God (See Maharal, *Gur Aryeh, Bereshit* 9:21). Man came into being when the *neshama*, the *tzelem Elokim*, was invested in him. At that moment he awoke to self-consciousness and understanding. Adam experienced his deepest self and so was aware that man is an extension and expression of God. But we have the free will to act and to understand ourselves and the world in ways that structure our awareness differently. We can focus on aspects of our personality that block our actualization of God and our consciousness of Him as the root of our being. Torah is our guide to centering ourselves in the aspects that do actualize our connection to God and, potentially, make us aware of Him.
25. *Shulḥan Arukh, Oraḥ Ḥayim* 47:7.
26. Ex. 24:7.
27. By contrast Jacob, when the apparent death of Joseph gave him the impression that his relationship with God was over, continued to practice Torah as before. This is because Jacob's spiritual insight allowed him to see that the aspect of his humanity that connects to God is his deepest and essential self. Whether or not God reciprocated, this was who he was.

## RELATIONSHIP YES, BUT WHERE WAS THE TORAH?

By learning to recognize the miracles that saved us in Persia, we saw that our unique relationship with God still continued. But what of the actual Torah, our ongoing communication with Him? Our post-exile sense that the lines of communication had been cut was not based solely on our assumption that God no longer wanted us. There was also the fact that prophecy, the mainstay of Torah until that time, had disappeared.

Prophecy was a phenomenon of the land of Israel.[28] Exile brought a virtual end to the prophetic Torah we knew – that is, to God's direct conversation with us.[29] Though the prophet Ezekiel extended prophecy into the early years of the exile, he was the exception that proved the rule.[30] Daniel had visions of what would be in the distant future throughout his tenure in Babylon and Persia, but he was not a prophet.[31] He only saw the future through inspiration and did not merge his understanding with the Divine in the manner of prophecy. He did not chastise us and tell us what to do, as the prophets had always done, so he was not acting as a conduit for God's half of a conversation. A frightening silence had fallen over the relationship. Even with the Megilla showing us we were still together, where was the actual communication?

---

28. Moed Katan 25a; *Sifrei, Shoftim* 32.
29. Bava Batra 12b: "From the day the (First) Temple was destroyed prophecy was taken from the prophets...."
30. In Moed Katan 25a Rav Ḥisda explains that Ezekiel had prophecy outside of the land of Israel only because his prophecy began in the land of Israel. Midrashic sources cite different opinions among the *Tanna'im* on this point.
31. Megilla 3a.

*Chapter 4*

# Oral Torah in a Changed Environment

The events recorded in the book of Esther revealed that God was still involved in our national life. The Megilla taught us the skills of detecting hidden miracles, returning our awareness of God's ongoing commitment to us despite its more subtle expression. But if we have relationship with God there must be Torah, which is its medium. Where was the Torah? Prophecy was basically over.

The book of Esther also returned Torah to the Jewish people. By accepting the authority of the Sages to command us to read the Megilla annually, we recognized that they had replaced the prophets as the conduits of the divine will, inaugurating a new era of Torah.

In this new environment it was the Oral Torah that came to the fore. The Oral Torah was originally given prophetically on Mount Sinai along with the Torah that was to be written down. The Written Torah contained the actual commandments while the Oral Torah supplemented it with the details relating to the specific practice of the commandments. Along with the original received tradition of the Oral Torah came the responsibility for analyzing existing halakhot and past prophecies to ferret out the will of God implicit in them.[1] But as long as there was ongoing prophecy this was just an adjunct to an essentially prophetic connection. With the fading of prophecy, however, we could longer get God's side of the conversation directly from Him.

Application of the analytical methods of the Sages expanded to fill the vacuum, becoming the means for determining what God wanted from us. Because this rabbinic-centered Oral Torah was achieved through active derivation in contrast to the passivity of received prophecy, it paralleled the change in our relationship with miracles. Just as we became responsible for discovering God's hidden miracles, we became responsible for deducing His half of our conversation with the Divine.

This was not a mere adjustment in our relationship with God. The Talmud sees in our acceptance of the decree to read the Megilla a comprehensive renewal of our covenant of Torah on a level comparable to our original acceptance of Torah at Sinai![2] By recognizing the authority of the rabbis to obligate us, we implicitly recognized the legitimacy of the entire Torah, for Torah is the sole basis of rabbinic authority.[3]

But we implicitly acknowledge the authority of Torah every time we do a mitzva, and we acknowledge the authority of the Sages every time we accept one of their rulings. What was different here?

By elevating the significance of this acceptance, the Talmud was not telling us about *its* uniqueness. Rather, it was indicating the uniqueness of the context in which it took place – that there was a need for a new covenant. The appearance of this need at this time showed that the effects of exile had nullified our original acceptance of Torah. We must understand this change, as it will help us appreciate the depth of the new challenges facing our *emuna*. To do so it will be helpful to look at what the Sages actually said about this new covenant.

---

1. Temura 16a.
2. Shabbat 88a.
3. Deut. 17:11. See Berakhot 19b and Rambam, *Hilkhot Mamrim* 1:2.

## RENEWING THE COVENANT

"And they stood *in* the bottom of the mountain [Mount Sinai at the giving of the Torah]."[4] Rav Avdimi son of Ḥama son of Ḥasa said, "This teaches us that God inverted the mountain over their heads like a barrel and said to them, 'If you accept the Torah – good! But if you do not, there will be your burial.'" Rav Aḥa son of Yaakov said, "This gives the Jews a claim against the Torah." Rava said, "Even so, they returned and accepted it voluntarily in the time of Ahasuerus. We see this from the verse [in the book of Esther] 'the Jews upheld and accepted…,'[5] which implies they upheld that which they had accepted at a previous time."[6]

In this passage the Talmud tells us that when God offered the Jews the Torah on Mount Sinai He held a mountain over their heads, threatening them if they did not accept. The Sages compare the acceptance of Torah at Sinai to a wedding.[7] So it *seems* they want us to view that original acceptance as a bride being forced to accept her groom's offer of marriage – think of a groom proposing, then pulling out a revolver before his bride can answer and suggesting it would be a very good idea if she said yes. Even though we did say yes, we had "a claim against the Torah." This claim lasted until it was remedied by the Jews' voluntary acceptance of Torah after the events of Purim.

This interpretation of the passage is not viable. The comparison to a groom's revolver would not create a mere "claim" against the Torah; it would completely invalidate the Jews' acceptance and all its contingent responsibilities. It would imply that the Jews had no accountability to the Torah for the first thousand years of our history. Among other things, this would deny God the authority to punish us with the Babylonian and Persian exiles, since those exiles preceded the rededication at Purim.[8]

---

4. Ex. 19:17.
5. Est. 9:27.
6. Shabbat 88a.
7. For example, Mishna Taanit 4:8 according to many commentaries.
8. The approach to this aggada which I am developing is based on a lecture heard from Rav Moshe Shapiro.

*Part 1: Gateway to the Exodus*

The key to understanding this passage is the specific manner in which the compulsion at Sinai is described – "God inverted the mountain over their heads like a barrel." The idea of a "mountain over their heads" means that the weight of existence pressed upon them, necessitating their acceptance. They were shown with absolute clarity that the Torah is true and that it is the basis of reality.[9] They were not threatened with being physically killed. Rather, they realized that if they did not accept it they would be cut off from life – that is, their life would not be a life.

This explains the otherwise strange image of an inverted *barrel*. Barrels are hollow, so they are not used to crush things. The Talmud implies that if they did not accept the Torah they would be encased as in a barrel, trapped in an enclosed space cut off from the fullness of reality. This also explains the language "there will be your burial" instead of the expected "there you will die." They were threatened with living out their lives in the equivalent of a grave – that as, in a manner comparable to being dead.

Why is the specific nature of the compulsion so important? Had they been coerced with the equivalent of a revolver, it would mean that the free will of the Jews was relevant to the matter, but was artificially excluded. This would invalidate their "decision" because the defining component of self, their free will, would not have been party to the acceptance.

Actualizing free will in a decision, however, requires two conditions: the capacity to choose and the genuine existence of a choice – that is, of viable options. Absolute clarity about the truth of Torah removed this second condition; refusing the Torah was revealed to be the equivalent of death. It was not that our free will was excluded from this decision, but that there simply was nothing to decide. All components of our personality that existed in relation to this decision were present in the decision; there was nothing missing. Therefore it was binding.

If we want to compare Sinai to a wedding, instead of a revolver the proper metaphor would have the heavens opening above the *ḥuppa* (wedding canopy) and our bride hearing the voice of God say, "He is the

---

9. See *Midrash Tanḥuma,* Gen. 1.

right one for you, your one and only." Though she would feel *compelled* to accept the groom's proposal, we would not question the validity of the marriage because of it.

But such an acceptance of Torah could only be binding so long as the Jews had continued clarity about the truth of Torah and the necessity of upholding it, so that the exercise of choice continued to be irrelevant to their connection to Torah. Once that clarity was lost, the need for an active choice was introduced, and they then had to accept Torah out of their own volition in order for it to obligate them.

Clarity about the necessity of the Torah faded when the Jews went into exile, so only then did they need to reaccept the Torah. This was done when the Jews in Persia accepted the rabbinic decree to read the Megilla on Purim.

This adds to the losses of prophecy and obvious miracles that characterized these times the loss of a sense for the absolute truth of Torah. To fully appreciate the need for a new covenant of Torah and the challenges exile brought to our *emuna* we need to understand more deeply what these losses really mean.

## OUR FADING AWARENESS OF GOD

When we arrived in Persia we had nearly a thousand years of prophetic experience behind us. Though we have records of only fifty-five men and women who prophesied, this is because they were the ones who gave messages relevant for all generations. But prophets were actually common.[10] Prophecy, then, was not an occasional event in a generation. Rather, direct communication with God was an ongoing aspect of everyday experience for at least a portion of the Jewish people, making it a continuous part on our national relationship with God.

Prophecy requires a societal context of heightened awareness of God.[11] Pervasive prophecy among the Jewish people before the exile meant that this heightened awareness permeated the nation.[12] The cessation of prophecy then, rather than an isolated loss for specific

---
10. Megilla 14a.
11. See the commentary of the Vilna Gaon on *Seder Olam* 30.
12. Berakhot 32a.

*Part 1: Gateway to the Exodus*

individuals, was indicative of a compromise of our national spiritual depth. It showed itself in the passing of our clear awareness of existence as emanating from God. It became possible to view the world as a detached and empty physical reality.

Since Torah is a guide to understanding the world and self in the context of relationship with God, this was identical with losing clarity of the truth of Torah. When it became possible to relate to reality as physically based, it became possible to reject Torah. This does not mean that we began reaching for idolatrous alternatives – this was a loss of our instinct for spirituality of any sort. We no longer sensed any divine relationship defining our world. At least the inner *compulsion* to understand reality as creation and interpret life as an opportunity to serve was lost. Torah was no longer essential; it had become one possible option.

This obviously intensified all the *emuna* challenges we were facing. When we were aware of the divine as an integral part of our experience, we might question the "Who" and the "how" of it, but the fact of that presence and the need to relate to it was a given. This faded with the onset of exile. And it did not return when we came back to the land after the exile. Though there was prophecy after the return, it was only to a few individuals for a very limited time.[13]

In the thirty-fourth year of the Second Temple, the last prophets died, and the human capacity for prophecy became a rapidly fading memory.[14] The general thinning of spiritual sensitivity that came with exile had become a permanent feature of human awareness. But as we will see in the next chapter, this decline was only the beginning.

---

13. The last prophets were Haggai, Zechariah, Malachi, and Ezra. See also the Vilna Gaon's statement, in his commentary on *Seder Olam* 30, that prophecy ended with the ascendancy of Alexander the Great in the early years of the Second Temple.
14. *Seder Olam Zuta*, chapter 7.

*Chapter 5*

# Assault on the Miraculous

The book of Esther taught us to discern God's now hidden hand and inaugurated the Sages as the new arbiters of Torah, reconstituting our relationship with God. But the decline in spiritual awareness that forced these changes was just a harbinger of what was to come. Greece, the first Western society to define civilization, soon replaced Persia as the masters of the empire. Because Greece presented a new kind of challenge to our *emuna* we will need to go more deeply into its culture to understand it. We will start with an overview of what made Greece different and then go into more detail.

The exile to Babylon and Persia saw us replace the spiritual intimacy of the First Temple with a more aloof and subtle relationship with God. But though by the end of our time in Persia we no longer compellingly experienced our world as a creation, at least the sense of Divinity involved with the world continued to characterize our cultural context.

Under Greece, however, man's defining engagement with the external world shifted from the immediacy of physical experience to detached, abstract understanding. By channeling reality through our rational faculty, we lost the sense of awe and wonder that are the core of

*Part 1: Gateway to the Exodus*

spiritual experience.[1] Though intellectual proofs pushed the Greek philosophers to recognize that there must be an Entity that drives existence, the concept of God that emerged from their abstract rational frame was, not surprisingly, purely abstract.[2] This was a lifeless Divinity that just *was*, oblivious to the particulars of physical existence and incapable of reciprocal relationship.

This view put our vision of God and His involved relationship with the world under extreme pressure. It intensified the challenge of preserving the third pillar of *emuna* – communication based on our special relationship with God. In the Persian exile this relationship was obscured and only needed to be found. In the Greek world we now occupied, the very concept of that relationship was deemed impossible.

But the Greek outlook also opened a new front against *emuna*. It undermined the second pillar of our belief: that God performs miracles. In Persia the Jews did not question God's *ability* to do miracles; we merely lost sight of Him actually performing them for us. But Greek philosophy's view of God as an abstract Entity precluded Him from any purposeful intervention in history whatsoever. According to the Greeks, miracles simply could not happen.

---

1. On awe and wonder as the basis of religious experience, see Shabbat 31a; Rudolf Otto, *The Idea of the Holy: An Inquiry into the Non-Rational Factor in the Idea of the Divine and Its Relation to the Rational* (Oxford: Oxford University Press, 1958), 1–7. On rational processing as an obstacle to this, see Ernst Cassirer, *Language and Myth* (New York: Dover Publications, 1953), 32–33. Though in Torah we wed the two, this comes through a process of alternating from one to other as we go through level after level of experience and understanding: rational analysis leads to awe leads to rational analysis, etc.
2. There were two primary strains to Greek thought: the irrational/mystical epitomized by Pythagoras and his followers, and the rational that reached its ultimate expression in Aristotle (Cornford, *From Religion to Philosophy*, vi). In this book we will only be dealing with the rational, which became dominant as Greece spread its empire (Aristotle was Alexander the Great's tutor). And though Plato, who combined both strains, shaped the early development of Christian metaphysics, the rationality of Greece profoundly influenced civilization and continues to profoundly influence it, challenging our *emuna* all the while.

## Assault on the Miraculous

But it was not just that the Greeks brought a new aspect of our *emuna* under challenge. More important, they challenged it in a new way. Our exiles to Babylon and Persia were a consequence of succumbing to the weakening of our spiritual experience. We had our externally anchored physical experience; we had our internally anchored spiritual experience. Over time, as was true for humanity generally, the intensity of our spiritual awareness diminished. But as long as the spiritual aspect continued to dominate, we interpreted our physical experience in a spiritual context. As that domination ebbed, however, the physical dimension began to influence our overall understanding of reality more and more.

For example, the idolatry that destroyed the first Temple was a consequence of spirituality tinged by physical experience, with the transcendent Source of existence confused with a more tangible deity. When the punishment of exile snapped us out of our illusions, idolatry lost its attractiveness.[3] We saw it as compromised spirituality stemming from a weakness of spirit, so we were confident in the superiority of Torah. For this reason we do not find that there were any mass conversions to idolatry in Babylon or Persia.

Similarly, the inability to perceive miracles came from experiencing reality from a more physical perspective. We lacked the strength to engage and apply our deeper spiritual awareness. If we experienced a natural world, then that was what we experienced. But we understood it to be coming from our own shortcomings; it was nothing to be proud of. The increasing emptiness of the world we lived in was a source of national embarrassment.

Greek culture, however, did not view the experience of a natural world as an inadequate form of spirituality. Rather, it was the projection of an alternate, intellectual interpretation of the nature of internal experience – one that claimed to be truer and more noble than the spirituality of Torah. The Greek worldview framed *Torah* as the perspective born of weakness – a weakness to accept a colder but true reality. This challenged us with a doubt that was new for us.

---

3. For an example of how punishment does this, see the reaction of the Jews to the decree of exile after the sin of the spies in Num. 14:34–40.

## Part 1: Gateway to the Exodus

In other words, when we were in Babylon and Persia we understood that we could do better than the culture our hosts displayed – that with Torah we could reach a higher and purer engagement of reality if we had the strength. The Babylonians and Persians would claim events showed that their gods were in ascendance, but there was nothing absurd about the Jewish position.

The Greek worldview, however, suggested that rather than reaching higher, Torah was reaching for straws. Our experience of physical reality as purely natural, rather than coming from weakness, was now understood to support the Greek view. In the context of the more spiritually opaque world we occupied, the Greek argument was sufficiently powerful that for the first time we find many Jews adopting the culture of our enemies.

It is imperative that we understand this new Greek reality. Greece transformed our world from a civilization determined by Near Eastern views and ideals to one determined by Western attitudes. As such, it is the root of the culture we find ourselves in today and the pressures we face. To understand Greece – its challenge and how to deal with it – we need to look closely at this new Greek experience and interpretation of human awareness and how it contrasts with Torah.

### A NEW APPROACH TO THE GODS

The vast gulf between Greek/Western culture and that of the East is seen in the differences between their approaches to spirituality and worship. Though the Greeks recognized the existence of gods and mentioned them constantly in their writings, the Greeks showed an easy familiarity with the gods that was new and "disorienting." The Greeks believed the gods to be much closer to humanity in their nature and being than would have been admitted in Egypt, Babylon, or Persia.[4]

In the literature of the Golden Age of Greece the gods were presented like comic-book super heroes (or super-villains). They were completely

---

4. Henri Frankfort, H. A. Frankfort, John A. Wilson, Thorkild Jacobsen, and William A. Irwin, *The Intellectual Adventure of Ancient Man: An Essay of Speculative Thought in the Ancient Near East* (Chicago: The University of Chicago Press, 1977), 374; Jean Bottero, *Religion in Ancient Mesopotamia* (Chicago and London: University of Chicago Press, 2004), 37–39.

## Assault on the Miraculous

interested and involved in the doings of man, differing from their human counterparts only by having some supernatural power. By way of contrast, in Babylon man understood that he was created for the sole purpose of relieving the gods of the necessity of work; it was an absolute master-slave relationship,[5] with service to the gods the basis and purpose of man's existence.

Some sense of the all-encompassing nature of the subservience that Mesopotamians felt toward their gods is conveyed by the fact that they viewed their cities as private estates of gods. Each city belonged to a principal deity, and an enormous percentage of its land and wealth was controlled by the temples.[6] In a sense, then, one's home had a status similar to that of a servant's quarters.

While in the Near East service of the gods was motivated by existential fear, the Greeks, though they accepted the importance of giving the gods their due, did so primarily out of a sense of custom and propriety.[7] Aristotle, who recognized a Supreme Being, took it a step further, denying any efficacy to worship other than its psychological impact on the worshipper.[8] At least one major modern authority on Greece characterized the whole Greek belief in the gods as an unfortunate detour in the overall course of Greek cultural development – a mere "episode."[9] One cannot imagine any expert making a comparable

---

5. See the Bronze Age Babylonian creation epic *Enuma Elish*, Tablet 6. James B. Pritchard ed., *The Ancient Near East: An Anthology of Texts and Pictures* (Princeton: Princeton University Press, 2001), 33.
6. See Thorkild Jacobsen, "Mesopotamia: The Function of the State," in Frankfort et al., *The Intellectual Adventure of Ancient Man*, 185–202.
7. E. R. Dodds, *The Greeks and the Irrational* (Berkeley, Los Angeles, London: University of California Press, 1951), 242–44. See also Plato's dialogue *Timaeus*, where Timaeus says, "All men, Socrates, who have any degree of right feeling, at the beginning of every enterprise, whether small or great, always call upon God." Service to the gods is here seen as something appropriate. The Talmud states that from the time of Greek hegemony onwards (Yoma 69b) the idolatry of the nations was "*minhag avoteihem b'yadeihem*," a tradition of their forefathers rather than a personal passion (Ḥullin 13b). The Romans during the pagan period similarly viewed ritual as a matter of propriety (Dodds, 244).
8. Robert Mayhew, "Aristotle on Prayer," *Rhizai: A Journal for Ancient Philosophy and Science* 2 (2007): 295–309.
9. Cornford, *From Religion to Philosophy*, for example 39–43.

*Part 1: Gateway to the Exodus*

statement about the ancient Near Eastern societies. There, the relationship with the gods was definitive of human experience and purpose.

### REALITY MEDIATED BY THE INTELLECT

By the time Greece achieved empire, a deep respect for and reliance upon rational intellect had emerged as the defining energy of its culture.[10] Plato with his theory of forms identified a specific category of ideas as the only true reality; from Aristotle we inherit the concept of man as the "rational animal."[11] These views represented a shift in the focus of human personality and (with some modifications under Rome) form the basis of the Western cultural ethos.

One consequence of this was the belief among Greek philosophers that the world is fundamentally understandable.[12] Their focus on rational, abstract understanding de-emphasized the messy particulars of physical reality that make events and objects unique to extract concepts and laws that were generally applicable and fully intelligible.[13] Since the only point of interest to the Greeks was that which the intellect understood, they were constantly reaffirmed in their belief that all of existence was comprehensible. That included the gods, which reduced their distance from man.

Academics view the principal achievement of Greek culture as the emancipation of thought from physical experience, which allows man to process reality through unrestricted abstraction, substituting philosophy and science for religious mythology.[14] This does not mean

---

10. Dodds, 238–43.
11. The specific term was not used by Aristotle but is implied in the Nicomachean Ethics 1:13 and in De Anima 3:11. The term comes from medieval scholastic philosophy based on the Aristotelian view that rationality distinguishes man. By way of contrast, no Mesopotamian definition of man would have failed to focus on his obligation to worship.
12. Frankfort, *The Intellectual Adventure of Ancient Man*, 377.
13. Cassirer distinguishes rational/theoretical from mythico/religious thinking: theoretical thinking moves from the particular to abstract categories whereas mythical thinking is based on full engagement with the particularity of the moment. Cassirer, *Language and Myth*, 24–28, 32–33.
14. Frankfort, *The Intellectual Adventure of Ancient Man*, 376–87. There were significant limitations to this breakthrough; the Greek philosophers still carried the baggage of more ancient Greek religious categorizations and understanding in the assumptions

that abstraction was invented by the Greeks. Abstraction was something humanity achieved early on and over time it became a growing aspect of human awareness. But the Greeks took their involvement and reliance on it to an unprecedented level, rejecting the relevance of the particulars of physical existence to understanding reality.[15]

Their reliance on intellect ushered in the Greek confusion of reality-as-man-understood-it with reality itself. Aristotle, representing fully developed Greek intellectualism, "denied the existence of anything other than what he could perceive, and…thought that any matter that he could not reach through his own logic was not true."[16]

Torah, on the other hand, sees the depth of existence in the marriage of the abstract with specific material reality. We praise God for "doing wonders" when He combines the soul with the body.[17] That is to say, the combining of spiritual with physical is greater than either spiritual or physical reality alone and is "wondrous"; it is beyond our comprehension and we celebrate this incomprehensibility.

In Western thought the integration of spiritual and physical, rather than defining reality, presents an inscrutable mystery that challenges the Greek vision of a comprehensible universe. The modern version of this difficulty is called the mind/body problem. Two and a half thousand years of philosophy and five hundred years of science have been unable to adequately answer how consciousness with its freedom

---

that formed the basis of their perception of the world (in the language of Durkheim, their "collective representations"). Still, their approach was speculative and led over time to increasing awareness of those assumptions and a tendency to attack them. See Cornford, *From Religion to Philosophy*, 40–46.

15. Frankfort accepts that the first major cultural advance toward abstraction was made by "the Hebrews" with their vision of the transcendent God. But, in his view, it was not taken far enough. Complete abstraction awaited the arrival of Greece. See *The Intellectual Adventure of Ancient Man*, 373.

16. See Ramban's commentary on Lev. 16:8. This description of Aristotle's view sounds exaggerated. But it is actually a penetrating understanding of the intellectual position, with Aristotle's confident pronouncement precisely reflected in modern academic attitudes. As we will see soon, the presumption that man understands everything distorts our view of reality; it led Aristotle to deny the possibility of creation. See note 26 for a modern example of this attitude and its resultant distortion.

17. Rabbi Jacob ben Asher, *Oraḥ Ḥayim* 6:1; Rav Yitzhak Hutner, *Paḥad Yitzḥak*, Pesaḥ 15.

connects with causally determined physical reality.[18] Though some consider this *the* question of modern philosophy, few take it to the next step of seeing in our inability to resolve the issue a need to reconsider the whole Greek construct.[19]

Man's intellect is humbled by this synthesis. To bring it to a more immediate level, as challenging as it is to conceive of the soul of man – an abstract, spiritual entity – when we witness the dawning of comprehension in the flesh-and-blood eyes of a two-year-old we are utterly dumbstruck if we consider what we are seeing. The deepest reality we can access, the *tzelem Elokim* (image of God), is encountered through the unfathomable creative uniqueness of individuality, not in the abstract category "man."[20]

This awareness and acceptance of wonder, of what cannot be comprehended, opens the way to the Jewish perception of intellect as a vessel to receive understanding from beyond. It also allows for prophecy, not merely as a vehicle to know the future or hidden facts but, more important, to gain insight that is beyond the grasp and limitations of the human mind. Most importantly, as we will see soon, it leads to worship.

## THE GREEK CONCEPT OF DIVINITY

The exclusive focus on abstraction by the Greeks affected their concept of God. We already mentioned that this focus led them to believe that everything is *truly* comprehensible – that is, in its essence. In fact, they believed that this understanding or idea of the essence of something *is*

---

18. The emphasis in this sentence should be placed on the word "adequately," as the Greek assumption that the world is understandable has led to extreme proposals to answer the difficulty. In the past the preferred path was to deny the reality of physical existence. More recently the direction has been to deny the significance, or even the existence, of consciousness.
19. In *Mind and Cosmos: Why the Materialist Neo-Darwinian Conception of Nature Is Almost Certainly False* (Oxford: Oxford University Press, 2012), Thomas Nagel at least recognizes the significance of this quandary. The next step for him, however, is a complete rethink of our understanding of reality rather than questioning the limits of human understanding.
20. See, for example, Rabbi Meir Simḥa of Dvinsk, *Meshekh Ḥokhma, Bereshit* 1:26, who equates man's free choice (the basis of individuality) with his *tzelem Elokim*.

its true existence.[21] Once reason forced them to recognize a Supreme Being that underlies reality, the necessary next step was to conceive of that Being as the ultimate, rational, thinking Being Who upholds existence by thinking the understandings and ideas that compose the essence of all that exists.[22]

But since man can comprehend the world also, this implies that the philosopher can think the thoughts that "the One" thinks in His capacity as upholder of existence. Greek rationality, then, led the Greeks to assume that man can emulate God on the most essential level![23]

Greece connected man to God by raising man up and accentuating one of man's most elevated capabilities, his intellect. But at the same time, this connection diminished the greatness of God. If "the One" upholds the world through His comprehension of it and we can also comprehend it, then despite all the greatness the Greeks ascribed to "the One," they regarded Him as effectively bound by the limitations of human understanding, contained in a reality determined by human logic.

One ramification of this can be seen in Aristotle's rejection of the idea that existence has a beginning – creation *ex nihilo*. Because creation was not logical *to him*, he held that physical existence *must* be eternal.[24] God *could not* have created existence through a specific act because it did not make sense to Aristotle, who understood himself to be the arbiter of human understanding (and many agreed).[25] God was therefore limited

---

21. As mentioned earlier, this is the centerpiece of Plato's theory of forms.
22. There is extensive scholarly debate when the Forms came to be understood as the thoughts of God. The concept is brought in Philo, but its origins are in an earlier generation of Neoplatonists. See "The Ideas as Thoughts of God," Jon Dillon, *Etudes Platoniciennes* 8 (2011): 31–42.
23. "For Zeno, man's intellect was not merely akin to God, it *was* God, a portion of the divine substance in its pure or active state" (Dodds, 238).
24. Rambam summarizes Aristotle's position in *Moreh Nevukhim* II:13. Rav Kapach in his edition of *Moreh Nevukhim* in that chapter footnote 13 points out that Rambam attributes the summary to Aristotle "and his students," implying that Aristotle's position is not fully explicated in his own writings. The entirety of *Physics* Book 8 is concerned with the eternity of the universe.
25. Rambam refers to Aristotle as "the head of the philosophers" (*Moreh Nevukhim* I:5) and much of *Moreh Nevukhim* cites his opinions, with Rambam often agreeing with them. Much of medieval philosophy, both European and Islamic, builds on or reacts to Aristotle.

*Part 1: Gateway to the Exodus*

by man's logical understanding.[26] God's transcendence, then, was merely an extension from this world and wholly contained in it.

## THE IMPOSSIBILITY OF MIRACLES

The cultural context established by Greece exerted great pressure to diminish the greatness of God in the minds of the Jews. In a sense, our faith was pulled toward the wrong God, or at least the wrong concept of God. But not only did the Greek conception of "the One" provide a false alternative vision of God, it also denied the existence of the path to discover the true Creator.

As we determined earlier, true appreciation of the greatness of the Creator must grow from understanding the miracles of the Exodus. Once exile began and open miracles ceased, we needed to connect to the miracles of the Exodus by developing the skill to recognize hidden miracles. But Greece's intellectual concept of God threw a tremendous obstacle in the path of that project. The more advanced form of this intellectual vision developed by Aristotle denied the possibility of miracles altogether, whether revealed or hidden. We already mentioned that the

---

26. The Greek conviction that reality is fully comprehensible to man remains a major influence on modern thinking. A current example of the severe distortions this introduces into our view of reality is modern philosophy's response to the mind/body problem we mentioned earlier. We are still unable to adequately explain how non-physical consciousness with its freedom syncs with physical reality, which we understand to be bound by physical causation. Since we believe that we can understand everything, anything that cannot be understood must be wrong. This has led to the now widely held position that all of reality is physical, thus eliminating the problem. In the extreme case philosophers deny the genuine existence of first-person-experience consciousness! For example, Daniel Dennett, a highly decorated Professor of Philosophy at Tufts and author of *Consciousness Explained*. describes himself as a "teleofunctionalist," which is a belief that the reality of mental states lies *entirely in their functional role!* The assumption that "we can know everything" also easily morphs into "we must already know everything" or "we must already be on the direct path to knowing everything." This attitude results in overblown confidence in present scientific theories (see Simon Conway Morris, *Life's Solution: Inevitable Humans in a Lonely Universe* [Cambridge: Cambridge University Press, 2008], 314–26), and contributes to the halting character of scientific advance observed in Thomas Kuhn's *Structure of Scientific Revolutions,* 3$^{rd}$ ed. (Chicago : The University of Chicago Press, 1996), 62–65, 126–35.

Greek conception of God as an abstract entity meant He was removed from and oblivious to the changing specifics of physical reality and history. This implied miraculous intervention was impossible.

Furthermore, God is perfect. Human rationality understands this to imply that He cannot change, which among other things means that He cannot change His course or the manner of His expression into the world at all, let alone in response to human action or petition. This precludes miraculous intervention in history. Furthermore God's perfection means, according to human reason, that His creation must also be perfect and therefore does not need alterations or interventions.[27] These arguments were the basis of Aristotle's attack on the concept of creation *ex nihilo* that we mentioned earlier.[28]

During the Babylonian/Persian exile God's miracles became hidden. But the possibility of miracles was an integral part of the Near Eastern outlook, so they merely needed to be found. Under Greece there seemed no point in searching for them, because they could not exist! This distinction allows us to understand why after the Hanukka rebellion the skills taught by the book of Esther were not enough to guide us to recognize the military victories against the Greeks as hidden miracles. Because of Greek cultural influences we needed the added force of the obvious miracle of the Menora's flames to establish that miracles were occurring.[29]

## LOSING THE NEED TO WORSHIP

But the denial of the possibility of miracles was only part of the problem. Under Greek rule not only did it seem pointless to try to search for them, we also felt no compelling *need* to look. For Greece undermined the general human impulse for relationship with God.

---

27. See chapter 1, note 34. Rambam states that the Sages reasoned that all "miracles" were built into the natural order from the beginning of creation (*Perush HaMishnayot Avot* 5:6; see, for instance, Genesis Rabba 5:5) and attributes their position to a reaction to this Greek idea (*Moreh Nevukhim* II:29). Whether or not this was Rambam's final position on the matter is debated among the commentaries. See also Rabbi Yosef Yehudah Leib Bloch, *Shiurei Daat I, Nisim veTeva*, 108–38.
28. See note 24.
29. See chapter 2.

*Part 1: Gateway to the Exodus*

Greek dedication to abstract understanding freed the mind from the limitations imposed by the particularity of specific experience. They focused on formulating generally applicable categories of understanding and identifying universally active forces. Intellect achieved tremendous penetration, and the possibility of controlling physical reality expanded.

But this came at a price: reality was mediated through understanding rather than being encountered in the immediacy of experience. It is immediacy that is the basis of spiritual awareness and the need for worship. To be spiritually aware is to be overwhelmed by the specific event rather than abstracting it into just one more case of a general idea; that is, to be nullified before that which is outside the self rather than defining, containing, and controlling it through the abstract categories of understanding.[30] It was the immediacy experienced by ancient Near Eastern peoples that fostered their civilizations of awestruck worship.

Granted, this immediacy had limitations. The inability to disengage awareness and understanding from physical immediacy led to an identification of spiritual power with the specific forces and objects through which they were encountered. This led to polytheism and idolatry. These were only overcome when Abraham achieved abstraction and applied it to the immediacy of Near Eastern awareness. This combination of abstraction with immediacy allowed him to soar above idolatry and reach the unitary transcendent Creator.[31]

The Greeks, however, adopted abstraction wholesale, denying any significance to immediacy. They denuded reality of any spiritual strength by exclusively identifying the truth of awareness with the unfolding of abstract ideas, which is something wholly contained within and controlled by man. Though the philosophers could prove the existence of God, He could only be a necessary intellectual construct rather than a

---

30. Cassirer, *Language and Myth*, 23–43. Cassirer is building on Hermann Usener's book on divine names *Gotternamen: Versuch einer Lehre von der religiosen Begriffsbildung* (Divine Names: An Essay Toward a Science of Religious Conceptions). But the classic source that discusses the centrality of awe to religious faith is Rudolf Otto's *The Idea of the Holy*, cited in note 1 of this chapter.
31. This will be explained in chapter 9.

## Assault on the Miraculous

Being whose presence overwhelmed. Our Sages describe this dulling of spiritual sense as a loss of all internal compulsion to worship.[32]

The sense of being overwhelmed captures the essential response of the worshipful self to the external environment. The Greek mindset undercut this sense. But there is also a specific form of self that is a prerequisite for true worship that was lost under Greece. We can derive this from the Hebrew term for worship: *avoda*.

*Avoda* shares its root with the word for slave, *eved*. This implies that worship in the ancient sense, the worship that came to the world from the Near East, involved a dedication of self that was tantamount to the loss of individuality found in enslavement.

However, there is an important difference between slavery and worship. In slavery the individual has lost his self-*expression*. His actions obey the will of his master, but internally he may desire to do something else reflective of being someone else. Worship, however, is something that is not externally compelled. The very *self* is dedicated in that the worshipper does not merely do what he is commanded to do, but also accepts the obligation to find the aspect of self within him that wants to do what he is commanded to do and identify with it.

The individuality of the worshipper still persists in each person's distinctive experience of the numinous – the facets of reality through which he encounters it, the uniqueness of his personality through which he realizes it, and the contribution he finds to make in its service. But some choice and individuality are circumscribed. Today, we perceive our individuality as our most precious possession – it is us. We need

---

32. In Yoma 69b there is a passage beginning with the verse "And they cried to the Lord their God with a great voice" (Neh. 9:4) and continuing: "What did they cry? 'Oi, oi (the evil inclination to worship idols) that destroyed the Temple and burned the hall and killed all the righteous and exiled Israel from their land, it still dances among us. It was only given to us to earn reward. We don't need it and we don't need its reward.' A tablet fell from the heavens upon which was written, 'True.' ...They sat in fasting three days and three nights, and (the evil inclination) was handed over to them. There went out from the Holy of Holies a lion-cub of fire. The prophet said to Israel, 'That is the inclination to worship idols.'" An evil inclination is a corruption of a positive energy. The inclination to worship idols is a corruption of the inclination to worship. The elimination of the inclination to worship idols can only be accomplished through the elimination of the inclination to worship. See the appendix and *The Choice to Be*, 257–59.

to invest real effort to see spiritual greatness in surrendering any aspect of this individuality; to us the surrender seems at first like a shirking of personal responsibility or suicide of identity. Only after contemplation do we realize the goal is a superseding of self rather than a relinquishing of it. But this is a subtle distinction that is hard for us to imagine any but the rarest of individuals achieving with genuine integrity. Yet in the ancient Near East *avoda* was universally practiced!

We can only understand this by presuming that the experience of selfhood in the ancient world was radically different from our experience today. What sort of internal environment could explain the universality of this kind of worship? Only a sense of self that is *found* in this dedication rather than sacrificed. That would be an awareness of self as a tributary of some transcendent river or a branch of a great tree. Existence was experienced as emanating from a higher source; and that source was the center of our aliveness and more significant to us than our individual being, more me than I am. The independence of self we so value today would have seemed to the ancients as tantamount to a person damming up his source river or cutting his branch from its tree – that is, like death.

This sense of my being emerging from somewhere or someone outside myself is the pre-Western form of self, which in seeing its reflection in the world, perceives the world as created and has the potential for prophecy. We have as much difficulty imagining this form of self as the ancients would have had imagining the (for them) bizarre form of autonomous awareness that characterizes our inner experience.

This ancient self faded as we became increasingly centered in our intellect. For the intellect understands and therefore determines its world. This makes intellect the basis of the world it perceives, centering us in our autonomous identity independent of any higher source. The replacement of the earlier experience of self with one more ego-based came, then, with the loss of the immediacy of our engagement with the world. Together, these changes eliminated our compulsion to worship.

As previously noted, Greek culture was not exclusively responsible for this transformation. The Greeks certainly accelerated this shift in humanity by creating an entire culture around human reason. But intellect was part of man's consciousness from early on in the development of culture and, with time, increasingly dominated understanding. So the changes we are describing were a civilization-wide phenomenon, part of a larger process in motion long before the arrival of Greece.

This was seen in a slow deterioration of the vitality of Near Eastern worship stretching back nearly a millennium before Greek hegemony. Over that period an increasing brutalization of the relationship with the gods was clearly evident.[33] Our loss of prophecy and intuitive spiritual awareness should also be viewed in this larger context – not the brutalization but the weakening of spirituality at its core – as we were an integral part of this Near Eastern world. Though our losses came toward the end of this process, they had a history that parallels the timing of this general weakening of spirituality.

Our connection to God had also been weakening continually for a millennium, beginning with the transition of leadership from Moses to Joshua[34] and continuing with the demand of the Jewish people to replace the prophet with a king as their principal intermediary to God,[35] the increasing simplification of Torah beginning with King David and stretching through the prophetic period,[36] and the rise of idolatry among the Jews.

Still, a clear watershed was passed when intellect came to define rather than enhance man's engagement of reality, undercutting our basic compulsion to worship.[37] This coincided with the return of the Jews to their land, the building of the Second Temple, the end of prophecy, and the transition of civilization from Persia to Greece.

When Alexander swept the Persian Empire away and remade civilization in the image of the West, only the Jews with their Torah and its purified monotheism survived culturally to carry forward the kernel of the Near Eastern vision of man as essentially a worshipper. But the Jews would be hard-pressed to develop their vision of humanity with genuine vitality while planted in the spiritually barren soil of a Greek cultural context – especially since we also were subject to the increasing

---

33. Jacobsen, *The Treasures of Darkness*, 223, 226–32.
34. Baba Batra 75a: "The face of Moses was like that of the sun, the face of Joshua was like of the moon."
35. I Sam. 12.
36. Makkot 24a.
37. Yoma 69b. See note 30.

ego-focus now characterizing human experience. If Persia had forced adjustments to our relationship with God, all the more so the advent of Greek hegemony required the harnessing of new resources.

The event in which our conflict with Greece came to its fullest expression was the war commemorated by Hanukka. The decree we have from the Sages to light the Hanukka candles, then, represents the discovery and application of those resources.[38] We must now try to understand the significance of those flames.

---

38. The requirement to sing Hallel is not a decree specific to Hanukka. Rather, it is the application of a pre-existing halakhic principle to sing the praises of God when we experience a miraculous, national salvation.

*Chapter 6*

# Breaking Through the Bubble

The Greek conquest of the land of Israel brought the Jews under the rule of Alexander the Great. His approach to governance was to respect local customs. Therefore the Greeks at first were respectful of the Jews and their Torah; aggressive Hellenization would only be attempted much later. But influence from the new overlords was inevitable. They brought with them their practices, attitudes, and values, all of which reflected their intellectually based engagement with reality. This had the effect of drawing our internal center closer to our intellect. Human personality was already moving in that direction – a contributing factor to the success of Greece. But our direct exposure to the Greeks accelerated the process for us.

As we discussed in the previous chapters, man's continuing shift toward an intellectual and ego-centered experience of reality had already silenced prophecy. While still in Persia we countered by adopting the Oral Torah, the discipline of analyzing prophecies of the past in order to recover our conversation with God. But the arrival of Greece made it obvious that our embrace of the Oral Torah was not only a response to Persian circumstances; it was also a case of *makdim refua lemakka*, God giving us the cure for a disease that was about to strike. When the Greeks came and pulled us even more into our intellect, we had already learned to harness it in the service of the Creator instead of following the Greek philosophers who used it to usurp God's role of determining reality.

**AN INCOMPLETE SOLUTION**

Though the Oral Torah addressed this central challenge posed by Greece, it was not a complete solution. We already mentioned in the last chapter that there are intrinsic problems with processing reality through the intellect. It alters both our perception of and relationship with God. Unrestrained, intellect perceives God as a detached and static thinking Being constrained by rationality. So our increasing focus on our intellect put pressure on our recognition of the limitless, transcendent God that brought us out of Egypt. And the intellectual engagement with reality filtered out consciousness of what we cannot know, undermining our sense of awe – the foundation of worship. This inclined us toward more of an awareness of God in place of real relationship, dependence, and service.

But our intellectual focus also created problems for Torah itself. Though the Oral Torah allowed us to channel intellect into our relationship with God, Torah and intellect are not easy bedfellows. Intellect, if we direct it at the world in place of at God, has the potential to make us masters of our world in the manner of the Greeks. Therefore its use always carries with it the temptation to turn away from God.

Furthermore, even when applying intellect to Torah with its prophetic foundation, the whole nature of intellect is to understand independently. So intellect was structurally in some conflict with the received prophecy it was analyzing, tending to distort its conclusions toward a vision of reality as known from our perspective and determined by us – that is, Greek style.

The intrinsic independence of intellect also tends to foster pride, whether in one's individual ability or in humanity's capacity for understanding. Pride reinforces all these distorting tendencies of intellect. For the Oral Torah is distinct from philosophy and theology (that is, from a human perspective) because it is informed by divine inspiration. This requires genuine humility, with understanding taking the role of a supplicant seeking gifts of higher perception. The experience of pride, however, accentuates the "from myself" aspect of understanding, blocking the "from God" aspect. Torah from myself may resemble Torah, but it is actually a shallow façade that is disconnected from its ineffable essence and infinite Source.

By analogy think of looking at a face. If I restrict myself to observing what I can actively see with my eyes, my slow perusal of the face reveals something aesthetically beautiful. But if I accept it as a window on the human soul and open myself to a different level of experience – one that I cannot control – I become aware of something extraordinary. I do not merely see the face; rather, through it I engage something much deeper. A corpse can be beautiful, but it is not attractive. It cannot grab me the way the life sparkling in the eyes of a mischievous three-year-old can.

Torah cannot be contained in a prideful person, because while Torah is infinite, the ego is not. So long as the ego is forcefully present, the clearly demarcated self is too confined a space for the infinite Torah. It can only hold an incomplete piece which, severed from the larger whole, is distorted. The boundaries of the self must dissolve through humility for an individual to attach himself to the boundless Torah.[1] The intellectual basis of the Oral Torah made this humility a constant challenge.

**A NEED TO ACT**

Though the Oral Torah expanded dramatically under the rule of Greece, vulnerabilities began to show as cracks appeared in the tradition. Arguments began to arise in law, showing that we had lost our grasp on the deepest levels of truth, those that come from the realm that unifies all perspectives.[2] More worrying was the emergence of the *Tzedokim* (Sadducees) and *Beitusim*, sects founded by heretical scholars who rejected the concept of reward in the next world in alignment with

---

1. Maharal, "Drush Na'e LeShabbat Hagadol," in *Haggada shel Pesaḥ* (Bnei Brak: "Yahadut," 1980), and "Netiv HaTorah," chapter 2, in *Netivot Olam* I. See also Rabbi Hayim of Volozhin, *Nefesh HaḤayim* 4:5.
2. The first unresolved argument ever to arise in halakha (see Mishna Ḥagiga 2:2) was between Yosi ben Yoezer of Tzreida and Yosi ben Yoḥanan of Jerusalem (Rashi, Ḥagiga 16a). Yosi ben Yoezer was killed by the Greeks (Genesis Rabba 65:22).

*Part 1: Gateway to the Exodus*

Aristotelian ideas.³ We needed a counterweight to keep our intellect in check and protect us from its forceful tendencies.

But as Greek domination wore on, intellect's influence only strengthened. The Jewish people were falling further and further away from the Creator. We needed to forcefully repudiate the independence of the human mind on a national scale. But our cultural environment was only making that more and more difficult.

As occurred in Persia, matters came to a head, forcing the issue. Antiochus IV, ruler of the Seleucid state which was one of the successors to Alexander's empire, made an aggressive and violent effort to Hellenize the Jews, spurred on by Jewish Hellenists.⁴ Rebellion ensued, and God led us to miraculous victories. We were saved once again, and the Sages created the festival of Hanukka to mark the event.

Torah holidays are never mere commemorations. Each one fortifies a distinct and essential facet of our relationship with God. The mitzvot of each holiday actualize the aspect of our personality through which we build the associated facet. The fact that the Sages instituted a new festival indicates that we merited salvation from the Greeks by using some previously untapped capability.

Since we had managed for over a thousand years of history without Hanukka, this new capability was presumably one that became essential only as a result of the rise of Greece. The festival was established to allow us to annually revitalize that strength. This was necessary because just as it allowed us to defend ourselves from the first Greek onslaught, we need it to defend against the continuing pressure of Greek cultural influence. What is this capability and how do the Hanukka candles bring it out?

**FACING THE IMPOSSIBLE**

When Alexander first swept through Israel, Greece was the foremost military power on earth. By the time the Jews rebelled, Rome was already on

---

3. Contemporaries of Yosi ben Yoezer and Yosi ben Yochanan, mentioned in note 2. They were all students of Antigonos of Sokho.
4. Hersh Goldwurm and Meir Holder, *History of the Jews: The Second Temple Era* (New York: Mesorah Publications, 1986), 59–66. See also Flavius Josephus, *The Wars of the Jews* 1:1.

# Breaking Through the Bubble

the rise and the Greek empire was divided. Still, each individual Greek kingdom was a formidable military power in its own right. The Seleucid kings, who then controlled Israel, could quickly raise seasoned and well-equipped professional armies numbering in the tens of thousands. The Jews, on the other hand, had lacked sovereignty for centuries and possessed no trained fighting force. When Antiochus IV tried to Hellenize his subjects, the Jews faced imminent cultural extinction. But they were defenseless; revolt appeared suicidal.

It was under these circumstances that the high priest Mattityahu and his sons were moved to act.[5] There followed a series of miraculous victories on the battlefield that pushed the Greeks from Israel, saving the unique Jewish relationship with God. Yet the Sages focus our attention on the minor miracle that occurred with the Menora at the rededication of the Temple. The commentaries explain that we focus on the Menora because it was indisputably miraculous. Recognizing miracles on the battlefield is tricky, and the Sages wanted to ensure that there would be no doubt that the hand of God was driving events.[6]

In this, Hanukka appears as a variation on the theme of Purim – that we need to recognize God's involvement in events occurring within the confines of nature. The miracle of the Menora takes the place of the Megilla's guidance for directing our understanding of events. Apparently the Megilla was not sufficient because the challenge of recognizing hidden miracles under Greece was more difficult than when we were under Persian dominion. More than guidance was needed; we had to see some obvious break in nature.

## A NEW LIGHT

Since we had passed the era of open violations of nature, the miracle took place in the inner sanctuary of the Temple, somewhat removed from this world. But when the flames of the Temple Menora burned for eight days on one day's worth of oil, it still gave enough light to reveal the existence of miracles. For those who were paying attention, it utterly

---

5. See the *Megillat Antiochus*.
6. Maharal, *Ner Mitzva*, in *Ner Mitzva/Or Ḥadash* (Bnei Brak: "Yahadut," n.d.), 22. See the earlier discussion of Hanukka in chapter 2.

*Part 1: Gateway to the Exodus*

refuted Greek understanding. In combination with the lessons we could still derive from the book of Esther, it helped us to see our military victory over Greece for what it was and to recover the ability to perceive God's involvement in world affairs generally.

But what do we take from Hanukka for the future that is new? In what way did we go beyond the achievements of Purim? For that matter, what did we accomplish that was of such magnitude that it merited the miracle of the Menora – a violation of nature in a time when such occurrences had already passed from human experience?

On Purim the Jewish people were saved through prayer.[7] One is hard pressed when reading the Megilla to find any initiative taken by the Jews to save themselves. The only effort was Esther's supplication to Ahasuerus, which, according to the Sages, was essentially a disguised prayer to God.[8] In the Purim story God played the role of savior, with our only responsibility to ask, recognize, and appreciate His efforts.

On Hanukka the challenge was very different because the Jews themselves had to act, engaging the Greeks in combat. The Jews needed to recognize the Creator's hand in the achievements of *their* actions – to appreciate on some level that *all* results belong to God. This required a qualitatively different level of clarity about God's total mastery: that there is no source of control in existence other than God[9] – that even our ability to freely choose our actions and goals does not change the fact that all accomplishments are His. This is *yiḥud Hashem*, the deepest level of God's relationship to reality – one that is profoundly difficult to comprehend,[10] and the full revelation of which is the purpose of history.[11] We will discuss *yiḥud Hashem* in more detail in the second half of this book.

This was precisely the insight we needed to overcome the influences of Greece on Torah. We had been forced to channel our Torah relationship with the Creator through the intellect of the Oral Torah.

---

7. Maharal, *Or Ḥadash*, 68.
8. Est. 7:3–6; *Midrash Abba ben Gurion*, chapter 1. See *The Choice to Be*, chapter 20.
9. Ramchal, *Daat Tevunot* 36.
10. Rambam, *Hilkhot Teshuva* 5:5.
11. Ramchal, *Daat Tevunot* 34.

But the pridefulness characteristic of intellectualism pulled at us constantly to view what understandings we achieved as our own, threatening to turn our Torah into philosophy. The battlefield taught us otherwise.

Though combat, with its threat of death, excites *our* greatest effort, we reached clarity that our successes were a gift of God. We then extended this awareness of our dependence to our Torah study. Though we expend effort – even terrific effort – to understand, we do not create the insights that follow.[12] Rather, through our exertions we effectively request inspiration from God, with our efforts providing the sacrifice that merits receiving that insight. Only this humility allows divine inspiration to flow through us unhindered by our egos. We break out of the rationally based perspective of Greece with its limitations and shrunken vision of God and connect to an expansive realm that allows the possibility of miracle and the ability to reach toward the truly transcendent God.

Breaking the boundaries of rationality was actually central to the military victories. The decision to rebel was sheer insanity; logically speaking it was impossible for the Jews to win. They had to reject this conclusion and accept that human intellect, as powerful as it is, exists within a larger context to which it is subservient. The fact that reason sees a goal as impossible does not mean it should not be attempted. The relevant question is not whether something is possible, but whether it is necessary in order to further God's will. We only need to ask ourselves whether the action before us is what God requires of us at this time.[13] The results are up to Him. If it is a time for success and we are meritorious, success will come. And just as our efforts in the world are not the actual cause of the outcomes that follow, so also our Torah insights are gifts in response to our study, not its products.

The forcefulness of the Maccabees' conviction in this matter was demonstrated by their willingness to put their own lives on the line for the cause. But more than merely demonstrating commitment, this willingness to sacrifice self was also the essence of what they were committing to. The "I," whose independence and autonomy was hardening

---

12. Ramban, Bava Batra 12a.
13. When an action is optional rather than morally incumbent upon us, we do need to consider the likelihood of success. See Berakhot 3b.

through our increasing focus on intellect, seems to be all we are, all we have. We must recognize that our autonomous experience of self is actually a thin slice of a much deeper entity based beyond the individual. The "I" is not the sum of our person but rather the medium and instrument of our service to God.[14]

This awareness is a prerequisite to self-sacrifice, and the actions of the Maccabees actualized this attitude in them. In fact, so decisive was their choice that it penetrated to a depth of self that transcended their individuality and their generation. Their sacrifice made a change in the spiritual substrate out of which all Jews emerge, making this awareness available to the Jewish people for all time.[15] This is the reason for the annually recurring festival of Hanukka.

This choice by the Maccabees to fight a suicidal, unwinnable war was the greatest possible repudiation of the Greek worldview. By actualizing this vision in themselves through their actions, the Hasmoneans linked this world to the next sufficiently to allow the open miracle of the Menora to break through to a level of physical actuality – at least within the confines of the temple. Self-sacrifice, then, is our response to the intellectual focus that Greece brought to humanity. Through it we check intellect's prideful tendencies toward individual isolation and connect our limited individual awareness to our greater self and its larger context.[16]

---

14. Maharal, *Tiferet Yisrael*, chapter 29.
15. Rav Eliahu Dessler, *Mikhtav MeEliahu*, 11th ed., vol. 2 (Jerusalem: The Committee for the Publication of the Writings of Rabbi E. L. Dessler, 1978), 111.
16. The Jews do not have a monopoly on self-sacrifice. But the deep individuality of the Maccabees combined with the complete selflessness with which they sacrificed themselves gave their actions supreme significance. This contrasts with, for example, Greek self sacrifice in battle such as the famous suicide mission of the Greeks at Thermopylae to stop the Persian conquest of Greece. In line with the classic Greek attitude toward courage in battle, they acted in order to exhibit and be identified with personal valor. See Herodotus 8:26, translated by A. D. Godley (Cambridge: Harvard University Press, 1920): "Mardonius, what kind of men are these that you have pitted us against? It is not for money they contend but for glory of achievement!" Their self-sacrifice was not a giving up of self so much as an accentuation of self. The opposite extreme would be the Japanese kamikaze, who effaced themselves before their emperor before they gave their lives. Their sacrifice was not a giving of self for they no longer had a self to give.

## A LIGHT FOR THE AGES

But we do not find ourselves at war in every generation, while the limiting vision of Greece is a continuing pressure. How can the achievement of the Maccabees protect us today? Where is our opportunity for self-sacrifice on an ongoing basis? The answer is in the very intellectualism that created the danger requiring this sacrifice in the first place. The only way we can successfully involve our intellect in the creation of Torah is through dedication amounting to self-sacrifice – at least in the post Greek world. Only with this sacrifice in the pursuit of truth can we avoid the prideful barriers of ego that our intellect otherwise puts up and reach the Divine inspiration that is the living root of the Oral Torah.[17]

Thus the Sages teach us: "The Oral Torah is not found in one who seeks the pleasures of this world – physical desires, honor, and greatness. Rather it is found in one who kills himself (in the tents of Torah)."[18] What do they mean by "kills himself"? It cannot be meant literally; we are obligated to guard our lives! Rather, by putting the unwavering pursuit of truth ahead of any selfish attachments to physical reality, we burn out those aspects of our personality that are not dedicated to God. That is, we eliminate ("kill") the self of mixed motives, anchoring ourselves instead in a deeper part of our being and becoming a pure vessel for Torah.[19]

In some ways this is a more challenging form of self-sacrifice than that found on the battlefield. True, self-sacrifice on the battlefield means the sacrifice of one's entire life. However, the danger in which

---

17. See Rava, Shabbat 88a. In the previous note we described the characteristics that make the self sacrifice we oppose to Greece significant. Those characteristics are particularly true of the self-sacrifice that comes in dedicated Torah study. In Torah learning the creative individuality of the person is actualized to its maximum in the very act of self-sacrifice.
18. *Midrash Tanḥuma*, Noah 3; Berakhot 63b.
19. In Shabbat 88b we see how this process of purification works when powered by God's revelation rather than man's efforts. The Talmud states that when the Jews heard God speak each of the first two commandments on Mount Sinai they all died and were brought back to life. That is, they were connected to that aspect of themselves that was totally in line with the will of God to the point that their souls actually cleaved to God to the exclusion of their individual existence. Each purified soul was then reunited with its body in individual existence through Torah (Sefat Emet, *Bamidbar LeShavuot* 631).

*Part 1: Gateway to the Exodus*

he places himself lasts only for a time, and the actual sacrifice is done by someone or something external to him. One who *lives* for truth, on the other hand, must himself do the sacrificing, and he must do it constantly day after day.

It is unrealistic to think that the entire nation can achieve this. But the few who do, connect beyond this world, unleashing a flow of divine inspiration that brings true Torah to our otherwise orphaned people and links the whole nation back to God. And though the rest of us may not reach the level of purity attained by the greats of Torah, we can still maintain a vital connection to it.

This comes through our respect, support, and relationships with these exceptional individuals and also through the small sacrifices we all make, each according to his or her ability. Whether it be rising early to learn or running out of the house to give to the community, relinquishing ego to maintain equilibrium in the midst of chaotic children's play, sending a spouse to a class even when the kids are difficult, or supporting Torah, self-sacrifice is an ongoing and integral part of Jewish experience that connects us to a reality beyond the one accessible by the Greek intellect.

**THE SYMBOLISM OF THE MENORA**

We light the Hanukka menora every year to revitalize this connection. On the simplest level it recalls the miracle of the Temple Menora, reminding us that miracles can, indeed, happen. On a deeper level, light, which allows us to see, symbolizes wisdom, which allows us to understand.[20] The flame of the Hanukka menora is a flame that we must ignite. In this respect the light we create resembles the Oral Torah, which is wisdom we are responsible to develop.[21] But though we ignite the candle, the flame only burns because of the oil.

The Hebrew term for oil is *shemen*, which is related to the word for eight, *shemona*. Eight is the number associated with things beyond nature, for nature was created in seven days.[22] Moreover, physical reality

---

20. Prov. 6:23. See *Numbers Rabba* 14:10 and 15:5.
21. Rabbi Tzadok, *Pri Tzaddik Shemot, Pikudei* 7.
22. Maharal, *Ner Mitzva*, 23.

is structured around seven: all things physical extend in six directions – forward, backward, right, left, up, and down. The idea of the object is the seventh facet of natural reality – it unites the otherwise disparate six dimensions into a coherent whole.[23] Eight goes beyond this seven of natural physical reality.

The connection between *shemen* and the supernatural *shemona* comes from the inexplicable (at least, to the eye) transformation of a viscous liquid into light. This is suggestive of how the light of true wisdom comes to us from a realm beyond. All wisdom begins with an intuition that arises from an unknowable source. We have become oblivious to this fact and its significance, which isolates our thoughts in the shallow waters of consciousness. Torah, however, can be Torah only so long as we remember that it does not belong to us but rather comes to us as a gift from beyond. Light coming from the oil of our Hanukka lamp reminds us of this. To emphasize this, the oil of the Menora burned for a supernatural eight days, which we recall with our eight days of lighting.

I don't mean to imply by this that the effectiveness of this mitzva is dependent upon contemplating these somewhat esoteric ideas. Like all mitzvot, this one is symbolic. I mean that in the strong sense. Light, flame, oil, even the number eight – as much as these are realities in our mundane world, they connect to templates of ancient origin buried deep in our souls. Like a key opening a lock, they unleash energies and associations within us of which we may or may not be conscious. We can enhance the effect through conscious understanding, but we are affected regardless.

We can, however, take the mitzva further than this symbolism by consciously adding a layer of context. The oil whose miraculous burning we commemorate came from the one container whose seal of purity remained unbroken. The fact that the oil came from one vessel rather than the many vessels that would have been needed under normal circumstances suggests a link to the unitary realm which is the source of Torah and all miracle. The seal that guaranteed the purity of the oil was that of the *kohen gadol*, the high priest. He is the one person who is allowed to enter the place in this world that connects to that hidden

---

23. The Maharal explains this in many places, e.g., *Tiferet Yisrael*, chapter 7.

*Part 1: Gateway to the Exodus*

unitary realm – the *Kodesh Kedoshim*, the Holy of Holies in the Temple, where physical law was transcended.[24]

The self-sacrifice aspect of Hanukka is nested in the remembrance of the miracles the Sages added to our prayers. By recalling the sacrifice of the Maccabees in the context of the miracles we experienced – "the strong in the hands of the weak, the many in the hands of the few" – and by putting it in prayer, we avoid any confusion of sacrifice with mere valor.

**TRANSITIONING TO ROME**

Though we live in a Greek-influenced world, we no longer live in a Greek world. Greece was eventually conquered by Rome. And though Greece and Rome are culturally related, they are not the same. Rome brought a new focus to our engagement of reality, different from the intellectual one that characterized Greece.

Perhaps even today those fully immersed in Torah can still anchor themselves in their intellect and rely on the self-sacrifice of Torah study to reach beyond this world to God. The rest of us, who live more in the world, will have to understand how Rome changes us and how we can overcome its influence to build genuine *emuna* even today.

---

24. The ark took up no physical space. See Maharal, *Ner Mitzva*, 22–23.

*Chapter 7*

# Rome and Christianity

The culture of self-sacrifice through Torah learning that we developed while under Greek rule allowed us to break through the rational shell introduced by Greek intellectualism. However, Greece was soon replaced by Rome as masters of civilization and the Jews. Though Rome was a Western power like Greece and borrowed extensively from Greek culture, Rome was different in fundamental ways and added new layers of challenge to our *emuna*.

It is tricky to identify the essential challenge of the Roman exile, because it has lasted for over two thousand years. For reasons that will soon become apparent, we are still considered to be in the cultural web of Rome. During this expanse of time, the social milieu fostered by Rome has undergone profound changes. When Rome conquered us, it was pagan. Three hundred years later it was declared Christian. Two hundred and fifty years after that, it began to be identified with a militant Christian doctrine that was punitively intolerant of any other religious practice. And today we consider Western society essentially secular. The obstacles to maintaining and developing *emuna* in a belligerently Christian society would seem to be very different from those we face when trying to maintain it in an agnostic and sometimes aggressively anti-religious environment. What is the underlying commonality of all

*Part 1: Gateway to the Exodus*

these cultural forms, and what continuity is there in the way our *emuna* is challenged and our response?

We can begin by contrasting Rome with Greece. While the Greeks filtered reality through the intellect and therefore valued thought and reflection, the Romans were much more focused on immediate reality and functionally minded. Where the Greek might become a theorizing scientist, the Roman was an engineer, seeking solutions to this-worldly problems. The Romans eventually became enamored of Greek culture.[1] But they selectively absorbed it according to their taste, dispensing with much of its intellectual flair in favor of those aspects that resonated with their more practical nature.[2]

With regard to philosophy, for example, the Romans embraced Greek ethics with its emphasis on attitude and conduct while showing little stomach for Greek metaphysics.[3] They were primarily attracted to the ethics of Stoicism and Epicureanism, both philosophies that were, in the words of one scholar, "strong reactions against the abstractions of Plato and Aristotle, and would tolerate nothing but concrete reality."[4] It is telling that one of the most famous and influential works of Stoicism – the *Meditations* of Marcus Aurelius – was written by a Roman emperor on campaign. It was typical of the Roman outlook that Marcus Aurelius rejected the primacy of contemplation as an end unto itself so beloved by Greek Platonists, replacing it with duty as man's highest responsibility.[5]

---

1. This took some time. In 161 BC the senate forbade philosophers to take up residence in Rome! William Turner, *History of Philosophy* (Boston and London: Ginn and Company Publishers, 1903), 190.
2. Ibid.
3. "In accepting the philosophy of Greece, the Roman spirit asserted its practical tendency, selecting what was more easily assimilated, and modifying what it accepted, by importing to it a more practical character. Thus it was the ethical philosophy of the Epicureans and Stoics and the Eclectic systems of later times, rather than the philosophy of Plato and Aristotle, that throve when transplanted to Roman soil" (ibid.).
4. St. George Stock, *A Guide to Stoicism* (Lexington, KY: Feather Trail Press, 2010), 7. This is a reprint of a 1908 classic.
5. Marcus Aurelius, *Meditations* 6:22. The singular importance of duty comes up over and over again in *Meditations*. Duty includes thought and reason, but always focused on how a person must be in the world – both his attitudes and actions.

That Romans replaced contemplation with action as the ultimate human activity indicated that they saw reality as anchored in material existence, in contrast to the Greeks, who saw reality as anchored in ideas. The significance of this metaphysical shift for us lies less in the intellectual change it represents than as an indicator of a change from the Greeks in the nature of self experienced by the Romans.

We determine what is real by reference to our inner experience because our only contact with what something is, as opposed to how it appears, is our experience of self. So if under Rome what was identified as the locus of reality changed, this necessarily reflected a change in the center of personality and inner experience. Roman identification of reality with the concrete, material realm showed that their sense of self was heavily influenced by their physical bodies.

The spiritual realm is unitary. It is only because we have bodies that we are capable of individual awareness. We would expect the body's governing influence on us to result in a consciousness dominated by awareness of autonomous individuality. In fact, social historians of the period see just such a transition unfolding during the Roman empire. Writings from the period reveal that for many the once-easy integration with the world and its affairs began to break down, as people became more detached and absorbed in themselves as isolated individuals.[6] Traditional forms of action and public service lost their meaning. Increased focus on self was also reflected in the spending of the moneyed classes. The great wealth they had once invested in communal religious events and public buildings was instead directed toward their private residences and displays of personal status.[7]

This sense of isolation seems to us like an obvious description of internal life; it is difficult for us to imagine any alternative. But this is only because we are the cultural descendants of Rome. In the ancient Near East, by contrast, we experienced self as an extension of a higher

---

6. "After generations of apparently satisfying public activity, it was as if a current that had passed smoothly from men's inner experience into the outside world had been cut. The warmth drained from the familiar environment" (Peter Brown, *The World of Late Antiquity AD 150–750* [London: Thames and Hudson, 2013], 51).
7. Ibid., 67.

being. And under Greece we located ourselves in a larger context of ideas. It is this isolated individuality with all its consequences that is the defining characteristic of Roman culture, the consistent thread that ties together the disparate societies that it dominated, and is our essential continuity with Rome.

## A DIFFERENT CLASS OF EXILE

Despite the fact that Rome continued the Western tradition begun by Greece, the Sages saw something exceptional in Rome, something that put it in a category all its own. They conveyed this in a midrash that associates the empires with non-kosher animals. For an animal to be kosher it must have two characteristics: it must chew its cud and have cloven hoofs. The Torah lists four animals that have only one of these characteristics and associates each of the four empires with one of them. Babylon, Persia, and Greece were all joined to animals that chew the cud but do not have fully cloven hooves – that is, they have the internal, hidden sign of *kashrut* but not the external, visible one. Only Rome was associated with an animal that has cloven hooves but does not chew the cud – an animal that appears to be kosher on the outside but is not on the inside – the pig.[8] What are the Sages telling us by this?

To create an empire a nation must have the capability of unifying disparate peoples. Unity is a spiritual quality, ultimately belonging to and emanating only from the One God.[9] Therefore, no nation can succeed to empire without being connected to God so that it conveys His quality of unity into the world.[10] Signs or elements of *kashrut* are indicative of connection to God.[11] An empire, then, must have the equivalent of an element of *kashrut*. But because the empires were not completely connected to God – they did not convey His unity into the world in its fullness – they could not have both elements of *kashrut*.

---

8. Leviticus Rabba 13:5.
9. Deut. 6:4.
10. Kings are usually seen to rule with the authority of a deity – representing or being that deity. In Europe that eventually expressed itself in the concept of "the divine right of kings."
11. I understood this interpretation of the midrash from a lecture of Rav Moshe Shapiro.

Which sign is associated with each empire is indicative of how it connected to God and conveyed His unity. The first three empires had an internal connection but they lacked the external connection. Externally it was obvious they were not dedicated to the One transcendent God – to the extent that they worshipped they worshipped idols. But internally, their sense of connection to some divinity with roots leading back to the transcendent Creator was real. Notably, for all of our criticism of Greece, in this regard the Sages still group it with the Near Eastern empires when compared to Rome – there was some authenticity in their intellectual relationship with God.[12] Rome, however, was different. It "had cloven hooves" – externally it gave expression to the One God. But something was critically missing internally – Rome did not "chew the cud."

In this same midrash the Sages illustrate what they are saying about Rome with the simile of a Roman judge who condemned an adulterer, a magician, and a thief to death. As these criminals were being led to execution, the judge leaned over to the prosecutor and whispered, "I did worse than all three of them in a single day."[13] Rome's cloven hoof, then, was its legal system – Rome was famous for its legal codexes and court systems. The consistent application of law across the breadth of the empire both unified it and was expressive of God's external connection to creation – His structuring of reality through the laws of nature and the moral code of Torah.[14] But Rome did not "chew the cud" because its internal connection was missing. The Romans themselves did not feel any moral compulsion to obey the laws.[15]

---

12. There are, however, numerous midrashim that group Bavel and Persia together, with Greece and Rome together in a separate category. See, for example, Numbers Rabba 16:22.
13. Leviticus Rabba 13:5.
14. These both actualize God's trait of *din* (judgment) associated with His name *Elokim* – His "external" trait, the one through which he structures creation, as opposed to God's more essential trait associated with His four letter name through which He gives existence to creation.
15. The same midrash also gives another interpretation of what it means that Rome did not chew the cud: Romans "are prideful, rob, and steal, under the guise of expressing justice." According this understanding the internal lack was reflected in their actual

*Part 1: Gateway to the Exodus*

The Divine unity that bound Rome together was only on a surface level without any true internal basis.[16] Though we observed that Romans were focused on themselves, the Roman self lacked the depth to integrate with transcendent moral structure, so it lacked substance and any sense of moral necessity.

This midrash also clearly conveys another important characteristic of Roman society: it gave value to external appearance over internal content or basis. This, at first, seems paradoxical. If Romans were so internally focused, why such concern for appearances?

In fact the Roman desire for external approval and esteem shows how empty was their internal world. When we said Romans were internally focused, we emphasized that they experienced individuality as something that was *isolated*. In contrast to the Near Eastern societies where man experienced himself as an extension or expression of a larger whole, and Greek culture where man existed as part of a larger reality of ideas, under Rome we experienced self as something cut off from any more expansive or deeper reality. The self instead of being a conduit or stepping stone to the divine, transcendent depth of our humanity – our *tzelem Elokim* – was instead cut off and contained within itself, an endpoint of internal reality rather than a way station. The resulting self was too impoverished to serve as a basis of personal value or genuine self-esteem – that is, to justify to the Romans themselves their own existence. They therefore turned to the opinion of others. Because they could not find value in themselves they strove to have others impute value to them.

Consistent with the Sages' contention that we are still in the Roman exile, these insights into the nature of Roman selfhood are uncomfortably descriptive of our own experience. The emphasis on appearances and dependence on the opinions of others finds extreme expression in our Facebook, social-media generation.

---

laws. They were structured to give the Romans what they wanted rather than to apply some objective form of justice – a different kind of insincerity.

16. When Rome turned Christian, the comparison to the pig remains apt but takes on a different meaning. The worship was presented as being to the One transcendent God; but, as we will discuss, people's devotion was compromised and was directed to a Being whose Oneness was compromised.

It was not just the Roman self that was shallow. Romans projected their internal isolation on their world, resulting in an empty reality where what they could see was all there was. They lived in a flat physical world of material being without significance. Just as the Roman self is familiar to us, so this Roman world. Though over time we may have increased the resolution of our vision, perceiving physical structure in ever-finer detail, as heirs of Rome we still do not recognize any additional dimensions or depth to our world. It is this shallowness of self and world that distinguishes Rome from all the empires that preceded it and makes clear we are still in the Roman exile.

## SPIRITUAL BACKLASH

It is easy enough to understand how the Roman mindset translates into our present day secular materialist worldview with its denial of God. But things are clearly not so simple, as it took two thousand years for Roman society to reach today's monolithic materialism. It first passed from scrupulous adherence to pagan tradition through an intense and aggressive dedication to Christianity. If man is becoming increasingly anchored in his ego consciousness and physical being over time how do we explain the emergence of Christianity with its commitment to the One God? This question is best answered in the context of general patterns of cultural development.

Society provides the context within which we live out our lives. We exist through the merging of a finite, bounded physical body with an infinite, boundless spiritual *neshama* (soul), and society needs to allow both of these elements to thrive. Just as society must give us the opportunity to meet our physical needs it must also allow us to give expression to our *neshama*.

There is a clearly recognizable pattern that recurs through history where over time cultures becomes increasingly defined and tightly structured followed by a kind of breakdown or readjustment that sees the emergence of free-flowing, non-rational movements. Why is this? While the hardening of the culture need not interfere with its citizens fulfilling their physical needs and often expands their wealth, the increasingly restrictive environment represses the *neshama*, choking off its ability to actualize itself. The subsequent breakdown is the push back from the *neshama*.

*Part 1: Gateway to the Exodus*

Something like this happened in Greece in the second century BC. We spoke in the last chapter about Greek rationalism and its attempt to clearly articulate and precisely define reality. Though this was the aspect of Greece that its empire brought to the world, there were other elements to Greek society. In the second century, however, rationalism began to approach complete dominance in Greece, threatening to eliminate alternative expressions. This set off an eruption of interest in the irrational – magic, the occult, and mysticism.[17] Though this reaction had some disturbing characteristics, its occurrence was a consequence of the irrepressible nature of the boundless *neshama* rebelling against its containment. The impulse to rebel against repression is often a sign of health; but the form the reaction takes is not always healthy.

The emergence of Christianity under Rome reflects a version of this same pattern spread over a much longer stretch of time. We have been discussing in this book how man became increasingly isolated in the shallowness of his bounded physical being over the course of history which more and more constricted the soul's expression. Under Rome this reached the point of strangulation, leaving Romans with a pervasive sense of loss of self, purposelessness, disquiet, and ennui. This was a consequence of the soul's reaction to the paltry level human experience had reached in the Roman era and provided a basis for the emergence of Christianity.[18] In other words the increased interest in the occult in second century Greece that we mentioned was a local expression of the same cultural pattern as the emergence of Christianity, but in the case

---

17. Dodds, 242–48. Dodds mourns this backlash as the forces of irrationality rolling back the gains of rationality. Though irrationality may have been the result in this case, we recognize the underlying cause as the healthy refusal of the spiritual to be marginalized by the physical. Another example of the irrational undoing the gains of rationality cited by Dodds is the Romantic movement in English literature arising in reaction to the rational Enlightenment. Here, also, others view it differently, seeing Romanticism as a reaction to the deadening of the human spirit by the Industrial Revolution.
18. Christianity was the Roman response to this void. Maharal states that for the Jewish people this vacuum will ultimately bring the messianic redemption (*Ner Mitzva*, 18). This is hinted at in the last line of the midrash we were discussing about the signs of *kashrut* (Leviticus Rabba 13:5).

of Christianity the pattern was expressing itself in the context of the full sweep of humanity's historical experience.

## THE EMERGENCE OF CHRISTIANITY

Ironically, the internal isolation that contributed so much to the emptiness of Rome also opened an avenue that seemed to fill it. Alone with themselves, the Romans were forced into an intense engagement with whatever level they could reach of their *tzelem Elokim*, the Image of God within. People confused this with personal revelation and direct connection to transcendence, occasioning overnight conversions and fanatical devotion to various gods and sects.[19] Mystery cults proliferated, and Christianity also took root in this fertile soil.

Since this awakening came through the unitary self, the experience mirrored monotheism, favoring its attraction in the long run over the inertial connection to idolatry. Monotheism was also more intellectually satisfying than polytheism. We will see later that the intellectual assault on polytheism was central to the Christian campaign for conversion of the pagans.[20] Even though the Greeks were great thinkers and also polytheists, this was because their worship was a carryover from their past. It continued parallel to their philosophical tradition rather than as an integral part of it, with numerous intellectuals rejecting it.[21]

The attraction of monotheism initially led to intense interest in Judaism.[22] The Torah approach, however, was not a viable option for most Romans. The slow path to God of doing mitzvot to uncover the deeper aspects of self that transcend individuality and genuinely emanate from the One God was difficult and set a very high bar. It took time to

---

19. Brown, *The World of Late Antiquity*, 51–53.
20. See note 23. It is worth noting that many of the Christian disputes with the Neoplatonists centered on the Trinity, an aspect of Christianity that actually compromises its monotheism. The Christians touted the Trinity as a superior version of the multilevel reality Plato described in the *Timaeus*.
21. We mentioned earlier from Robert Mayhew that Aristotle, the epitome of Greek rationalism, recognized only the one supreme Being and saw Him as utterly removed from any awareness of the particulars of existence. This left no place for worship. Aristotle recognized in it only psychological benefit. See chapter 5, note 8.
22. Louis H. Feldman, *Jew and Gentile in the Ancient World* (Princeton: Princeton University Press, 1993), 342–82.

achieve any sense of connection, the mitzvot were a big responsibility, and circumcision was a real barrier. All but the most dedicated were put off. When Christianity jettisoned all this, it presented a workable and attractive alternative for the masses.

Furthermore, there was something in Christianity that resonated strongly with the Romans: the concept of the Trinity.[23] Romans located primary reality in the individual self. So once they were introduced to the concept of the unitary Creator – Who is theoretically the locus of reality – the distinction was blurred between man and God. When combined with the fact that it was through the self that they encountered any semblance of spirituality, the distinction between man and God broke down completely. By joining man to God, the Christian Trinity spoke to this defining confusion. It allowed Christian monotheism to fit smoothly with Roman metaphysics and to graft naturally onto the empire. But the price was a profoundly diminished concept of God: He was transformed into something that was part of physical reality.

**THE CHRISTIAN GOD: ASSAULT ON TRANSCENDENCE**

We might have expected that the early days of Rome, when the Romans adopted Christianity and the biblical God, would offer the Jews some respite from the pressures Greece placed on our *emuna*. This was not the case. The Christian vision of the Trinity did even more violence to the omnipotence of the Creator than had the Greeks. The specific understanding of the Trinity accepted by the Roman Empire when it first adopted Christianity saw the Christian savior and God Himself as coequal facets of God.

It is important to understand the extent to which the official Church of the Roman Empire associated physical being with God in its early days. Though more moderate views prevailed during the fourth century, by the time of the Council of Ephesus in 431 the official position

---

23. The engine driving conversion of the masses was miracle-working and exorcism (Ramsay MacMullen, *Paganism in the Roman Empire* [New Haven: Yale University Press, 1981], 95–98; Brown, *The World of Late Antiquity*, 55). But, as MacMullen points out, the pagans also acquired adherents through performing miracles and oracles. So it remains legitimate to ask what favored the adoption of Christian doctrine over the many pagan alternatives.

of the Church was that God had died on the cross. According to Peter Brown, the distinguished Princeton historian of this period, the bishops pressed for this because ordinary Christians needed to know that God actually experienced death so that they could be confident that He would empathize fully with their situation![24]

At that time, an opposing patriarch observed: "The ignorant populace of Constantinople danced around bonfires, chanting, 'God has been crucified. God is dead.'"[25] Though at the Council of Chalcedon, twenty years later, the doctrinal excesses of these earlier councils were blunted, the depth to which these ideas penetrated the Roman psyche was evident in the fact that even the slight modifications that were made led to controversy lasting hundreds of years and split the Church.[26]

My aim here is not to characterize the position of present-day Christianity, a multifaceted and diverse religion espousing many different visions and filling the spiritual needs of a great many people. Rather, my aim is to understand its roots and how they reflect on the nature of Rome and our experience of exile in Rome and its cultural descendants. The original church position effectively undid our forefather Abraham's primary innovation of separating God's Being from physical reality. Thus even in the early stages of Christianity, our belief in the existence of the *truly transcendent*, unitary Creator was under attack.

But as challenging as this compromised vision of God was to our *emuna* there were other aspects to Rome that were equally difficult for us and for our *emuna*.

---

24. Brown, *The Rise of Western Christendom*, 117–20.
25. Ibid.
26. Ibid., 120–21.

*Chapter 8*

# Materialism and the Shallow Self

Though the concept of the Trinity diminished God by confusing Him with man, we might have expected this same confusion to bolster the significance of man. Strengthening this expectation is the fact that it was the experience of self that Rome had interpreted as a connection to spirituality. How do we put this together with the Sages' identification of Rome with inner emptiness and our own experience under Rome of a critically compromised self?[1]

Though in the early days of Christianity individuals may have been drawn in by the newness of their experience of self, it had its limits. There was a reason why they confused the God they thought they were encountering with physical being: this self was shallow and isolated from truly transcendent depth. When the newness of the encounter wore off, it was not necessarily so exciting.

---

1. Rav Moshe Shapiro, in describing the weakness of self in modern times observed that our self is so weak that we lose our consciousness of it in our awareness of the world – the observer is forgotten in his observations.

## Part 1: Gateway to the Exodus

Whatever greatness of self early Christians may have sensed, when the church built the foundations of its empire it turned instead to preaching a path of extreme asceticism, humility, and submission.[2] It embraced the emptiness in men, leveraging their ennui by directing people to run away from themselves in the false hope that this would lead to God. Confusing man with God may have been an elevation of man, but it did not elevate men.

In building on this weak self, Christianity came to view reality as primarily spiritual. What had been a Roman attachment to physical reality disconnected from any spiritual root flipped into its opposite: reality was viewed as essentially spiritual, while the physical dimension of this world was held to be unredeemable and therefore to be dispensed with.[3] This attitude was the underlying basis of the Christian rejection of the necessity for the mitzvot, the means by which the Jews sanctify physical being.[4]

This purely spiritual approach, however, was unrealistic, because reality is a combination of physical and spiritual. Indeed, it is dominated by the physical. Genuine spirituality can only be reached *through* our physical being. What was presented by Christians as a complete attachment of self to spiritual reality was actually an unrealistic flight from self in the false hope that this would lead to God. What it achieved instead was a deeper internal vacuum.

The illusion inherent in the approach became fully revealed when the culture flipped yet again into its opposite, with Western Christianity morphing into the purely secular vision of modern Western society that rejects spirituality entirely, regarding reality as only physical – a more natural expression of its essentially Roman root. In the long run Christianity did not succeed in sanctifying the material realm by combining God and physical being. Instead it robbed anything beyond the material of any sense of reality.

---

2. Brown, *The World of Late Antiquity*, 96–103. Though holy men, monks, and nuns never comprised a large percentage of the Christian population, they played a critical role in peoples' imaginations.
3. See Lamentations Rabba 24:9 and Rabbi Tzadok, *Maḥshavot Ḥarutz* 1.
4. See the commentary of the Vilna Gaon on Song of Songs 1:3.

## THE EMPTYING OF SELF

The modern materialist outlook no longer conflates our hollow inner experience with God, identifying it as the basis for reality. Instead, we associate reality with our bodies, locating it in material existence. Not that material existence has more significance or meaning – it is perceived as being empty, like the self perceiving it. But at least material has substance. It is *demonstrably* real, something the conscious self cannot claim.

With the passage of time this identification of reality with matter only intensifies. It is increasingly common to repudiate the reality of everything else, such as spirituality, ideals, or morals. There are even those who deny the genuine existence of conscious, first-person experience because it is not tangible! Academics taking this position are both popular and decorated.[5] The diffusion of these attitudes is reflected in the increasing affirmation among college students of moral relativity.

Our focus on the material realm has yielded vast knowledge of its structure, bringing technological progress and power over nature. Among other advances, it has brought devices that have broadened the scope and availability of communication with others. In the past, social interaction has provided an important vehicle for deepening our humanity and appreciation of God though encounters with *tzelem Elokim* (the Image of God) in us all. But today's ballooning, device-mediated communication has instead profoundly diminished the depth of communication, only accelerating the emptying-out of our humanity People's weak sense of self inclines them to those formats that minimize real connection, like texting, blogging, and posting in place of conversation; it takes too much effort to genuinely engage the self.[6] Technology thus allows us to hide from one another under the guise of socializing.[7] As more and more communication is mediated this way, our true social abilities atrophy.[8]

---

5. E.g., Daniel Dennett (see chapter 5, note 26).
6. See Sherry Turkle, *Alone Together* (New York: Basic Books, 2011), 187–209.
7. Ibid. 154: "Networked we are together, but so lessened are our expectations of each other that we can feel utterly alone."
8. Yalda T. Uhls et al., "Five days at outdoor education camp without screens improves preteen skills with nonverbal emotion cues," *Computers in Human Behavior* 39 (October 2014): 387–92.

*Part 1: Gateway to the Exodus*

How far this dehumanization can go is seen in the increasing acceptance of and even preference for social robots as caregivers or objects of care and affection. This may sound like science fiction because in the West we are still some years away from this becoming a widespread practice. But in Japan it is already happening.[9] And the West is preparing to follow suit. Robots are expected to take an increasingly prominent role in child care and elder care in the not-so-distant future.

The usefulness of these robots in performing physical tasks is not surprising. What is deeply disturbing is that studies consistently show the ease with which people accept and even *prefer* them as partners for emotional relationships, even quite personal ones![10] With robots, there *really* is no inner experience. And yet people either have difficulty recognizing that, allow themselves to be fooled about it, or feel it just doesn't matter. If we can accept objects as people, then people cannot be much more to us than objects.[11] In this we see Rome approaching the unadulterated expression of its cultural essence: reality becomes synonymous with one-dimensional material existence to the extent that we no longer distinguish our own humanity from material function.

**SOCIETY UNDER ROME**

This extreme thinning-out of our experience of self profoundly complicates our pursuit of *emuna*. We spoke before of how our understanding of reality is a projection of our internal experience. If we are empty inside, how can we conceive of the existence of God? But it also has tremendous social implications which compound this complication.

We would expect an inner experience of emptiness to lead to social alienation – it is difficult to truly join with others when one feels inadequate. Moreover, meaningful relationships with our fellows are ultimately grounded in our ability to genuinely value them, which requires engaging their *tzelem Elokim*. We cannot find in others what we cannot find in ourselves. So quite apart from today's increasingly fractured

---

9. Turkle, *Alone Together*, 146–47.
10. Ibid., 127–33.
11. "We seem determined to give human qualities to objects and content to treat each other as things" (ibid., iv).

forms of communication, social alienation has always been a defining characteristic of Rome and its exile.[12]

This social alienation further undermines our *emuna* because our ability to recognize *Elokut* – Godliness – is supported by our sensitivity to the *tzelem Elokim* of our fellows. It is no coincidence that Abraham, who discovered the transcendent God, was renowned for his kindness to people.[13]

And this social support for *emuna* becomes increasingly important even as it becomes increasingly difficult. Over the course of history we become centered more and more in our physical dimension. As that happens, those aspects of our relationship with God that we experience through the context of physical reality become more central the relationship. These are the mitzvot between man and his fellow, where we encounter God indirectly through *tzelem Elokim*. Thus while the First Temple was destroyed by Babylon on account of idolatry (a corruption of man's direct relationship with God), the Second Temple was destroyed by Rome on account of baseless hatred (a violation of the relationship between man and his fellow man).[14] So our alienation from one another cripples our relationship with God.

## THE CHRISTIAN CHURCH: ASSAULT ON CHOSENNESS

We have discussed how Christianity and Rome compromise our concept of the transcendent God. We have discussed how Christianity and Rome undermine our sense of significant self and significant others. Christianity also undermines our nationhood. For Christianity also intensified the attacks of earlier exiles on the concept of Jewish chosenness.

The Persian exile had obscured our uniqueness as a people before God. Greece had denied the possibility of any uniqueness before God. Christianity embraced the concept of uniqueness but declared, "We are the new Israel and ours is the new Word!" They accepted that we *had*

---

12. Dan. 2:43.
13. See Rashi, Gen. 18:3 and *The Choice to Be*, 37–42.
14. Yoma 9b.

*Part 1: Gateway to the Exodus*

been the chosen people. However, they forcefully proclaimed that God had permanently rejected us and transferred our role to them![15]

When we spoke earlier about the importance of the unique relationship of the Jewish people to God we said that anything undermining it compromised specifically our *emuna* in God's communication with man. In the context of this exile, however, the Christian usurpation of chosenness was a frontal attack on every aspect of our emuna as it was used often violently as a weapon to force conversion to Christian beliefs.

To appreciate the depth of the challenge we faced it is important to note that the Church did not put itself forward as one particular group (the Christians) replacing another particular group (the Jews). Rather, Christianity claimed to be *the* universal religion of all of humanity.

In the third century, when their doctrine was being formulated, the Church fathers were conscious that they would not succeed in converting the pagan masses without winning over the intellectuals. They therefore developed their theology along Neoplatonic lines, claiming to be the only reliable guardians of the Greek philosophical heritage.[16] They argued that with their doctrine, universal rationality had finally become fully expressed in spiritual terms, that they had achieved the synthesis of Greece and Rome.[17] Even Thomas Aquinas, who a thousand years later put faith squarely above reason and challenged Aristotle on various points, thought that when Aristotle came to conclusions that conflicted with Christian dogma it was because Aristotle, lacking the guidance of

---

15. Ramchal, *Daat Tevunot* 36.
16. See Brown, *The World of Late Antiquity*, 82–84, 134; also Thomas Williams, "Augustine and the Platonists" (lecture given at Christ College, Valparaiso University, October 23, 2003).
17. The Greek embrace of abstract reason led them to exclude from truth anything that was a particular expression rather than an all-embracing generality. We discussed earlier that this was at odds with the Jewish concept of the unique relationship of the Jewish people with God. Frankfort, in his essay significantly entitled "The Emancipation of Thought from Myth," credits the Jews with having made great strides over the earlier cultures of the Near East toward this "emancipation," but regards our *emuna* in ourselves as the Chosen People, as a mythic holdover; the completion of the "emancipation" had to await the arrival of Greece (Frankfort, *The Intellectual Adventure of Ancient Man*, 369–73). The Christians avoided the charge of "myth" by claiming that Christianity was a truth intrinsic to the place of humanity in existence.

revelation, had made *mistakes in reasoning*.[18] This identification of Christianity with objective rationalism would lead the philosopher Immanuel Kant in the eighteenth century to recommend what he termed "the euthanasia of Judaism": Jews should voluntarily adopt Christianity so as not to be at odds with universal idealism.[19]

In actuality, the root of Christian universalism lies in Roman materialism rather than Greek idealism. To understand this we must first understand the concept of a chosen people.

The role of a chosen people exists in the scheme of creation because while reality combines both physical and spiritual dimensions, they are not equally present. The basis of our reality is material, so everything shares that evenly. Spirituality, however, is like a root that connects to and enlivens that physical foundation. Though all of physical reality benefits from its life-giving force, not everything has equal proximity to the root.[20] The image of reality as an upside-down tree with its roots in the heavens is used by the commentaries.[21]

Think of an individual person as a model of this idea. Though the *neshama* is the root and essence of the individual and gives life to the whole person, it is not equally expressed in all aspects of the personality. That we have a soul is strongly expressed in our consciousness and thinking, associated with the head and in our emotional awareness, associated with the heart. But we also have hands. These are capable of effecting expressions of our *tzelem Elokim*, but in and of themselves represent it less.

While the differences among peoples are not as great as the difference between the head or heart and the hand, the peoples of mankind are each centered in a different facet of human personality. Each is characterized by different talents and strengths. Each is capable of expressing

---

18. Hava Tirosh-Rothschild, *Between Worlds: The Life and Thought of Rabbi David ben Judah Messer Leon* (Albany: State University of New York Press), 114–15.
19. Immanuel Kant, *The Conflict of the Faculties*, trans. Mary J. Gregor (Lincoln and London: University of Nebraska Press, 1992), 95.
20. Maharal, *Tiferet Yisrael*, chapter 1.
21. Maharal, *Gur Aryeh, Bereshit* 9:21. Maharal speaks there about man, but it is equally true of creation in its entirety, which is modeled after man (See Malbim, *Seder Ramzei HaMishkan, Sefer Shemot, Parashat Teruma*).

*Part 1: Gateway to the Exodus*

God in the world in an essential manner unique to that people. All were created for that purpose and all are needed for God to be fully expressed in creation. But some roles leave a people more directly connected to the Creator than others.

The particular role of the Jews is evident in our having conveyed the prophecies of monotheism to mankind. As a result of the Exodus, we have heightened responsibilities to God.

Despite Christian claims to the contrary, our role has not changed.[22] Now as before, we are obligated to set an example of a people *totally* committed to the Creator. That is, we must fully integrate Him into every aspect of our lives. This is accomplished through the mitzvot and halakha. Each person must also bring his own individual creativity to the process. But halakha guides and structures our internal sense of self, our relationships with others, and our direct connection to the Creator, harnessing every element of our personality in the process. The purity with which we accomplish this task today is painfully imperfect. But we are in exile, so we do not expect ourselves to be fully realized or our achievements to necessarily take on full expression in the world. Our successes often come in the form of relative accomplishments and are usually internal and largely hidden. Still, we are doing our part to move the world toward its goal.

Anyone can choose to leave his people with its particular task and join us to share in our particular task. But it is not necessary to do so in order to have a relationship with God and a meaningful role in creation. The total focus expected of us is not the only way, nor is it required of everyone. Though all have a place, it is not the same place. It doesn't make sense that it would be, as we are all different.

Christian Rome, by viewing God as actually having a physical component, blurred the distinction between the physical and spiritual realms. This allowed for the idea that spirituality could be uniformly expressed in creation, leaving no place for distinct peoples, each having a unique role in humanity's spiritual project of connecting God to His world. But this was as illusory as mistaking a head for a hand. Christian

---

22. See Rashi, Deut. 29:12.

universalism, rather than an abstract ideal of bringing everyone to their true humanity, was simply an attempt to make everyone like them.

This explains why the Christians developed their universalist vision. But how do we understand the violence with which they sought to impose it? The answer to this question is contained in the point we just made – that Christians wanted everyone to be "like them." We discussed how the Roman self, centered in material reality, is profoundly lacking with an underlying sense of inadequacy, whether conscious or not. A person with a sense of inadequacy finds the presence of a strong other existentially threatening.[23] The inadequate person has an amplified, even crushing awareness of his inadequacies when faced with a solid self, and either dissolves or attacks. The attack can either be to eliminate the other or to subsume the other in himself so that the other is no longer other.

Imperial Rome became imperial Rome because it attacked.[24] Before Rome became Christian, however, the Jews were only other when they were an independent and rebellious country. Once the Roman legions put an end to Jewish sovereignty, Jews were basically tolerated as part of the empire and to an extent prospered. Judaism was a recognized and legally protected religion. When Rome became Christian, however, the Jews became other by virtue of being Jewish and the persecutions began.[25] The Christians needed to eliminate that otherness. Thus the vigor with which they pursued either the liquidation or conversion of the Jews and, failing that, degraded them to the point that even the inadequate Roman self felt superior in the presence of Jews.

## MODERNITY AND ITS CONTINUING ATTACK ON JEWISH UNIQUENESS

The war against Jewish uniqueness survived the modern secular revolution to be born again in a new form. A substitute for Christianity, or perhaps a holdover from it, is the potent vision of a united mankind, understood to mean humanity without the distinct identities that create national or tribal divisions. This is projected as an objective moral good,

---

23. See Maharal, *Or Ḥadash*, 130–31.
24. *The Choice to Be*, 145–54, 181–84.
25. Brown, *The World of Late Antiquity*, 104, 174.

## Part 1: Gateway to the Exodus

relegating the Jews, insofar as they cling to their faith, to their traditional status as impediments to universal idealism.[26]

This secular Western "ideal" of unity, however, is no less compromised than the Christian ideal it replaced. Another way of saying "without identities that create divisions" is "with uniformity," a rephrasing that removes the romantic ring from the concept. Here the cultural imperialism of the Christian version survived, made painfully obvious by the specific form this "universal man" takes. Consistently it is a projection of the vision of the ideal person in vogue in the West at the time, swinging with the vagaries of society's whims.

The particularity and arrogance underlying this seeming universal – whether the Christian version or the secular one – has been unmasked by the rising prominence of Islam with its inconveniently different universal vision. It is worth noting that the intensifying conflict between the East and the West has not softened the rhetoric of many modern ideologues toward what they still consider "the Jewish problem." They still identify the Jews as a primary obstacle to their universalist ideals. Considering the size of the other peoples who resist inclusion in their very particular version of humanity, the absurdity of the obsession reveals its basis in blatant anti-Semitism.[27]

### STUCK IN THE PHYSICAL WORLD

Today we find ourselves deeply absorbed in this spiritually barren modern Western iteration of Rome. It obviates the need for a Creator by viewing physical reality as always having existed. This had been a central tenet of Greek tradition due to Greece's uncompromising faith in human rationality, as we mentioned earlier. So when science repudiated the biblical doctrine of a beginning and adopted a vision of physical

---

26. See Jayne Svenungsson, "Enlightened Prejudices: Anti-Jewish Tropes in Modern Philosophy," in Hans Ruin and Andrus Ers, eds., *Rethinking Time: Essays on History, Memory, and Representation* (Huddinge, Sweden: Södertörns högskola, 2011), 280, 286–89.
27. Ibid.

## Materialism and the Shallow Self

eternity,[28] this "new" cosmology was actually a return to the original roots of Western culture rather than a nullification of them.

So although a vision of reality as purely physical is relatively new, having come into full focus only during the last few hundred years, it is really the latest version of a vision that we have been struggling with for over 2,300 years. From the time civilization was defined by the culture of Greece, it has been moving inexorably toward it. For though the Greeks were enamored of intellect, human intellect, as we pointed out earlier, is not transcendent. Rather, it is an extension of the physical realm we inhabit. And though it has taken over two thousand years to clarify the unadulterated implications of Greece's radical rationalism, this was its unrealized core from the beginning: a world of matter, pointlessly moving forward according to the inexorable play of physical laws, potentially fully comprehensible and controllable by man through the expansion and application of science, and with morality a mere utilitarian convenience.

But even though it is a direct extension of Greek ideas, the extreme naturalism that emerges under our modern iteration of Rome isolates us even more starkly from spirituality than occurred under Greece itself. Greece at least had a concept of a higher Being. And even though what Greece related to as their equivalent of a spiritual realm was actually an extension of physical reality, at least the Greeks sought to attach themselves to something beyond immediate material existence. Reality was not completely empty.

Today our argument with Rome is over whether any non-material reality exists at all. Our faith is confronted with unprecedented challenges and needs new support beyond what is provided by Purim and Hanukka. But we have no historical salvation to guide us in how to deal with these problems on a national level, for salvation from Rome has yet to come.

---

28. There is no significant difference in this regard between the steady state theory of cosmology and the Big Bang theory. Most versions of the Big Bang presume the existence of something before the bang.

*Part 1: Gateway to the Exodus*

### SOMETHING TO WORK ON

There is, however, an aspect of this new challenge that can be addressed through our individual rather than our national experience. We mentioned earlier that our modern vision is a consequence of our consciousness becoming increasingly centered in our individual ego-experience of reality. The natural/scientific view is premised on the concept that each person, through logic and observation, can understand the world entirely from himself – at least, given enough equipment and guidance.[29] It is by building entirely from the individual that modern culture dispenses with tradition and God. The instincts about truth which this breeds in us can only be satisfied if each one of us as individuals takes personal initiative to develop his own basic *emuna*.

We have pointed out that one of the underlying principles unifying exile under Rome is the confusion of material existence with reality, whether in the Christian version that attributes physical being to God or the secular version that only recognizes the existence of matter. The *emuna* we are searching for, then, is one that accentuates God's complete independence of physical existence – His utter transcendence. Based on our earlier suggestion that the Christian critique of Jewish uniqueness is a consequence of compromising the transcendence of God, this *emuna* should also result in a strengthened appreciation for the distinct identity of the Jewish people and Torah.

The Greeks used intellect to create a substitute for the biblical God; we responded by using that same intellect to bind ourselves to God, recovering relationship with Him through the analytics of the Oral Torah. Similarly, we can use the defining trait of Rome that so complicates our relationship with God – its radical individualization of experience – in the service of that relationship. We can use the personal isolation that is the basis from which Rome creates a vision of reality independent of God to create an independent relationship with God. If modern society has trained us to respect only that which we deduce on our own, let us deduce our faith![30]

---

29. See Descartes, *Discourse on Method*, discourses 2 and 4.
30. There has always been great value in this. In his introduction to *Ḥovot HaLevavot* (Duties of the Heart), Rabbenu Baḥya exhorts us to go beyond our trust in the

## Materialism and the Shallow Self

But how are we to do this? To whom can we look for guidance?

There was one person in our history who succeeded on his own in achieving faith in the unitary Creator from within a world that had utterly forgotten Him – our forefather Abraham. It makes sense to turn to him for guidance in the spirit of *maaseh avot siman lebanim* – the deeds of the fathers are signs for their children.

True, Abraham lived in idolatrous times, when everyone recognized a source or sources to existence. However, his primary innovation was to recognize the utter transcendence of the Creator. So, though our circumstances are different from his, his discovery is relevant to our specific needs. We can learn from him how each one of us can achieve personal conviction in the existence of the *transcendent* Creator. If we can follow his example, even today, in the midst of the Roman exile, we can achieve faith – at least a faith that provides a basis from which to build on the Exodus to a deeper faith.

As we move forward, however, it will be important to keep in mind the limitations of our approach. Building so heavily on the autonomous self holds the danger of severing our reliance on God, even when used in the pursuit of *emuna*. We faced a similar problem under Greece. With the Oral Torah we co-opted the Greek tool of autonomous intellect to the service of Torah, but then the Oral Torah began to break down. Only when through self-sacrifice we repudiated the independent power of the intellect could we fully benefit from the Oral Torah's potential to connect us to God.

Similarly, we can build to a limited extent on the Roman sense of the autonomous self; in the next chapter we will discuss how we as individuals can build *emuna*. This, however, is not a complete solution; we will eventually need to repudiate the independent power of the self. And just as under Greece the spiritual breakthrough came at a time of national deliverance, so it must eventually be with Rome. In the meantime, however, we need some check on the excesses of autonomy. An

---

statements of the wise – to work through their words, make them our own and come to our own personal certainty of the truth of their statements. In our times, however, personal conviction rather than just deepening our faith has become *essential* to its viability.

*Part 1: Gateway to the Exodus*

attitude of humility and repentance with their inherent sense of dependence will have to suffice as a frame for our individual efforts to create *emuna* and relationship with God.

We now turn to Abraham for direction on how to do that.

*Chapter 9*

# The Path to the Creator

In the last chapter we recognized that because we live in the cultural context of Rome, we each must achieve some level of *emuna* on our own. We also recognized that we need guidance on how to do this, and identified Abraham as the appropriate person to turn to because he, living among idolatrous peoples, found the Creator without any outside assistance. But when we try to learn from his example we run into a problem. Despite the obvious centrality of Abraham's *emuna* to everything the Torah is about, we do not find there any description of how Abraham did it.

The text cites a few details of Abraham's early life – his birth, his father, his marriage, his family's journey from Ur Kasdim to Ḥaran.[1] But from there it jumps to Abraham's first prophecy at the age of seventy-five.[2] No mention is made of the events leading up to the prophecy.[3]

---

1. Gen. 11:26–32.
2. Gen. 12:1.
3. There are midrashim that understand that the "covenant between the pieces" (Gen. 15:1–21) occurred before the prophecy of *Lekh Lekha* during a prior trip of Abraham to the land of Israel when he was seventy (*Seder Olam Rabba*, chapter 1). But this merely shortens the gap of silence, still leaving us with the same questions.

## Part 1: Gateway to the Exodus

There must be some background story to why God spoke to Abraham. And we certainly would not expect God to reveal Himself to someone who did not recognize His existence. But though we do find veiled references later in the text to other incidents in Abraham's early life,[4] an account of how he came to his *emuna* is absent.

The commentaries speculate on the reason for this strange silence.[5] For our purposes, the reason doesn't matter. We want to understand Abraham's path, and in this the Torah text does not assist us. We also have no physical evidence from Abraham's time that helps us in this regard. Our only source of information is midrash.

We have already had an opportunity to work with midrash in this book. For example, in the previous chapter we analyzed the midrash which compared the empires to animals with one kosher sign. That experience showed us how an arcane comparison expressed in a few cryptic words turned out to be a highly efficient language for conveying profound insight into our situation. That experience should give us a healthy respect for the depth of midrash.

But for help with Abraham we must turn to midrashim that we might think fall into a different category – those that describe historical events. As we look at them, however, we will benefit from remembering that the same authors who wrote the aggadic midrashim wrote these historical ones. More important, they wrote them for the same purpose – to convey deep understanding rather than to record what we call today history.

This is clear from the seemingly random and historically irrelevant details that are often included in these midrashim. If their purpose is

---

4. For example, Gen. 15:7 with *Tana Debei Eliahu Zuta* 25.
5. Maharal in *Netzaḥ Yisrael*, chapter 11, for example, explains that if we knew what Abraham did to merit his relationship with God we would think that it was an example of *ahava sheteluya bedavar* (love which is dependent on something, in this case Abraham's righteousness). If so, then "once that something is gone, the love also disappears" (Avot 5:16). By implication we would understand that our relationship to God – which we inherited from Abraham – is dependent on our continuing in Abraham's righteous path. But if we fall away from that righteousness (as we did), we lose our unique relationship with God (basically the Christian argument). This is not the case – our special connection to God is a permanent part of creation. But to avoid this destructive misunderstanding, Abraham's early merits are hidden from us.

merely to record historical facts, why use valuable ink to preserve extraneous material when far more important aspects of events are ignored and forgotten forever? The significance of these details is only to be found in the meaningful conceptual insights they give.[6]

This is supported by the otherwise-disturbing frequency of arguments between midrashim over these seemingly innocuous details. If they are inconsequential, why fill the tradition with unnecessary contradictions? But the arguments between midrashim are not over "facts." They are arguments over conceptual understanding, and the existence of arguments in midrash is, in this regard, no different from the existence of halakhic arguments in the Talmud, which generally are also over concepts rather than facts.[7]

There are those who will understand some historical basis to these kind of midrashim and there are those who will not differentiate between these historical midrashim and those that are purely conceptual, like the one we discussed linking the empires to the partially kosher animals. This dispute is irrelevant to us because everyone agrees the point of the midrash is not to convey the actual events but, rather, to convey the deeper truths coming through them. To determine these we need to approach the details of these midrashim as if they were projections based on a conceptual framework – a vision of how things might have occurred to actualize the deeper reality that the author of the midrash understood was coming into the world. This will help us ask the kinds of questions that will ferret out the concepts we seek.[8]

---

6. See Rambam, *Perush HaMishnayot*, Sanhedrin, chapter 10.
7. A general assumption we apply to the arguments of the Sages is that they do not have *maḥloket bemetziut* (an argument over facts). Rather, they argue over understanding. Commenting on Ketubbot 57a, Rashi explains that we take this approach because otherwise we cannot apply the principle *eilu ve'eilu divrei Elokim ḥayim* ("both are the words of the living God").
8. Maharal, *Beer HaGola*, Beer 6 Rabbi Tzvi Hirsch Ḥayes, *Mevo HaTalmud*, chapter 29. Maharal states that the exclusive intent of the Sages of the Oral Torah was to convey spiritual essences and truths, with their stories supplying the clothing in which the concepts are delivered. He discusses there an aggada from Gittin 56b that tells of a gnat that flew up Emperor Titus' nose and knocked on his brain for seven years. When he died they split his skull and found a two pound bird with a beak of brass and claws of iron. Maharal explains the concept being conveyed by each detail of

*Part 1: Gateway to the Exodus*

To us as children of modern Western civilization, this use of history is very foreign. We have been schooled exclusively in Thucydides' scientific approach, where our first responsibility is to determine the facts of what actually happened and then analyze them for understanding. This fits well with our Roman metaphysic that identifies reality with the material realm and views understanding as adding our interpretation to the reality of physical events. Torah, however, comes from another era and looks at things quite differently.

Torah teaches us that spiritual truths are the deepest realities, with the physical world and history their medium of expression. This point was forcefully brought home to me by a conversation I once had with Rav Zevulun Schwartzman. I was asking him about a subtlety in how Moses had experienced the revelation on Mount Sinai which was not explicitly brought out in the Torah text. I had the conceptual understanding of the event clear but was unsure in which of two possible ways this expressed itself. He answered that the question was irrelevant. The thing that counted was the spiritual principle involved, not the specific way it became realized. I was shocked! How could the question of what actually happened be irrelevant, or even of secondary importance?! Those are the facts!

I subsequently understood that this highlighted how different the Western tradition of understanding is from that of Torah – how much these two systems comprehend reality from differing metaphysical perspectives.

---

the story and its specific relevance to Titus based on his role in history. He states that how Titus actually died is irrelevant to the truth of the aggada, because the Sages are not concerned with the actual events. Rather, their sole interest in their words is to convey the essential truths that occurred regardless of which specific events were the vessel of their expression in physical reality. The Sages' interest is to construct a story to convey these truths accurately and, for those who know how to read it, clearly. Rav Moshe Shapiro was passionate about the importance of this point of Maharal. Rav Shapiro would not even consider a psychological explanation of aggadot, for the Sages' exclusive focus is essential truths. In *Mevo HaTalmud* Rav Hayes applies this even to aggadot recording conversations between historical figures – more standard historical midrashim. The Sages were not party to the conversations, and we do not expect them to have a tradition recording them. Rather, the Sages understood what was happening in the world spiritually, and they constructed a conversation that conveys these truths.

## The Path to the Creator

The Western tradition – at least from Rome onwards – sees reality as anchored in material being and gives first priority to what is actually happening in the world, for that is the medium of reality. Torah apportions significance in exactly the opposite way. Primary reality lies in the spiritual dimension. Which of several possible ways a spiritual truth actualizes itself in the world is of passing consequence. My question to Rav Schwartzman about what actually happened to Moses was like asking someone about the color of an envelope in which an essential letter was delivered – a fact of no real consequence. It is important to realize that this way of looking at things does not do away with the concept of history; rather, it changes its focus – what is deemed significant and worth remembering.

But if the point is to convey the relevant concept, why do the Sages speak in this opaque language rather than directly discussing the abstract concepts? For one thing, as we have seen, if you know how to understand the language it is an extraordinarily compact way to communicate deep and complex ideas. That the uninitiated cannot understand what is being said is actually viewed as a significant benefit, perhaps even the primary one. For unless these ideas are understood in the full context of the tradition, they can be both misunderstood and abused.[9]

A related reason is that Torah – including the midrashic tradition – understands spiritual and physical reality to be deeply intertwined with one another. In fact, Torah can be viewed as a guide to acting in such a manner as to retain their integration. As we already said, physical reality exists only to provide a medium through which the truly significant spiritual truths can be expressed. The last thing we want is that the physical world should diverge from directly expressing its spiritual foundations. This separation is the root of evil. But to keep the physical attached to the abstract realm, we must keep the abstract realm connected to the physical. Therefore, the Sages do not speak in a purely abstract language. Rather, concepts are conveyed through the language of events.[10] We will achieve a more authentic reading of midrash if we remain true to this approach.

---

9. Ramḥal, *Maamar al HaHaggadot*.
10. Another related reason why midrash speaks through events, one directly relevant to the topics covered in this book, is that the Sages respect the Torah as a tradition

## Part 1: Gateway to the Exodus

We will begin now with a midrash that recounts the process by which Abraham came to his *emuna*. In the text and footnotes I will give a few examples of alternate midrashim to give a sense of the diverse conceptual approaches to the event.

> When Abraham was born a star rose in the east and swallowed four stars in the four directions of the sky. The advisors of Nimrod (the King of Babylon that supervised the building of the famous tower) said to him, "At this moment a son was born to Terah from whom will eventually issue a people who will inherit this world and the next. Give his father a house full of silver and gold and kill the child." …Terah hid his son in a cave for three years, while the Holy One prepared two windows for him, from one of which came oil and from the other flour. When he was three years old he left the cave and asked himself, "Who created the heavens and the earth and me?" He prayed all day to the sun, but in the evening the sun set in the west and the moon rose in the east. Abraham said, "Neither of these have dominion. There is a master above them – to him will I pray and to him will I bow." He went to his father and asked him, "Father, who created the heavens and the earth and me?" His father answered, "My gods created the heavens and the earth and all this." Abraham said, "Show me your gods. Perhaps they have the capability of creating all this." Immediately, his father brought his gods to show to Abraham. Abraham went to his mother and asked, "Mother, make me fine food and I will bring it to my father's gods; perhaps they will accept my offering." She immediately made some for him and he brought it, placing it before the biggest of his father's idols. But there was no response. He returned to his mother and asked her to make even better food. She did and he brought it once again before his father's idol, and again there was no response. Immediately, the *Shekhina* (Divine Presence) rested upon him (he experienced *ruaḥ hakodesh*, divine inspiration) and he cried out

---

reaching back to the pre-Greek era, when human thought did not separate concepts from their physical expression. The advantage of that, as we said, is that it retains the intimate connection between meaning and reality.

regarding the idols, "They have mouths but they do not speak, they have eyes but they do not see…" (Ps. 115:5). He took a torch and burned them. He brought the largest idol outside and placed the torch in his hand. When his father returned home and saw that his gods were burned he asked Abraham, "My son, why did you burn my gods?" He answered, "I did not burn them. The big idol got angry with the others and burned them." He said back, "My son, you are an idiot. Does this idol have strength or life that it could do such a thing?! I made them from wood!" Abraham said back, "Let your ears hear your own words. If they have no strength, why did you tell me they created the heavens and the earth?"[11]

The ancient Mesopotamian society into which Abraham was born, and where much of civilization was concentrated, was relentlessly idolatrous and polytheistic. God was effectively unknown.[12] By Abraham's time, the Mesopotamian tradition of idolatry was a developed and complex vision. It was not, however, based on a speculative theology; it could not be, as the capacity for abstraction was not yet an integral component of human thinking. Rather, idolatry was a natural outgrowth of man's experience of reality in the early days of civilization.[13]

Before abstract reason came to dominate human consciousness, our center of self was located outside our individual being.[14] This awakened a powerful need to maintain connection with that source through worship. Whom and what to worship emerged from the complex interaction between our inner awareness and our dependencies upon and vulnerabilities to our external environment.

## ABRAHAM'S BREAK WITH MESOPOTAMIA

Our midrash presents a vision of how Abraham grew beyond the idolatry of his age. According to our midrash, Abraham began his break with

---

11. Rabbenu Baḥya on Gen. 15:7 quoting a midrash (author's translation).
12. Genesis Rabba 39:7 and Maharal, *Gur Aryeh, Bereshit* 11:32.
13. Jean Bottero, *Religion in Ancient Mesopotamia* (Chicago: The University of Chicago Press, 2004), 44–47. This will be explained later in this chapter. See also the appendix.
14. See chapter 5 and the appendix.

tradition at the age of three when he first asked a simple yet profound question: Who created the world and me? It seems surprising that so revolutionary a discovery as that of the unitary Creator should begin with such a seemingly obvious question. Had no one asked this before?

We need to understand what Abraham was really asking. We tend to identify Abraham's primary achievement as the recognition that physical reality must have a source, which would mean his question was headed in that direction. This is because we confuse Abraham's situation with our own, in which the dominant culture is secular, viewing reality as exclusively physical. But Abraham's world was idolatrous – *everyone* knew there was a source. Abraham's actual accomplishment was to break through the false visions of the nature of that Source which dominated his time. His innovation lay not in asking where everything came from, but in asking the question in a new way.

When the Mesopotamians asked questions about creation they were not concerned with the here and now. It was a question of history, of origin. In their effort to comprehend their world their understanding could not be complete without some explanation of how things came to be.[15] But there was no sense of immediate relevance to the question.

Abraham's search for the Creator was different. When he asked who his Creator was he was asking not a history question but an existential question: How can there be existence? in the sense of what sustains it now? The clue to the uniqueness and depth of Abraham's question is contained in its last two words. He asked, "Who created the heavens and the earth *and me?*"

Someone working purely within the Mesopotamian frame would not have added the words "and me."[16] For in Mesopotamian idolatry the creator god had no direct connection to the present. The existence of any individual asking a question about creation would be seen as coming from his parents. The gods controlled reality; they did not uphold its continuing existence. The words "and me" in Abraham's question, however, revealed that he was searching for a Creator whose support

---

15. See Bottero, *Religion in Ancient Mesopotamia*, 44, 72, 81–82.
16. Note that in our midrash, when Terah mirrored Abraham's question he left out the words "and me."

of existence was ongoing, implying a very different kind of power than that attributed to gods by the average Mesopotamian. At first, in all innocence, Abraham sought to identify the idolatrous force to which he owed primary allegiance. It would only become apparent later that his question challenged idolatry to its core and implied its destruction.

What so distinguished Abraham from the rest of his world at the tender age of three? Our midrash tells us that the astrologers of Babylon's king Nimrod had seen a sign in the stars that a son was born to Terah who would upend Nimrod's world. They advised killing the child. To save him, Terah secreted the infant away in a cave. The midrash tells us that Abraham first left that cave at the age of three.

What does the midrash wish to convey by this detail? We might think that Abraham's isolation shielded him from the idolatrous vision of Mesopotamian culture so that he was able to formulate an understanding of the world built from his innate humanity rather than the distortions of his cultural context. That could be an aspect of what our midrash intends. But another version of this midrash has Abraham spending the first thirteen years of his life hidden in a darkened room of his family home;[17] according to this version he would have been exposed to Mesopotamian culture. What both versions have in common is that by the time Abraham saw the world for the first time, he had already reached a basic level of intellectual capability.[18] What was gained by this timing?

We might ask ourselves what an extraordinary three-year-old would think on emerging for the first time from the dull grayness of a cave into the light and color of day. In the case of Abraham the midrash tells us. He asked, "Where did all this come from?" In the language of the midrash: "Who created the heavens and earth and me?"[19]

---

17. *Pirkei DeRabbi Eliezer* 26.
18. The ages of three and of thirteen are both noteworthy as marking transitions to another level of maturity and understanding. Three is when understanding begins. Thirteen is when a male reaches *daat*, a new level of understanding. So though the midrashim argue over what level of maturity in understanding was required for Abraham to begin his process, they agree that the emergence of understanding was an essential ingredient.
19. Anyone with any psychological sophistication might ask at this point how it is possible that Abraham emerged from the cave sane. A child growing up alone in a closet

*Part 1: Gateway to the Exodus*

The Ḥovot HaLevavot notes that an adult who is taken in and sheltered by others feels more appreciation than does a child adopted at infancy, although the child receives more care than the adult. The child becomes accustomed to his new parents' giving before he is aware of how remarkable it is; he takes it for granted before he can recognize his indebtedness. The adult understands from the beginning what he is receiving from his patrons; therefore he feels appreciation and wants to reciprocate, if only by saying "thank you."[20] Most of us relate to the gifts of existence like an adopted infant. They were already in place for us when our consciousness awoke, so we take them for granted. Because Abraham was hidden in a cave until he reached a basic level of maturity, his circumstances gave him the sensitivities of an adult adoptee toward the kindness of the Creator; Abraham was able to appreciate the given-ness of existence before becoming inured to it.

We must combine this insight into Abraham's situation with our knowledge of the trait that animated his character throughout his life: *ḥesed* (giving, kindness).[21] As the childhood taunt has it, "It takes one to know one." One who is a giver recognizes the given-ness in any situation and searches for the giver to express thanks. Abraham was a giver by nature and was therefore primed to search for the giver of reality.

### A NEW LEVEL OF DEPTH

These considerations are sufficient to understand why Abraham was able to ask the question "Who created the world?" But what allowed him to ask his question with the existential bite that separated him from the rest of his world? What led him to add "and me?" To answer this we need to understand more precisely this trait of *ḥesed* and appreciate the purity with which Abraham possessed it.

---

does not develop normally. What we said earlier about the manner in which midrash communicates makes this question irrelevant. Details like Abraham's isolation are included only to convey some specific meaning. The relevant question when analyzing a midrash is: What are the Sages teaching us by adding the details they choose to mention?

20. Ḥovot HaLevavot, Introduction to *Shaar HaBeḥina*.
21. Mic. 7:20.

The term *ḥesed*, which we translate as "kindness," is distinct from *raḥamim*, which we translate as "mercy" or "compassion." *Raḥamim* is aroused by an external catalyst; we feel bad for another and therefore give to him. *Ḥesed*, on the other hand, is an internally generated desire to give – it is, as it were, an uncaused cause.

The ultimate paradigm for an act of *ḥesed* is God's creation. For at the time of creation there was no "other" outside of God to prompt His desire to give. God was alone, and His act was motivated entirely from within Him. Within the confines of creation it is rare to find circumstances which allow for a completely unadulterated act of *ḥesed*, but the trait remains a distinct one. When we say that Abraham possessed the characteristic of *ḥesed* we refer to this specific talent for *initiating* goodness and the corresponding sensitivity to the *initiation* of goodness.

While Abraham's *ḥesed* in the general sense of kindness was sufficient to occasion the question that launched Abraham's search for a Creator, the specific quality of this trait determined the depth of the question and the criteria by which an acceptable answer would be measured. For when Abraham asked, "Who created the world and me?" he could not be satisfied with identifying some intermediate cause or creator that was itself caused or created by someone or something else. The purity of his *ḥesed* gave him a sense for the act of *initiation* that is the true beginning of any process and he sought the initiator of existence. This was a critical distinction.

The difference between Abraham's question and that of his peers can be illustrated by a stereotypical debate between a poet-philosopher and a scientist. The poet, contemplating a beautiful wooded valley, is overcome by the enormity of existence and asks whimsically, "Where did all this come from?" The scientist answers, "Thousands of years of erosion by wind and rain created the soil that allowed this forest to grow." The poet responds, "That does not answer my question." The scientist responds, "Millions of years of subcontinental plates sliding against one another threw up these mountains and then the erosion began." The poet protests, "You are not speaking to my point." The scientist replies, "After billions of years gravity brought dust together and eventually there was continental drift...." The poet looks exasperated, to which the scientist adds triumphantly, "There was a Big Bang."

*Part 1: Gateway to the Exodus*

At this point our poet responds, "You have answered absolutely nothing! What, then, banged the Big Bang? Where did all the matter come from that banged?" It is clear from the pattern of the scientist's answers that any additional answer he gives will merely take things another step back, which will just lead to the next question. This is because the scientist is answering a different question from the one being asked by the poet. The scientist is explaining how things came to be in their present state, answering a chronology question, tracing a horizontal line in time. The poet, however, is actually asking how can there be existence at all. His is asking a metaphysical question, probing vertically for a different depth and significance of being.

While the scientist is answering from within the framework of our experience – that is, within the framework of time – the poet is asking a question that necessarily requires that we step beyond that box. The poet does not take physical existence for granted. He instinctively recognizes that the paltry existence characterizing the material reality that we are aware of cannot support or explain its own existence and searches for a greatness of Being that can. If it must be sustained – "given" – there must be a giver. Who or what is that Giver?!

To my knowledge, all Mesopotamian myths of creation, like our stereotypical scientist, viewed existence only within the framework of time. They all identify intentional creation with a god who is a chronologically intermediate figure that existed in a context outside himself – that is, a god that himself needed to come or be brought into existence.[22] This was also true of the pre-biblical myths of creation originating in Egypt, the other major cultural center of the time.[23] Abraham, because of his trait of ḥesed, was like the poet stepping out of the box seeking the true Creator, the ultimate Originator, about whom one could not ask,

---

22. See Bottero, *Religion in Ancient Mesopotamia*, 90.
23. Donald B. Redford, *The Ancient Gods Speak: A Guide to Egyptian Religion* (Oxford: Oxford University Press, 2002), 246–51. There is one complex of Egyptian myths that deals with creation on a level somewhat comparable to that of Abraham and the Torah, namely what is referred to as the Memphite theology. But this is now generally agreed among scholars to have been developed during the 25th Egyptian Dynasty (Redford, 249), making it contemporaneous with Solomon's Temple. This was long after Torah's transcendent monotheism was made known to the world.

"Who created this creator?"[24] Eventually, this could only take Abraham to one place – to what we call *Mukhraḥ HaMetziut*, Necessary Being. In other words, if we seek that which was not created we seek that which *must* exist. But in the era that Abraham lived this required a tremendous conceptual leap that took him decades to achieve.

## WHAT ABRAHAM DID NOT DO

Before we dissect our midrash to determine Abraham's path of discovery, it is worthwhile to avoid confusion by highlighting what we are *not* saying. In our analogy to the discussion between the poet and the scientist, it is the poet who represents Abraham's position. The poet models how a pure trait of ḥesed leaves one unsatisfied with incomplete, intermediary solutions to questions about existence. The analogy was not intended to suggest that Abraham, in the manner of the scientist, found the Creator through a series of solutions each reaching further into the past and then shown to be inadequate. Such a scenario would see Abraham finally realize that there is no end to the question "what came before that," which would lead him to conclude that the answer he sought could not lie in creation but must rather be transcendent.

We slip into such an assumption effortlessly because it would have Abraham following a line of reasoning that is almost intuitive to us, and which has been used in one form or another since Greek times. It is called the cosmological argument for the existence of a Creator, and it goes as follows: Every present has a past that caused it. But there cannot be an infinite number of pasts, for then we could never reach

---

24. We see here the fundamental importance of character and its development. Our understanding of our world is not determined by our intellect, but rather by the questions we ask in our efforts to understand that world. Those questions are determined by our character. Someone with a developed sense for ḥesed can recognize the given-ness of the world and will naturally ask who gave or made it. With enough persistence that person will eventually arrive at the Creator. Someone who lacks the internal space to become aware of the given-ness of the world will take it for granted and lack the impetus to ask who made it. Observing the causal chains that form his world, he is prone to ask how our world came to be as it is. But this form of the question is unlikely to bring him to recognize the Creator in any genuine sense. Such people, like the scientist in our analogy, are satisfied that they know all they need to know about the origins of existence once they have heard of the Big Bang.

*Part 1: Gateway to the Exodus*

the present.[25] Though we can abstractly conceive an infinite sequence of numbers, the idea that an infinite sequence of *actual* causes exists is inconceivable. Since each causative event requires some time, an infinite sequence would take forever to reach the present. Moreover, we need a beginning. Therefore there must be something outside of the sequence that started things – a First Cause. We thus must recognize the existence of a transcendent Creator.

Though logicians claim to have refuted the cosmological argument,[26] it still seems coherent to us and is, I think, the only classical argument that retains any persuasive power today. However, the argument is built by positing an infinite sequence against the direction of time and then recognizing that the very limitlessness of the sequence contradicts its possibility. To think in this manner requires several nested levels of abstraction. Since this was an age when achieving abstraction at all was a monumental accomplishment, it is difficult to imagine Abraham producing such an argument. In any case, we see no hint in the midrash that Abraham relied on this logic.

#### ABRAHAM'S PATH

What, then, does the midrash tell us about Abraham's path? We see that from the very beginning, Abraham had the intuition that there must be a source to existence – his only question was Who. We already discussed how his dominant trait of *ḥesed* was the basis of this instinct and how that trait, along with Abraham's insulation from the distorted understandings of his culture, protected him from accepting easy but inadequate answers to his question.

According to the midrash, Abraham first searched for creation's source in the physical world, which was the only arena directly accessible

---

25. This is a simplified version of the Aristotelean version of the argument, which is phrased in terms of causes: everything that exists was caused, and its cause was caused, etc. Presenting the argument it in terms of time does not work for Aristotle, who believed the universe existed eternally. The possibility of an infinite sequence in time was a point of contention between Aristotle and the Islamic philosophers. See Rambam, *Moreh Nevukhim*, introduction to part 2.
26. See chapter 1, note 45. There are also innumerable books and articles written by philosophers with the goal of refuting the argument.

to him. This naturally led him to focus on the sun, the physical sustainer of all life. But he rejected this as the basis of existence when the sun set, revealing that its mastery was limited to the daytime.

This shows that from the beginning Abraham also intuited that the source he was searching for was a single, unitary source. For this reason Abraham did not then turn to the moon. It could not be the moon, since Abraham had already seen that the sun was the unchallenged master of the day. Once the sun had set, it was clear that the source Abraham sought was not part of physical reality.

This meant that his target was not directly observable. So it was not something he was going to be able to find on his own, and he turned to his father to guide him in civilization's answer to the question. Abraham was directed by his father to the family idols, physical forms through which powers were manifest in the world. Given the choice among idols, Abraham chose the biggest one, so that there could be nothing lacking in the idol being worshipped. He gave it an offering, and when it was not accepted he gave an even better offering, so there could be nothing lacking in his gift. Still there was no reaction from the idol.

Abraham reacted to the idol's unresponsiveness by utterly rejecting idolatry. How did he come to this conclusion? If a god is manifest through an idol, it has a physical dimension. If it is physical it has needs – in Mesopotamia the belief was that man was created to provide the gods with food. Since the offerings were intended to fulfill the needs of the god, they should be accepted regardless of the merits of the one bringing the offering.[27] Since Abraham was confident there was nothing missing in either his offering or the idol he was worshipping, there was no explanation for the gift not being accepted other than that idolatry is false. Though it was traditional in the idolatrous societies of Mesopotamia and Egypt to make offerings to idols and then distribute the food to the priests, Abraham understood this to be a ruse.[28] The bankruptcy of idolatry was revealed; the gods of Mesopotamian society could not be the source that Abraham sought.

---

27. Maharal, *Netivot Olam, Netiv HaAvoda*, chapter 1.
28. This is called the reversion of the offering. See, for example, Redford, *The Ancient Gods Speak*, 281–82.

*Part 1: Gateway to the Exodus*

## ABRAHAM'S LEAP

At that point Abraham knew that he could not answer his question on his own, and society could not help him. There was nowhere to turn. When he reached this place of complete helplessness, his desperate desire to understand was answered. In a flash Abraham found himself propelled by divine inspiration to the concept of transcendence, the realization that the Creator is utterly removed from physical reality, the infinite Source of all possibility and existence.

It is important to appreciate that though it takes the midrash only a few lines to describe Abraham's search, it actually covers a significant stretch of Abraham's life. Though Abraham began asking the question "Who created the heavens and the earth and me?" at the age of three, it was only at the age of forty-eight that he achieved his breakthrough.[29] This means that he searched relentlessly for forty-five years. It was Abraham's dogged perseverance that merited his receiving inspiration at the age of forty-eight.[30]

Though inspiration has no direct cause that we can perceive, we can still recognize what primed Abraham for his breakthrough. Abraham's starting point was the realization that the reality that he had access to lacked sufficient greatness of being to explain its own existence. Since he did not take its existence for granted, it shouted out to Him that it must have a source. After he began seeking that source, he eventually realized that it was not any object he could see in the world. Further investigation led him to conclude that it could not be a force of physical reality either. What was left?

To our modern minds the next step was obvious. But when Abraham jumped to the conclusion that the Creator is utterly transcendent, he leapt beyond his epoch. He succeeded in conceiving of something with no physical component, a purely abstract thought. Discovering the transcendent Creator, an existence independent of any physical vessel or medium, required that Abraham think abstractly.

In Abraham's time reality was understood to be anchored in material being. People lived in a physical world. Everything that they

---

29. Genesis Rabba 64:4.
30. Rabbenu Bahya on Gen. 15:7 and the midrash quoted at the beginning of this chapter.

encountered they encountered through its physical expression. It was a given that everything that existed could only exist through its physical expression – this was the basis of idolatry. Such a view was a corollary of the general state of intellectual development and mode of thinking then. At that time people thought in terms of concrete objects. For example, in Mesopotamia they knew how to count. But though they could count seven bushels of wheat, the abstract number seven, independent of some specific realization, would have been challenging for them to grasp.

Thus in order to recognize the Creator, Abraham had to think in a way that ran counter to his generation's mode of thought and metaphysic. We learned earlier the remarkable innovations of Greek culture were anchored in a capacity for abstraction.[31] But Abraham lived long before the age of abstract speculation began in Greece. The dawn of the speculative outlook is somewhat arbitrarily associated with the year 585 BCE, when Thales, the first of the Milesian school of philosophers, predicted a solar eclipse.[32] Abraham's era was well over a thousand years earlier. Academics view the antiquity of the Jews' transcendent monotheism with wonder. In the era in which Abraham lived, his insight was both a radical departure and an extraordinary achievement.[33] Our midrash tells us it required divine inspiration.

We have difficulty realizing the magnitude of this departure because we naturally think in abstractions.[34] To understand Abraham's challenge, compare it to a small categorical leap that is more accessible

---

31. Pure abstraction catalyzes the *intellectual* advancement of civilization. For example, imagine trying to create calculus using word problems without abstracting them to symbolic equations, or doing long division without numbers.
32. Cornford, *From Religion to Philosophy*, 1.
33. Frankfort, *The Intellectual Adventure of Ancient Man*, 367–69, (367–69) is awestruck by the level of advancement represented by the Jew's recognition of the transcendent Creator. He is speaking there about the Jews generally, not specifically Abraham, who represents the leading edge of this advance.
34. Abraham's breakthrough was of such magnitude that according to the midrash (Genesis Rabba 39:7) after achieving it Abraham was absolved from the obligation of honoring his parents. The departure was so radical that he was no longer considered the child of his parents. He had become someone completely new. See also Maharal, *Gur Aryeh, Bereshit* 11:32. The midrash states that after this breakthrough there could never be another of comparable magnitude – no one else will ever be absolved from the obligation of honoring his parents.

to us. Picture a man living his whole life on the plains of Mesopotamia – flat as far as he can see in every direction, no mountain to climb to experience the optical illusion of the curvature of the earth. When he plans his canals he builds on the obvious fact that two lines that bisect a third line at the same angle cannot meet. That is his world; any alternative is inconceivable and would violate the very structure of what he perceives to be his reality (and would make a mess of his canals). One day he follows two "parallel lines" a quarter of the way around the earth and finds that they meet! What would it take for him to realize that his perception of what makes lines parallel only holds true on a flat plane but not on a curved sphere, and then accept the conclusion that, contrary to his perception, his world is not actually flat but is instead a sphere?[35]

## A PATH FOR OUR TIMES

We cannot rely on divine inspiration for our *emuna;* but we also don't need it in order to be able to conceive of the transcendent Creator, because we deal with abstract concepts all the time. But we do need a *reason* to believe in His existence. We can construct an argument for the existence of the Creator that will lead us along Abraham's path, without implying that it was the conscious structure of Abraham's intuition.

Our key first step is to refrain, like Abraham, from taking existence for granted. From there, we proceed to Abraham's conviction that material existence lacks the greatness of being to explain its own existence. Since it cannot exist on its own, there *must* be Someone/Something that supports it in existence. But Who or What?

At this point, for Abraham's divine inspiration we will substitute scaled down, Rambam-inspired proofs to the effect that the Creator is necessary, unitary, and transcendent. If you find the reasoning too technical, skip down three paragraphs. The reasoning goes as follows: This ultimate source is not itself supported in existence – if it were, it would be an intermediary, a part of creation, rather than the ultimate Creator we seek. If it is not created, it must come from itself. If it comes from itself, it could never have not existed because if so, "when" it didn't

---

35. Lines of longitude are perpendicular to the equator and appear parallel over short distances, but converge and meet at the poles.

exist it obviously could not have brought itself into existence – because *it* didn't exist "then." At this point we are tempted to say that because it cannot *not* exist therefore it *must* exist. But it is more accurate to say that because it exists without being created, existence is essential to its nature – its being has the quality of necessity.

It must also be unitary. For necessity defines a level or intensity of being – it is actually ultimate being. It is not a mere characteristic that can accidentally qualify another trait. "Being" is necessary as opposed to "beings" that have necessity. Necessary Being is unique. We call It God.[36]

Finally, because it is necessary it cannot be physical, for anything physical is a composite of form and matter. A composite is not necessary because its existence is dependent – dependent upon the maintenance of the unity of its elements.[37] So the Creator must be transcendent.

Who is this Being? Such a Being cannot be part of creation; that which is necessary must have always existed and, therefore, cannot be created. It also cannot exist within the confines of creation, for creation exists in time and space. A Being with necessity is not merely eternal; It exists beyond time. Finally, creation is physical and the Creator is transcendent.

Since we can only see that which is within creation, we cannot "identify" the Creator. But existence testifies to His existence, so we know there must be a Creator. Our question becomes our answer: Who is the necessary and unitary Creator? It is the necessary and unitary Creator – Whoever He is! Even without identifying Him in some specific way, we accept the necessity of worshipping Him.

---

36. See *Moreh Nevukhim* II:1 where Rambam proves through various logics that the Prime Mover exists, is necessary, must be unitary, and cannot be physical (the four qualities we are discussing here). Those arguments are extremely technical and difficult to get through; Rambam lays down 26 philosophical propositions before even beginning the proofs. The argument for unity I am using here is a pared-down version of the one advanced by Rambam after his fourth philosophical argument. In technical language if there are two Gods, they must have in common that which makes them God, i.e., necessity. And they must have a quality that distinguishes them – otherwise they are one and the same. Then they are composites, and composites are not necessary because they can dissolve.

37. See *Moreh Nevukhim* II:1 (the third philosophical argument). This is one of several proofs by Rambam that God is not physical – that is, the Creator is transcendent.

*Part 1: Gateway to the Exodus*

**THE UNDOING OF IDOLATRY**

Abraham's realization that the Creator cannot be *in* creation meant that idolatry (worshipping gods that have a physical anchor, as opposed to merely expressing themselves into creation) was false.[38] And God's unity requires that there cannot be other sources of existence. Thus Abraham's search for a true Creator who *initiates* creation from nothing, if taken far enough, leads inevitably to the recognition of the supreme and unique greatness of God – the monotheistic nullification of idolatrous polytheism. The depth of Abraham's question necessitated its revolutionary conclusion.

Abraham succeeded in separating God out from material existence. He recognized the utterly transcendent quality of God, even if he could not know anything specific about Him before he received prophecy some years after his discovery. It is by returning to the God Abraham found that we overcome the pressures specific to Roman exile that push us to merge God with material existence.

Yet for us as citizens of Rome, material existence sets the gold standard for what is real. Does relating to the transcendent God mean that we must lose any sense for His reality?! We spoke about this at the start of the book and concluded that when we discover God through His material creation – that is, in his role as Creator – it is physical reality that shouts out to us the existence of God. The reality of matter is not the reality of God. But the reality of matter gives real testimony to the existence of God.

In fact, Abraham inspired us to even greater conviction than that. From him we learned to ask, "Who created the heavens and the earth *and me?*" The reality of my own existence testifies to the existence of the Creator.

---

38. The existence of the necessary, unitary Creator does not rule out His creation of intermediaries or agents of His will (what the Torah calls *malakhim* [angels]). But once we recognize that the Creator continuously supports existence, an entity with genuinely independent authority – that is, one worthy of worship – is ruled out. Though polytheistic systems often recognized a supreme god – Zeus for the Greeks, Marduk for the Babylonians – the mythology of autonomous action and court intrigue to circumvent the will of this supreme god is incompatible with a unitary, transcendent Creator.

# The Path to the Creator

## WHAT WE LEARN FROM ABRAHAM

We began this book with the goal of strengthening our *emuna*. We turned to Abraham for guidance on how to do this and have learned how to retrace his steps. But what exactly is it that we learned?

At first glance it appears that in following our version of Abraham's path – substituting logic for divine inspiration – we have returned to Rambam's position, outlined in the introduction, that rational proof is the way to bolster our *emuna*.

This is a misunderstanding on two fundamental counts. First, Rambam requires rational proof because of his position that only logical deduction has the quality of necessity needed to qualify as emuna. We concluded that this set too high a bar for us. *Our* goal in retracing Abraham's path was not to attain absolute conviction through logical arguments, but only to drawn from them enough confidence in God's existence to accept the genuine possibility of miracles.

Second, and more fundamentally, any equation of Abraham's path to that of Rambam is based on a slight of hand. It is like saying because this one uses logic and that one uses logic therefore they both use logic in the same way. Logic does not play the same role in the two approaches. Rambam uses logic as his starting point. Though Abraham attempted to use reason in his search for God, and we with our familiarity with abstract thinking do use reason as a part of our search, the application of reason takes place in a larger context. *The starting point of the use of reason in Abraham's path was Rambam's end point!* Abraham *assumed* the very thing that Rambam was trying to prove – that there must be a Creator. Abraham only applied his intellect to that assumption in an effort to discover Who He is.

Rambam uses logical proofs to derive four things: God's necessity, His unity, His transcendence, and first and foremost His existence. We used logical derivations only to arrive at the qualities of necessity, unity, and transcendence. We did not attempt to prove God's existence, as this would deviate from Abraham's approach. True, we mentioned the cosmological proof in our imaginary dialogue between the poet and the scientist – but only to explain what Abraham was *not* relying on.

If we want to learn from Abraham how to gain *emuna* it is on his initial intuitive conviction that there must be a Creator that we need to focus. Where did that come from, and how can we also achieve that? We explained that it was a consequence of Abraham's *midda* (trait) of *ḥesed:* as a natural giver he recognized giving and sought out the giver in order to reciprocate. His *ḥesed* was of such purity that he sought the true initiator of existence.

*This is the key insight we gain from Abraham's process – that he worked through his* middot, *his character.* This makes sense given the principle of *maaseh avot siman lebanim* (the deeds of the forefathers are signs to guide us). The reason we turn to the acts of the forefathers to guide us is that they personified to an unparalleled degree of purity the very *middot* which are the stuff of our struggles and the focus of our purpose in life.

Abraham's conviction that there exists a Creator was not based on logic; but neither was it random, whimsical, or unanchored. It emerged from the objective foundations of human personality – the *middot*. We will learn in the next part of the book that there is an intrinsic structure to personality. When our *middot* are pure, our personality naturally conforms to this structure, which is one that lends itself to emuna.

## THE CENTRALITY OF *MIDDOT* TO *EMUNA*

From Abraham we learn, somewhat surprisingly, that the way to build *emuna* is to enhance the influence of our *middot* on our perception of the world. We who lack Abraham's fineness of character must also work on purifying those *middot* before engaging the world more fully through them.

This approach does not result in a proof of the existence of the Creator that is compelling in the manner of Rambam's logical argument. We do not experience a character-driven intuition as objective truth. However, it is important to recognize that in the time of Abraham it was otherwise. To Abraham this "argument from *middot*" brought absolute certainty – he allowed himself to be thrown into a fire rather than recant his beliefs.[39]

As we explained, the nature of human consciousness has evolved over historical time; when civilization first emerged we experienced

---

39. Genesis Rabba 38:13.

reality through our *middot*.[40] This was our reality and therefore our truth. In this earlier time purification of character *would* have been enough to bring certainty of the existence of the Creator. But this was before abstract reason's domination of consciousness. By the time Greece spread its empire, our experience had become mediated through our understanding, with ideas our deepest reality and truth. Because of this we treat intuitions born of character traits as untrustworthy at best. Today we are doubly removed from Abraham's time. For our consciousness has shifted yet again, to be anchored no longer in our intellect but in our sense of our own individual existence.

We said earlier that Rambam's rationally driven approach to *emuna* requires us to return the center of our personality to the intellect as in Greek times. We observed that for most of us this is unrealistic. How, then, does it make sense to argue the relevance of this *middot* approach which is even more removed from the nature of our consciousness?

Even if character is no longer the medium of our experience, it forever remains its foundation. The way our *middot* process reality determines the structuring of our awareness and understanding. This profoundly influences how our thoughts are formulated. By purifying our *middot*, we prime ourselves for *emuna*. The structure of our awareness becomes a fertile soil in which *emuna* can take firm root.

Abraham is the prime example of how this works. His *midda* of ḥesed – giving – structured his awareness in such a way that the world presented itself as *given*, implying the existence of a Giver. Similarly, in the Middle Ages as Jewish philosophy was developing and the *ḥakhamim* needed a Hebrew equivalent to the word "existence," they chose *metziut*, which effectively means "that which is brought forth." The language frames reality in such a way that it seems incomplete without recognizing a Creator. Creation becomes implicit in the way we view existence.[41]

This does not bring us to certainty in God's existence, as this implicit *emuna* remains in conflict with the ideas we inherit about the

---

40. We actually said that we experienced reality through its physical expression. This is equivalent to saying we experienced it through our *middot*, which are a more physical engagement of reality than intellect.
41. I understood this from a lecture of Rav Moshe Shapiro.

world from our surrounding culture. But when combined with the proofs from subjective experience that we discussed in chapter 1, this can give us sufficient confidence in the existence of God to trust in the actuality of our tradition of miracles and to build from the Exodus to the Torah's standard of *emuna*. This explains the extensive literature guiding people in these subjective, *middot*-based approaches to *emuna*, even though they do not result in an *emuna* that would satisfy the Torah requirements. We will have more to say on this point at the end of the book.

We will see in the second half of this book that the plagues, the miracles of the Exodus, also develop our *emuna* by developing our character. They, however, can produce another level of conviction because they work through the experience of miracles. But they also operate through the *middot*. Thus, by applying what we learned from Abraham and training our *middot*, we not only attain an intermediate level of *emuna* but also begin the process that will eventually lead to higher levels through our study of the Exodus.

It would be nice if in these last few pages we could learn from Abraham a proof of the existence of God that is compelling – something readers could study a few times like a challenging algebra proof and be on their way to fulfilling the mitzva of *emuna* in its fullness. Life is not so simple. Even Rambam, who held that *emuna* could be proven, acknowledged that a lifetime of personal work was required to prepare to internalize the rational argument in a meaningful way. Achieving *emuna*, the primary mitzva of the Torah, is a process that requires years of striving regardless of one's approach, especially in our times. There are no shortcuts to its genuine achievement. But there is also no goal more worthy of our efforts.

*Chapter 10*

# Summing Up and Moving On

In the ancient world man intuitively recognized the existence of gods, including a creator. Creation, however, was not of immediate concern. As an event that had been completed in the distant past, it was relevant only insofar as it rounded off people's understanding of their world. Abraham's innovation began with his realization that our reality requires ongoing support to exist. This gave the Creator immediate significance and also necessarily implied that the nature of His existence is greater than that of our reality. The qualities required of a Being able to create and sustain existence so dwarfed any other power that once Abraham recognized the transcendent Creator, He stood alone as the One God – at least for Abraham, who had full clarity about the implications of His transcendence.

When the Jewish people were reintroduced to God through the Exodus, He was again revealed as the power behind creation, so that our mitzva of *emuna* parallels Abraham's discovery. *Emuna* is the essence and basis of all the mitzvot, so if our mitzva of *emuna* is directed toward God in His role as Creator, then our whole relationship with Him is also built on this awareness.

## Part 1: Gateway to the Exodus

This is evident in God's primary name, the one that expresses His ultimate relationship with the world and that we read in our daily blessings and prayers. As we mentioned in the first chapter, it is composed of the four letters *yod heh vav heh*, which form a composite of the three tenses of being: *hayah, hoveh, yihyeh* – was, is, and will be.[1] This conveys the fact that God is past, present, and future – in other words, He *is* existence. Using the name implies a level of perception even beyond awareness of God as Creator and Sustainer of the world. For labeling God as the Creator implies that creation has a distinct existence, albeit supported by God. Recognizing Him as existence itself eliminates creation as a distinct entity, for whatever has existence necessarily derives it from Him.

We are supposed to strive toward this recognition when we recite the *Shema*. When we declare that God is One, among the many meanings of this declaration is our recognition that God is the only Entity that exists. The commentaries explain that when we say the word "One," during the *Shema* we should strive to experience ourselves as ceasing to exist – because we are saying that nothing, including ourselves, has existence separate from God. Rabbi Akiva died reciting the *Shema* because he reached such a clear recognition of this that he *actually* ceased to exist in this world![2] We obviously cannot function on an ongoing basis with anything close to this awareness. But it remains the deepest reality: God is the only true existence; creation is His instrument possessing no existence of its own.[3] The Sages refer to this as the vision of the *merkava* (chariot), where creation or some aspect of it is perceived as nothing more than God's vehicle of revelation.

We do not pronounce this primary name. That is, we do not express it into the phenomenal realm of time and space. Expressing it would imply that we have an actual connection to what this name implies, whereas in reality such clarity is beyond our reach in the world as we experience it today.[4] We can write the name – we recognize the

---

1. Rabbi Jacob ben Asher, *Tur Oraḥ Ḥayyim* 5.
2. Rabbi Tzadok HaKohen, *Or Zarua LaTzaddik, Alef Rabati*.
3. See Maharal, *Drush al Shabbat HaGadol*.
4. Rashi, Ex. 17:16, and Maharal, *Gur Aryeh* on the same verse.

truth of God's complete omnipotence. But it is a theoretical truth for us, not an actual one.

The actual intent we associate with this name is that God is the Source of our and all existence – in our language, the Creator.[5] Other characteristics of God are ancillary to this fundamental awareness. Relating to God first and foremost as Creator anchors our connection to Him in physical reality.

This is particularly important while we remain in our present, Roman exile, especially because of the continuing influence of Greece on intellectual life. We are being pulled in two contradictory directions simultaneously. While our Roman hosts identify reality with the material realm, the Greek penchant for abstraction led them to identify ideas as reality and God as an abstract Intellect. We did not accept their vision of God as a purely intellectual entity, but their influence still draws us today to relate to God in a manner that disassociates Him from material reality. We are particularly susceptible to this pressure because God is not physical and we studiously avoid connecting Him with physical things in order to steer clear of idolatry.

But though this more abstract relationship with God might have been adequate while we lived under the Greeks, nowadays it is not. Rome has moved our focus to material existence, so that this intellectualized relationship with God is experienced as something bordering on fantasy. In other words, the intellectual accommodation we made to Greece comes to haunt us in the context of Rome. Relating to both the transcendent and the creator aspects of God neatly skirts the problem.

**CONSCIOUS OF CONTEXT**

Our modern, abstract conception of God contrasts sharply with our ancient Mesopotamian heritage. Then, the gods had immediacy. Our perception of them was an outgrowth of the nature of our awareness at that stage in history: man was focused in material reality, unable to disengage understanding from the physical envelope that catalyzed our awareness. Therefore the gods were seen as the forces that populated our environment; their bodies consisted of the various elements of our

---

5. Rabbi Jacob ben Asher, *Tur Oraḥ Ḥayim* 5.

physical reality through which we experienced their power. The reality of the gods was identical with the reality of material existence.[6] A Mesopotamian would not need to prove the existence of his gods any more than he would need to prove the existence of his world.

Abraham's discovery of the transcendent Creator emerged from that environment. Despite the abstract quality of transcendence, Abraham's relationship with God did not lose its immediacy, for it sprang from his encounter with the material world. We are still supposed to relate to God in a comparable manner. Our awareness of the existence of the Creator should be one and the same with our awareness of existence itself, as it was with Abraham.[7]

If we focus on God as the Creator, we can correct some of the distortions that have crept into our relationship with God. Physical reality would then constantly testify to God's reality. Abraham asked, "Who created the heavens, the earth, *and me*." When he eventually answered "The Creator," the heavens, the earth, and himself were changed from questions to proofs. We need to work on relating to our reality in that manner. We cannot sacrifice full recognition of the transcendence of God. But so ethereal a concept needs something tangible to ground it. Creation provides that.

Abraham's investigation of the origin of the world brought him to an extraordinary level of conviction in the existence of the Creator. His legacy to us is not merely that conviction, but also his model of personal pursuit of that conviction. In this first half of the book we have traced mankind's slow but steady fall away from God, as civilization added layer upon layer of interpretation onto reality, complicating the task of *emuna*. We discussed the various mitzvot and approaches the Sages developed to aide us in surmounting these barriers – the writing of the book of Esther, the establishment of Purim and Hanukka, the development of a culture of self-sacrifice through Torah. But today, we find ourselves in

---

6. Jacobsen, *The Treasures of Darkness*, 5–13. In Mesopotamia the name of the god immanent in an object was sufficiently identified with the object that it was usually the same as the name of the object. For example, in Akkadian *šamšun* was both the word for "sun" and the name of the sun-god.
7. Maharal, *Tiferet Yisrael*, chapter 37. See also chapter 1 of this book.

the midst of an exile that requires us to go beyond rabbinic enactments and add personal initiative to our development of *emuna*.

This allows us to build on the peculiar and challenging nature of our experience of self under Rome – our sense of autonomy and isolation. While the isolation complicates the task of finding a genuine connection to God, the autonomy engenders an intuitive respect for understanding that we develop on our own. We can work with that.

We *can* as individuals engage our most essential selves in our relationship with God – our creative ability to understand and arrive at conclusions, to choose and recognize. It has always been important to harness these aspects of ourselves in the interest of faith, but it has become essential in our times.[8] Not only does such an effort speak to modern prejudices about the basis of truth, it also addresses directly the extreme isolation of self from God in our cultural milieu. We are most alone in the act of choice. When we choose *emuna*, we are alone with God, transforming isolation into intimacy. We will have a chance to develop these ideas more in the second half of the book when we explore the structure of personality.

Torah is an extraordinary guide to relationship with the Divine. But the times we live in place obstacles between the Torah we learn and our essential selves. Through activating our capacity for choice, decision-making, and creative understanding in a personal quest for the Creator, we bring our self into the center of the process.

As we each search out our own path to personal recognition of the Creator, many options present themselves; each person has to discover what resonates with him or her. Some will resonate with Abraham's perception that "the wondrousness of existence testifies that it must have a source." Others may accept the proposition that "the clear divinity evident in man proves that there is a God." (This appeals to those who are sensitive to moments when something otherworldly shines through our humanity in obvious testimony to a larger reality: the birth of an infant, the manifest unfolding of understanding in the face of a maturing child, contemplating self-consciousness and free will, the finding of a soul-mate.) People with a strong sense of right and wrong, a powerful

---

8. See chapter 8, note 30.

*Part 1: Gateway to the Exodus*

sense for objectively binding moral principles and ideals, may be convinced that "the compelling awareness of meaning testifies to a God."

Each of us have our own path and each of us needs to take the initiative to walk it. What Abraham teaches us is that whichever path we choose, we must walk it against a backdrop of work on character, harnessing our personality in the service of *emuna*. By accentuating our trait of *ḥesed,* we incline our intuition toward viewing reality as a creation, and we structure our personality to integrate *emuna* at the deepest levels.

Reality declares the existence of the Creator in so many ways. We each have our own way of hearing it. But we have to prepare ourselves to hear as well as put in the effort to listen. We don't need to reach objective clarity, just enough to be ready to move on in a meaningful way to the next stage of the process – the analysis of the miracles of the Exodus. It is now time for us to turn to that task.

# Part 2
## The Character of Faith

# Introduction

Our project with this book is to understand how to strengthen our *emuna*. In the first half we discussed the distinct approaches of Rambam and Ramban to the mitzva. Both hold that to fulfill the Torah obligation, our belief in the existence of the Creator must be objectively grounded. Rambam's position is that this must be achieved through reason, whereas Ramban's position is that it must be derived from our historical experience of the miracles of the Exodus, primarily the plagues.

In the cultural context in which we live, Ramban's approach is challenging because our extremely materialist perspective makes it difficult to integrate our tradition of miraculous experience into our historical awareness. But though Rambam's rational approach avoids this problem, we argued that exclusive reliance on human reason in our generation is unrealistic for the overwhelming majority of people. Thus we are left with Ramban's approach. But for an *emuna* built on miracles to be genuine we first need to confront the challenge materialism presents to viewing miracles as possible. That was the task of the first half of the book. Now we are ready to focus on the Exodus.

Our shift to the Exodus requires that we broaden our definition of *emuna*. In the first half we were primarily concerned with belief in the *existence* of the Creator. While obviously a crucial first step, such a belief

*Part 2: The Character of Faith*

cannot stand on its own. We tend to think otherwise, but only because our age is so spiritually depleted that our beliefs tend to be disconnected from our reality. If our belief in the existence of the Creator is genuine – meaning integrated – we are compelled to ask a host of questions. What is His purpose in creating? What is His relationship with His creation? What are our responsibilities toward Him? In other words, what are the *implications* of the Creator's existence for us and our world?

If these are not burning questions for us, then any claim to belief in the Creator is hollow. It would be like claiming to truly love someone whom we know only from a photograph. When it is genuine, love touches every aspect of our being. If we do not long for more relationship than what we have through a picture, then we are living an illusion, not experiencing love. *Emuna* also must fill our whole world. *As much as emuna is believing in the Creator, it is experiencing reality and self as creations.*

This translates into a belief that nothing can exist or function except as an expression of God's will. We call this *yiḥud Hashem*, the Oneness of God. Since in this half of the book we will be examining the plagues of the Exodus – God's expression into the world – we necessarily will be approaching *emuna* through *yiḥud Hashem*.

### THE MITZVA OF *YIḤUD HASHEM*

The mutual dependence between recognizing the existence of God and *yiḥud Hashem* is seen in Ramban from the fact that he considers them both aspects of the same mitzva.[1] He also derives both from the miracles of the Exodus,[2] so our expanded interest does not move our focus from the Exodus.

---

1. We explained in chapter 1 that Ramban derives *emuna* specifically from the miracles of the Exodus because he understands that the Jewish people's obligation of servitude to God as King is an integral aspect of the mitzva of *emuna* and God's kingship is a consequence of His saving the Jews from Egyptian slavery. Rambam teaches us that *yiḥud Hashem* is synonymous with God's kingship (Rambam, *Sefer HaMitzvot, mitzvat aseh* 2). Therefore Ramban, who combines *emuna* with God's kingship, necessarily also combines it with *yiḥud Hashem*.
2. Ramban, Ex. 13:16. Ramban states that from obvious miracles we can derive that there is no such thing as nature, only revealed miracles and hidden miracles – that is, God directly controls everything. This is *yiḥud Hashem*.

# Introduction

But even Rambam, who lists belief and *yiḥud Hashem* as two distinct mitzvot,[3] clearly sees them as mutually dependent. This is evident in his approach to the Ten Commandments. As we said earlier, Rambam understands that the first of the ten obligates us to believe specifically in the existence of the Creator. But though the second prohibits idolatry, Rambam states that its basis or essence is *yiḥud Hashem*, that nothing exists outside of God.[4] Unlike all other commandments, these two were given directly by God[5] *and were heard simultaneously*.[6] Their simultaneity indicates that neither stands without the other. Thus Rambam also understands that absolute clarity about God's existence cannot be real or integrated without absolute clarity about the fact that nothing can exist except as an expression of God's will.

---

3. Rambam, *Sefer HaMitzvot, mitzvat aseh* 2.
4. *Moreh Nevukhim* II:33. Rambam understands that the Jews on Mount Sinai did not hear the actual words of God when He spoke the first two commandments. Rather, they heard His voice and were filled with the clarity of the essential point of these two commandments. Rather than hearing the particular commandments against idolatry that are contained in the words of the second commandment, they understood the essence conveyed by the mitzva – that nothing exists except that which comes from God (*yiḥud Hashem*). This answers a difficulty raised by Ramban. The Talmud (Makkot 24a) states that there are 613 mitzvot, of which 611 were heard from Moses and two – the first two of the Ten Commandments – directly from God. But the second of the Ten Commandments contains four of the 613 mitzvot (*Sefer HaḤinukh* [published anonymously in thirteenth-century Spain], mitzvot 26–29), so it would seem we only heard 608 from Moses. Rambam's understanding answers this. The Jews did not hear the specifics of these two commandments but only perceived their essential truths: (1) God exists, and (2) nothing exists other than God. Thus from God they only heard two mitzvot: *emuna* and *yiḥud Hashem* (as heard from Rav Zevulun Schwartzman).
5. Makkot 24a.
6. *Pirkei DeRabbi Eliezer* 40 understands Ps. 62:12 – "God said one thing, I heard two" – to refer to the first two commandments of the Ten Commandments. *Mekhilta, Parashat Shira* 8 also states that this verse teaches that two things were said simultaneously. That these two commandments were said simultaneously is explicitly stated in Zohar II 81b.

*Part 2: The Character of Faith*

## DIFFERENT WAYS OF LEARNING

Though Ramban derives both the existence of the Creator and *yiḥud Hashem* from the miracles of the Exodus, they are ultimately derived in different ways. The existence of God is an abstract concept. And though Ramban learns it from actual events in the world – miracles – we don't need to know any of the details of the miracles. We just need to know that miracles occurred, and therefore miracles are a reality.[7] It is because the concept of the Creator's existence is an abstraction that Rambam is able to prove it through pure logic.[8]

Similarly, the *concept* of *yiḥud Hashem* – that everything in existence comes from God and serves His intent – is also abstract. Ramban again derives it from the mere fact that there are miracles,[9] and Rambam is able to prove it through rational argument.[10]

But in addition to the *concept, yiḥud Hashem* also has a practical dimension.[11] Since it involves God's relationship with the world, to fully grasp it we have to appreciate on a concrete, detailed level that all of reality comes from God. The mere possibility of miracles will not reveal this to Ramban, and abstract arguments cannot derive it for Rambam. Everyone will agree that this requires that we engage physical reality in all of its particularity.[12]

Miracles guide us in this, but only from looking at their concrete details. Our goal is not just to know that things have a Source, for understanding something as a creation redefines its significance. Everything must be comprehended in terms of the purpose it serves in furthering the

---

7. Ramban, Ex. 13:16.
8. *Moreh Nevukhim* II:1.
9. Ramban, Ex. 13:16.
10. *Moreh Nevukhim* II:1.
11. Ramḥal makes this distinction between abstract principles of faith and those which deal with God's practical interaction with the world in the introductory lines to his *Daat Tevunot* (5–7).
12. Rambam includes the Exodus in his discussion of the mitzva of *yiḥud Hashem* (Rambam, *Sefer HaMitzvot, mitzvat aseh* 2). The direct reason for this is that *yiḥud Hashem* is synonymous with kingship according to Rambam, and our specific obligation to accept God as our King derives from the Exodus (according to Ramban). The full mitzva, then, cannot be separated from engaging the particularity of this worldly experience.

goal of creation, which is man's full relationship with God. The plagues in all their grim and glorious detail were visited on Egypt to force this reinterpretation and guide its proper realization.

It will require a lot of work to understand what it is that we are supposed to get from all those details. But we learned a guiding principle in this regard as we finished off the first half of this book: transforming perception on this fundamental level requires development of character as well as intellectual change. Our understanding is not an isolated capacity but is rather embedded in the fullness of our personality. Even Rambam, for all his cerebral focus, states clearly: "Attainments in character are the means to intellectual achievements. It is not possible that a person should reach true understandings unless he is a person of supremely refined character...."[13]

As we saw in our discussion of Abraham, the significance of our *middot* (character traits) to understanding is not restricted to their effect on the clarity of our thinking. Our character traits actually prime us to look at things in certain ways. With Abraham we spoke of how his *midda* of *ḥesed* drove him beyond the idolatry of his generation to the general recognition of the existence of the transcendent Creator. But our interest in *yiḥud Hashem* requires us to understand the Creator's relationship with reality on a detailed level.

God created the different facets of existence through numerous acts. Each act of creation exhibited a distinct *midda* of God. We must purify our corresponding traits to be sensitive to the creative basis of each of these facets. So just as Abraham's recognition of the Creator was character-driven, our effort to recognize *yiḥud Hashem* must be character-driven, but in a much broader sense than what we discussed earlier. A fully integrated appreciation of our world as created requires a wholesale cleansing of character. Since the plagues came to develop this integrated *emuna*, they were necessarily directed at reforming our character.

In order to understand the specific ways in which the plagues affected our character, we will need to connect the plagues to our internal experience. That takes introspection as well as thought. We will also be connecting that internal experience to abstract ideas, which is difficult.

---

13. *Moreh Nevukhim* II:1, the fourth reason (author's translation).

*Part 2: The Character of Faith*

So though there is simpler preparatory work to do before we begin analyzing the plagues on this level, starting with chapter 13 there is challenging material ahead. These later chapters cannot be read passively and will probably require several readings to get straight. By way of encouragement I can only say that I have taught this approach to the plagues numerous times, and people have found it exciting. When we examine a part of Torah like the plagues, which are so familiar yet so strange, and discover that they yield penetrating insights that are as extraordinary as they are applicable, it is energizing and makes the Torah real for us.

*Chapter 11*

# Foundations of Faith

Our goal is to learn *emuna* from the miracles of the Exodus – principally the plagues. How do we do that? What exactly is it that we are to derive from them? We will begin our analysis by looking at the basic structure of the plagues as a series. Ten plagues struck Egypt:

1. The Nile was turned into blood.
2. Frogs rose from the Nile and swarmed over Egypt.
3. The dust of Egypt was transformed into lice.
4. Egypt (except for Goshen) was filled with wild animals.
5. Egyptian flocks were struck down by a plague.
6. Ash spread across Egypt and brought boils to the Egyptians.
7. A storm of thunder and hail with fire enveloped Egypt.
8. Egypt was attacked by locusts.
9. Egypt was filled with darkness.
10. The firstborn of Egypt were killed.

At first glance these appear to us as a random and bizarre sequence of assaults. Since the Creator has full control over all of reality, He could have used anything as His means of attacking Egypt. So it is legitimate

*Part 2: The Character of Faith*

to ask why these were selected. What was being demonstrated through this specific set of plagues?

We first observe that the plagues did not come upon the Egyptians as ten unrelated events. Rather, they were grouped. A study of the verses in Exodus reveals this clearly. Before the first plague Moses was commanded by God to meet Pharaoh early in the morning at the Nile and warn him that the Nile would turn to blood.[1] Before the second plague, the frogs, Moses was instructed *"Bo el Paro"* (Come to Pharaoh) to warn him of what was ahead.[2] The commentaries explain that *Bo el Paro* means "meet Pharaoh at his palace."[3] Before the third plague, the lice, Pharaoh received no warning.[4]

This pattern of warnings then repeats itself. Before the fourth plague Pharaoh was warned in the morning at the Nile;[5] before the fifth Moses was again instructed, *"Bo el Paro"* (Come meet Pharaoh at the palace to warn him);[6] there was no warning before the sixth plague.[7]

The pattern then repeats a third time: Pharaoh was warned before the seventh plague early in the morning on his way out of the palace,[8] before the eighth plague he was warned at the palace,[9] and before the ninth there was no warning.[10] This was followed by the final plague – the killing of the firstborn – for which, again, there was a warning.

This pattern divides the plagues into three groups and is the basis of the acronym mentioned in the Passover Haggada: *Datzakh, Adash, B'aḥav*. This acronym is composed of the first letters of each plague, grouped according to the pattern we have just identified: three, three, four.[11] The midrash tells us this acronym was etched into the staff that

---

1. Ex. 7:15.
2. Ibid. 7:26.
3. Hayim ben Moshe ibn Attar, *Or HaḤayim*, Ex. 9:1.
4. Ex. 8:12–13.
5. Ibid. 8:16.
6. Ibid. 9:1.
7. Ibid. 9:8–9.
8. Ibid. 9:13.
9. Ibid. 10:1.
10. Ibid. 10:21–22.
11. Maharal, *Gevurot Hashem*, chapter 33.

# Foundations of Faith

Moses used to bring the plagues.[12] A memory device was not needed to remember the plagues, of which there were only ten. It was there to indicate their proper grouping.

What is the significance of this pattern of warnings? Why first at the Nile, then at the palace, and then no warning?

## THE PATTERN OF THE PLAGUES

The purpose of the plagues was to reveal that God exists and that all of reality is dependent upon Him. That is to say, their purpose is educational.

Learning occurs in stages. First there is the introduction of a new idea. Then there is the understanding of how this new idea joins with previous knowledge. Then there is the assimilation of the new idea into a person's worldview. The plagues form a pedagogic process by which Pharaoh (and through him Egypt) and the Jewish people learn *emuna*.

There were barriers to bringing Pharaoh to recognize the existence of God the Creator, because that belief ran counter to the worldview of ancient Egypt. The Egyptians had many gods, so news of the existence of one more was not strange; when they learned of new gods from foreign peoples, they often assimilated them into their own pantheon.[13] But the Creator is not just another god.

The Creator is all-encompassing and transcendent, which was beyond even the *imagination* of Egyptians.[14] Though the full extent of

---

12. Exodus Rabba 5:6.
13. Redford, *Ancient Gods Speak*, 101.
14. My contention throughout this book has been that before Greece, when the capacity for pure abstraction became an integral part of human cognition, recognizing a truly transcendent Being would have been extraordinarily challenging without a received tradition. Rambam states this explicitly in *Moreh Nevukhim* I:63, "At that time it did not occur to anyone, with the exception of select individuals, that Hashem existed. All of their investigations did not go beyond the spheres, their forces and action, because they had not separated from their tangible senses and had not reached pure intellect." It was Abraham's great achievement to go beyond this. It is clearly evident that Egypt did not. Pharaoh – a physical being – was syncretized with the Egyptian creator god (Pharaoh was the son of Ra, the sun god, who in turn was syncretized with Atum, the creator god; see also Exodus Rabba 5:14). Furthermore, in all of Egypt's ancient mythologies (as opposed to the more modern Memphite

this characteristic did not become apparent until the last set of plagues, Moses asserted to Pharaoh that God was the Creator of reality at the beginning of the process, before the plagues began. Pharaoh's response was simply to throw Moses out of the palace.[15] Egypt could not accept that the Creator was not an Egyptian god manifest in the world through Pharaoh.[16]

In general, people have difficulty seeing things that are at odds with their expectations. Psychologists show this, for example, by rapidly flashing playing cards at test-subjects. When the researcher shows them a black ace of hearts, most people "see" the expected red ace of hearts. On a more profound level, Thomas Kuhn, in his famous work *The Structure of Scientific Revolutions*, observed that most people ignore the facts that do not conform to the theories they accept; this is why the progress of science is so slow. It is the rare individual who faces the contradictions as they mount and stands above convention to recognize new patterns and construct a theory that will truly account for the data. Most people simply do not assimilate things that contradict their assumptions and expectations of the world.

Therefore, under normal circumstances and without some preparation, Pharaoh would not have been capable of even hearing of the existence of God from Moses. Hence his initial reaction of ejecting Moses from the palace. But in the early morning on his way to the Nile, Pharaoh was vulnerable.

In Egypt Pharaoh was revered as a god. The midrash tells us that it was understood that Pharaoh, as a god, would not need to defecate.[17] Presumably the idea was that gods are a different level of being, with

---

theology whose origin is contemporaneous with the First Temple), the creator god comes into being in the midst of a preexisting reality. Moreover, the sun god – who is associated with the creator god – required protection during his journey through the underworld at night, attesting to the fact that this mightiest of gods was not fully omnipotent and therefore was not the transcendent author and basis of all existence.

15. Exodus Rabba 5:14.
16. Ibid.
17. Ibid. 9:8.

the realm of physical reality in its entirety existing only to sustain them. This understanding precluded anything being "indigestible" waste.[18]

But the reality was that Pharaoh was human and so had this physical need. Pharaoh's solution was to go for an early morning swim in the Nile and sort things out privately.[19] This is not to say that Pharaoh knew he was not a god and he was trying to deceive everyone. He presumably managed to rationalize the inconsistency, just as we all find ways to overlook our hypocrisies and live with them. But it does mean that in the early morning, as he was on his way to the Nile, Pharaoh was closest to awareness of the inadequacies of his worldview and therefore most vulnerable and open to looking at things in a new way. When, in that context, Moses proclaimed God's existence and followed the proclamation with the plague of blood, Pharaoh was able to hear it. From that moment on Moses' assertion that God exists was registered in Pharaoh's mind.

But that was only the first stage in Pharaoh's education. Moses then came to proclaim God's existence in Pharaoh's palace and warn Pharaoh of the second plague. The palace was the place where Pharaoh's false vision of reality found its fullest support. There, all his courtiers bowed before him. He sat on his throne, with his ornate attire and crown, and he possessed absolute and instant control over life and death. Moses could not have *initiated* recognition of God in such a place, as

---

18. This two-tiered vision actually revealed the limitations of the gods. They were not viewed as the basis of physical existence; rather, they fed on physical existence, which was understood to have existence independent of the gods with the gods dependent upon it (see Abraham's rejection of idolatry, chapter 9). The ultimate downfall of the idolatrous gods is seen as coming from their inability to separate out waste. See Isaiah 46:2 with Rashi. See also Rabbi Hayim of Volozhin, *Nefesh HaHayim* 2:7. The supreme greatness of God is that He is the basis of existence and not dependent upon it. Paradoxically, this is evident in the fact that His world contains evil that He can and eventually will remove, thus He does "expel waste." (See Maharal in many places, for example *Gevurot Hashem*, chapter 72.) Because God is the basis of existence, every detail is according to His will, even evil, which appears to be against Him. Evil does not possess independent existence but is merely a concealment of God's being, which is His means to allow man free will. The ultimate revelation of God's greatness comes when evil reveals that it only exists as a tool of God.
19. Exodus Rabba 9:8.

we saw from his first attempt before the start of the plagues. But after the existence of God was already introduced into Pharaoh's consciousness by the first plague, Pharaoh could hear Moses' statement that God exists even when Pharaoh was in the setting of his palace. And when the plague of frogs followed, Pharaoh was forced to become fully cognizant of God's existence even as he sat on his throne, personifying a vision that denied God's existence.

A student's education is only complete, however, when he internalizes an idea by understanding it on his own without the guidance of his teachers. In Hebrew this is called *bina*, deriving one thing from another.[20] This active learning integrates a person with his understanding, for it is now generated from himself. When the third plague came without warning and Pharaoh understood without Moses' direction that it proved the existence of God, God's existence was fully established in Pharaoh's mind and, through him, in the minds of all of Egypt.

This pattern of warnings – an early intercept on the way to the Nile, a visit to the palace, and a plague that Pharaoh had to interpret himself – demonstrates divine pedagogy. This is how to teach an idea to a student so that he will accept and internalize it even when he will find it profoundly jarring.

Each specific plague directly corroborated Moses' contention that God exists. In the first plague the Nile was turned to blood. To the Egyptians, the Nile was the most powerful reality on earth. Their entire sustenance was dependent upon it, and it filled their world – they even based their spatial orientation upon it.[21] Its significance was second only to that of the sun, an object not in this world but above it. Turning the Nile to blood indicated that God had power over the object that defined the world for Egypt.

The plague of the frogs advanced appreciation of God's power another step. For all the importance of the Nile, the Egyptians did not

---

20. Rashi, Exodus 31:2.
21. In the empire phase of Egyptian history, when Egyptians first encountered the river Euphrates they referred to it as the river that flows upstream when it is flowing downstream, because the Nile flows north whereas the Euphrates flows south. Wilson, *The Intellectual Adventure of Ancient Man*, 37.

live in it; they lived next to it on the land. The significance of the Nile lay in what it did to their land; its seasonal inundation brought water and rich mud to the fields, making them fertile and alive. Frogs seem to multiply in the mud and come up from the Nile onto the land just like the mud from the Nile, so inundating Egypt with frogs rather than watery mud indicated power over the Nile's ability to fertilize the land on which the Egyptians lived.[22]

The full awareness of God's existence, however, was only achieved when the third plague hit the very ground on which they stood as God turned the dust into lice. Unable to mimic this feat, Pharaoh's magicians admitted, "This is the finger of God." What was so remarkable about this plague that the magicians could not mimic it? Why did it so compellingly prove the existence of God?

The power of magic derives from a magician's ability to relate to objects as individual entities cut off from any larger reality. Isolation of the object in the sphere of the magician gives the magician power over it.[23] But a particle of dust is the epitome of insignificance. We cannot relate to it as an individual item; it can only be conceived as a part of the totality of reality. This means the only entity that can "control" dust is one that encompasses all of reality. No magician can do that. The plague of the dust proved that Moses was not a magician. Rather, he must represent a god.[24]

But not just any god. Changing dust particles to lice revealed that Moses' God was all-encompassing. We have already mentioned that the existence of such a god not identified with Pharaoh was unacceptable to Egypt. But it is also apparent that the Egyptians did not even have a concept of a truly all-encompassing god.[25] They had an overarching creator deity, but Egyptians understood this god to be very distant. Its power was only manifest through its association (syncretism) with other gods. Early in Egyptian history this creator god became tied to the all-powerful

---

22. Frog amulets were popular in Egypt as signs of fertility and resurrection because of their, "apparent self-generation from mud in teeming numbers." Redford, *Ancient Gods Speak*, p. 12.
23. Maharal, *Gur Aryeh*, Shemot 8:14.
24. Ibid.
25. See note 14.

sun god, which rules over the world. But despite the fact that Egyptians believed that this compound god had all hidden and all revealed power, the sun still had to battle forces of evil at night in its journey through the underworld and draft other gods to act as guards on the journey.[26]

This meant that, for all its power and reach, the sun remained an element in a larger context; it did not totally encompass reality. The plague of the lice revealed that God did – omnipotence of another order! When it came, we can imagine the shock and terror the Egyptians must have felt. We now gain some appreciation of the radical nature of the innovation Moses was introducing to Pharaoh and why Pharaoh had to hear about it first at the Nile. In any case, the lice established the existence of God for the Egyptians, and for the Jews also as they witnessed the unfolding process.

**THE SECOND SET OF PLAGUES**

But if the purpose of the plagues was *emuna*, and God's existence was established after the third plague, why were there more plagues? Clearly we are oversimplifying if we assume that the *emuna* to be derived from the Exodus was a simple recognition of God's existence. There must be more to it. And that "more" was as shattering to Egypt as recognizing God's existence, for the process of learning about it began once again from Pharaoh's vulnerability at the Nile.

The fourth plague – the attack by wild animals – introduced a new and, for the Egyptians, disquieting characteristic. Though the Jews themselves were unaffected by the first three plagues, the plagues did occur in their district along with the rest of Egypt.[27] They struck the

---

26. Redford, *Ancient Gods Speak*, 5 and 333.
27. Maharal, *Gur Aryeh, Shemot* 9:14. The Jews were unaffected because their personalities were anchored in a realm beyond the reach of the plagues. In later chapters we will explain how each plague emanated from a trait through which God creates existence, with each successive plague related to a more fundamental trait than the last. The defining facet of Jewish identity or personality derives from a deeper level of God's relationship to reality than these plagues, so the Jews were immune to them. The Jews were like an iron rod in a wood fire – though the fire reaches both the wood and the iron, the wood burns while the iron does not, because iron is impervious to the heat of an ordinary fire. So also there was no differentiation in the spread of the first three plagues, though there was in their effect. That differentiation was a

entire country without discrimination. For example, in the first plague the water in Goshen turned to blood as it did in the rest of Egypt. When the Jews drank it, however, for them it was water. With the fourth plague Pharaoh was specifically notified that though the animals would spread throughout Egypt, they would not enter the borders of Goshen where the Jews were concentrated.[28] This revealed that God controls the application of His power; He is not merely some force that can be turned on or off. Rather, God is an entity or personality applying force in a precise way to a specific end.

Polytheistic worship develops over historical time from conceiving gods as undifferentiated forces to identifying them as personalities.[29] Philosophers and etymologists understand this path to be intrinsic to the human mind's developing concepts of spirituality.[30] Egypt was already a very ancient kingdom by the time the Jews arrived there, and the Egyptians viewed their own gods as distinct personalities. The revelation that God also had this quality significantly advanced God's status in the eyes of Egypt and their appreciation of His capabilities. We can imagine the terror that would have seized them upon realizing that this immensely powerful God of Moses was not merely an amorphous force but rather a personality with a conscious agenda directed against them.

The extent of God's control over His power was demonstrated with the last plague of this set – the plague of boils. The wild animals had shown that God could contain the expression of His power, directing it

---

consequence of distinctions in the "receivers" of the plague as opposed to the discrimination of the "giver." It was not until the ninth plague – that of darkness – that Jews were in any way affected by a plague. The tenth and final plague that killed the firstborn – which emanated from the deepest level of God's relationship with creation – would have killed the Jews also had they not brought the Passover offering (Maharal, *Gevurot Hashem*, chapter 60). This will all become much clearer when we deal with the individual plagues beginning in chapter 14.

28. Ex. 8:18.
29. The process is well documented in the evolution of metaphors used to describe gods during the long history of Mesopotamian worship (Jacobsen, *The Treasures of Darkness*, 4–11, 20–21, 26, 79–80). For a more general formulation of the idea see Cassirer, *Language and Myth*, 62–83.
30. Cassirer, *Language and Myth*, 15–23, quoting extensively from the work of Gotternamen Usener, *Versuch Einer Lehre von der religiosen Begrffsbildung*.

*Part 2: The Character of Faith*

at a specific target. The plague of the domestic animals showed discernment of a different level as God distinguished between animals based on their ownership.[31] The boils demonstrated that God could also extend the expression of that power beyond the limiting factors of the physical structure of reality. Moses and Aaron were each instructed to fill both of their hands with ash. Moses then placed those four handfuls of ash in the palms of his two hands and threw the ash skyward. It then covered the entirety of Egypt.[32]

Two hands contained four handfuls – the smaller contained the larger; four handfuls covered all of Egypt – the smaller filled the larger. This made clear that the containment that characterizes physical reality in no way restricts God; He is independent of its strictures, and what God does is solely decided by His intention. Combined with what was revealed in the first set of plagues this demonstrated that He is the Author of reality's structure.[33]

The Egyptians would have found this deeply disturbing. They had a very strong concept of balance, order, and justice – what they called *maat*.[34] But though the maintenance of *maat* was the responsibility of Pharaoh and the gods, its content – proper order and structure – was *a priori* and objective. *Maat* was something the gods as well as man relied upon, not something they ordained.[35] To recognize God as the one who structures nature would be to attribute to Him a kind of omnipotence inconceivable to the Egyptians. This explains why the second set of plagues also had to begin at the Nile, where Pharaoh was vulnerable.

This demonstrated more than the raw power of God. If structure existed independent of God, then God would be part of a larger reality. His designation as Creator would have limited meaning; He might be the source of *our* universe and the most powerful force in it, but

---

31. Exodus Rabba 11:4.
32. Ibid. 11:5.
33. Understanding the connection between this revelation and boils requires taking the discussion to another level, which we will do in chapter 15.
34. Redford, *Ancient Gods Speak*, xi.
35. See, for example, Redford, *Ancient Gods Speak*, 65. The Greeks also had a concept of necessity that preceded and determined the gods; see Cornford, *From Religion to Philosophy*, 12.

His significance would be reduced to that of a department head rather than that of a true chairman.[36] Furthermore, if we identify God as the ultimate power, and if He is part of a larger whole, then by implication there is no true Creator in the sense of one who truly initiates existence. We would be left with some version of the ancient Greek vision of an eternal universe, within which God acts. These middle plagues eliminated that possibility.

In addition to His greatness, a fundamental characteristic of His specific conduct of the world was also established. The physical order of nature and the moral order of justice were both understood to be facets of one concept in the ancient world – structure.[37] When God was shown to determine structure, that necessarily included determining right and wrong, good and evil. Upholding God's will was then synonymous with righteousness, and opposing that will defined evil. When God struck specifically at the Egyptians, who were opposing His will, in order to save the Jews, who upheld His will, He was intervening in the world to punish evil and reward righteousness – establishing reward and punishment as the basis of His conduct of the world.

But even with all this, we apparently had not yet learned all there was to learn. For another set of plagues was still to come.

## THE THIRD SET OF PLAGUES

The final set of plagues again followed the customary pattern: the sequence began in the morning when Pharaoh was vulnerable, followed by a demonstration in the palace, and then by a plague without warning. That the plagues continued indicated that beyond God's existence and His acting in a specific manner unfettered by physical limitations, there was still something more that had to be understood about Him. Since

---

36. Placing such a limitation on the Creator is the root of evil and was the basis of the snake's temptation of Eve; see Genesis Rabba 19:4. Furthermore, if the objectivity of morality is independent of God anyone who merits life through strict judgment becomes independent of God because a system of justice independent of God necessitates that person's existence.
37. I mentioned the concept of *maat* in the previous paragraph. In Torah the name of God *Elokim* is used both with regard to structuring the natural order in creation and God's trait of strict justice.

*Part 2: The Character of Faith*

the series began in the morning when Pharaoh was leaving the palace, we see that this final lesson was equally shattering to Egypt's worldview.

This last series showed that God is *entirely* beyond comprehensible existence, a Being of an utterly unfathomable nature and capability. He does not merely encompass reality, as was seen in the first set of plagues. Nor is He just the author of structure, above its limitations, unhindered by considerations of space, time, and quantity as was seen in the second set. Rather, He is the unitary, transcendent, necessary Source and Determiner of being and existence. He is able to harmonize mutually exclusive opposites, unencumbered by and, therefore, determinant of the qualities of existence as well as their structure.[38]

In these last plagues God revealed Himself to be the Creator that Abraham had discovered through his decisive leap from the concrete thinking of his age to abstraction. Egypt was pushed to make that same break through this last set of plagues – to recognize a Being utterly independent of reality as we know it. Since in that ancient era abstraction was not yet an integral part of human thought, this had been virtually inconceivable to the Egyptians until then.[39]

How was this demonstrated through the last group of plagues? This series began with the seventh plague – hail. When the icy deluge rained down on Egypt, it was mixed with fire.[40] This was a resolution of opposites that demonstrated an omnipotence that was an order of magnitude beyond God's freedom from quantitative and spatial limitation seen in the sixth plague.[41]

The next plague was locusts. These swarms came to strip Egypt of all crops that survived the hail. But the verses describing this plague

---

38. This level of revelation is associated with the four-letter name of God, the יהוה.
39. See Maharal, *Gur Aryeh, Shemot* 9:14. See also Rambam, *Moreh Nevukhim* I:63 quoted in note 14. Though as we explained earlier in this chapter, Egypt had an overarching creator god that was not physical, the limitations they placed upon him showed that they could not conceive of him as truly transcendent of physical reality. We do see abstract cosmologies arising in Egypt, as evidenced by the Memphite Theology. But that is attributed to the period of the 25th dynasty, half a millennium later. See chapter 9 note 24.
40. Ex. 9:24.
41. Exodus Rabba 12:4. The mixture of fire and ice is described in the midrash as a *nes betokh nes* (a miracle within a miracle).

also highlight the fact that they *blinded* the Egyptians. Each locust was big enough to be perceived as a distinct creature, so that their multitude overwhelmed the Egyptians' ability to process information, leaving them to stumble in a haze. What was the significance of this blindness?

Our senses are constantly bombarded by an incomprehensible amount of information. The number of points of light which comprise a single visual image is vast, let alone the moving picture of our lives with its soundtrack, feeling, and smell. We understand our world by automatically grouping this information into a limited number of comprehensible entities, attributes, and concepts. But we do not just group the information coming to us through our senses; we also strive to unify our world through understanding. Only understanding that emanates from a transcendent origin can truly unify reality. Otherwise, what appears to be coherence is actually a consequence of ignoring the full picture.[42]

Egypt did not have access to this level of transcendence; therefore their understanding of the world gave a false impression of unity. The locusts gave expression to the true chaos that underlay Egypt's limited understanding – an incalculable amount of data lacking a truly unifying principle.

The third of this set, the ninth plague, was darkness. This was the plague that forced the Egyptians to internalize the awareness that their vision lacked a transcendent source and, therefore, any genuine reality. But darkness is something we experience every night. What was different about this darkness?

According to the midrash, the darkness that descended upon Egypt during this plague was from *Gehinnom* (purgatory).[43] *Gehinnom* is an aspect of the reality that exists beyond the illusions of physical existence; it is a part of the realm of truth. *Gehinnom* is a place where the individual experiences reality as he lived it in this world, but with full cognizance of the falseness he had allowed to corrupt his vision. He

---

42. I understood this from a lecture of Rav Moshe Shapiro. See Rambam, *Perush HaMishnayot laSanhedrin*, chapter 10, the first and second *yesod*. The second *yesod* speaks of God's ultimate Unity; the first refers to His ability to unify. Also see Song of Songs Rabba 1:12, which explains that God is called Shlomo because He is the *Melekh shehashalom shelo* (the King Who owns peace).
43. Exodus Rabba 14:2.

*Part 2: The Character of Faith*

experiences the non-being of the false reality he imagined, allowing him to reject its falseness, separate from it, and so move on to true reality as an integrated person. The darkness of *Gehinnom* that this plague brought to the Egyptians exposed them to the complete lack of true existence in the world as they lived it – a world without God. This established God as the transcendent Source of reality and existence.

**THE PLAGUE OF THE FIRSTBORN**

One plague remained: the striking-down of the firstborn. It was the *makka bepatish* (the completing blow) that demonstrated the full nature of God's relationship to creation. As the culmination of God's onslaught against Egypt, we might have expected this plague to wipe out all of Egypt. That, however, would have demonstrated merely God's omnipotent power. The actual lesson of this plague was more profound than that; it lay in its specific targeting of the firstborn.

The firstborn of any generation are the beginning of the next generation. They mark the transition between parent and child, creator and creation. By killing the firstborn God did not smash creation so much as cut it off at its root. He was not showing His power; He was proving His priority.

The Egyptians too would have experienced it in exactly this way. Though we tend to associate the suffering of this plague with the pain of parents mourning the loss of their children, this plague actually killed the adult firstborn as much as the children. Their significance to the Egyptians lay in their role as bridges to the ancestors. They were the leaders of the family by virtue of their inherited role as priests of the deceased family elders and so as conduits of blessing and legitimate authority.[44] Killing the firstborn cut Egypt off from the past and the all-important

---

44. See Abeer El-Shahawy, *The Funerary Art of Ancient Egypt* (Cairo: American University in Cairo Press, 2005), 90. In ancient Egypt the eldest son took over responsibility for the family when his father died, was responsible for the burial of his father, acted as a priest in the funeral, and was even occasionally pictured accompanying his father to the goddesses at the necropolis. The firstborn was central in ancient society generally. Before the sin of the Golden Calf, the firstborn of Israel had the role of priests. In ancient Rome the oldest male was known as the *pater familias* and had complete control over both estate and family, including authority over life and death.

dead. This would have brought a profound sense of existential aloneness and orphaned isolation to all Egyptians, a sense that their tie to their sources of existence was cut.

Since this plague struck at the root of creation and was applied by God, it demonstrated that He stands completely outside of creation – He is the context of existence. He was not merely demonstrating that He can take existence away from us; He was showing that without Him there is no existence, for He is its Basis.

## THE THREE PILLARS OF FAITH

The first three plagues established the existence of God. The last four revealed the transcendent nature of God. The middle three showed that God determines the structure of reality, acting in a specific and purposeful manner to accomplish His will. And since throughout the process Moses prophesied what was to come, the plagues also revealed that God communicates His will and intentions to man; He has expectations of us and lets us know what they are.

Taken together, these lessons cover what Rabbi Yosef Albo identifies as the three necessary and sufficient components of a complete system of *emuna* in God: (1) God exists and is transcendent; (2) He has a specific goal for creation and expectations of us that He communicates to us (there is a Torah of divine origin); and (3) He acts in the world to further that goal, including rewarding us for fulfilling our responsibilities and punishing us when we do not.[45]

When we say that the miracles and wonders of the Exodus – the plagues – foster *emuna* we do not mean a warm, fuzzy feeling that Someone is looking after us. We are talking about recognizing the existence of God along with a tightly structured understanding of His relationship to creation and our responsibilities to Him.

This is not to belittle the importance of the emotions that developed as we formed our relationship with God through this experience. King Solomon in the Song of Songs poignantly captures the sense of love and care that animated the event in his depiction of God calling to us to follow Him out of Egypt:

---

45. Rabbi Yosef Albo, *Sefer HaIkarim* 1:4; Maharal, *Gevurot Hashem*, chapter 47.

*Part 2: The Character of Faith*

> The fig tree puts forth her green figs, and the vines in blossom give forth their scent. Arise, my love, my beautiful one, and come away. O my dove, in the clefts of the rock, in the secret places of the cliff, let me see your countenance, let me hear your voice; for your voice is sweet, and your countenance is comely.[46]

But though there is a vital emotional component to the *emuna* that we derive from the Exodus, that *emuna* also has precision, structure, and obligation.

---

46. Song 2:13–14.

*Chapter 12*

# The Process of Creation

As a nation we originally achieved *emuna* through witnessing the plagues in Egypt. They demonstrated the three foundations of faith: that the unitary transcendent Source of all reality exists, that He communicates His will to man (the basis of recognizing Torah as divine), and that He acts in the world in a directed and specific manner to affect His will (the basis of reward and punishment). Once we have learned these, is there more to derive from the plagues? Do we need to look at them further?

The approach of grouping the plagues around three essential points leaves many details unexplained. We can appreciate why it would be appropriate to attack the Nile, a principle deity of Egypt, in order to demonstrate God's existence. But why turn it into blood? We can understand why the plague of frogs is an attack more specifically directed against the strength of the Nile (its seasonal inundation). But the midrash gives many seemingly superfluous details about this plague, such as that the frogs would enter houses by burrowing up through the floor stones and that they jumped down the throats of the Egyptians so that when the Egyptians tried to speak they croaked. As we mentioned earlier, when the Sages add these details they are not merely filling in the picture. They have something to communicate that is *essential*, conveying

*Part 2: The Character of Faith*

to us what spiritual reality is being actualized through events. What are they telling us through these specific details? Our current level of understanding leaves us with many questions of this sort. The plagues still seem arbitrary and strange.

But we have an even more pressing reason than these questions to search for more meaning in the plagues. The purpose of the plagues was to establish our *emuna*. Grounding *emuna* means more than just understanding its essential components, for *emuna* is not an isolated quality of mind or heart. Genuine *emuna* is definitive of our consciousness and must determine how we perceive ourselves and our world. Our *emuna* cannot be real to us unless it is integrated with our vision of reality. We therefore expect the plagues to give us guidance on how to understand the world and its functioning in such a way that our recognition of God emerges naturally from it.

We spoke about this in the introduction to this half. The command of *emuna* comes simultaneously with the command of *yihud Hashem*, which requires us to perceive every aspect of existence as a consequence of the will of God, because neither of these commands can stand without the other. If the plagues are to give us *emuna* in God then they must also give us concrete understanding of the world as a creation of God. How do we get from the plagues to this understanding?

There remains an obvious dimension of the plagues that we have not yet examined. Though we know what is to be learned from viewing them as three groups of plagues, we have not yet asked what we learn from them as ten individual events. What aspect of *emuna* is represented by the number ten?

We are commanded to recognize God specifically as Creator. If we turn to the Torah's account of creation, we find in the first chapter of Genesis that creation was accomplished through ten statements.[1] The parallelism between ten plagues that reveal the Creator and ten statements or stages of creation is suggestive. But to explore this further we will need to explain why creation is achieved through ten statements.

There is a mishna *Avot* that directly addresses this question:

---

1. Avot 5:1, Rosh HaShana 32a, Genesis Rabba 17:1, and a number of places in the Zohar.

## The Process of Creation

The world was created in ten statements. Why ten? It could have been accomplished in a single statement! It was to punish the evildoers who destroy the world which was created in ten statements and to give a good reward to the righteous who uphold the world which was created in ten statements.[2]

The mishna teaches that ten statements were needed "to give reward to the righteous who uphold the world which was created in ten statements." But how does this answer the question? Why not give reward to the righteous for upholding a world created in one statement?

Reward and punishment are a consequence of our being responsible for our actions – of the fact that we act out of choice. To say that we are rewarded and punished because the world was created in ten statements implies that only because the world was created in ten statements can we act as free agents. Why would that be?

Before the act of creation, if we allow ourselves to speak in such terms, God alone existed and everything was God. The infinity of God then had to retract to allow a place for finite creation. Each of the six days of creation begins with evening (withdrawal of the Creator to make space for creation) followed by morning (a positive filling of the void left over by the Creator's withdrawal). The necessary and infinite Being of God is the ultimate "something." Created existence by definition lacks the unfathomable quality of necessity; therefore, relative to God's level of existence, it is "nothing." Thus the creation of finite physical reality was actually the creation of nothing from something rather than the creation of something from nothing.[3] For this reason the Hebrew term for world, *olam*, means "hidden," for finite physical creation hides the infinite Creator.

Each of the ten statements by which God created existence brought an additional concretization of finite reality and therefore an additional concealment of the infinite Creator. Apparently ten statements make a creation that hides God to the extent that if we want to

---

2. Avot 5:1.
3. I heard this particular way of phrasing it from Rabbi Yaakov Shatz.

*Part 2: The Character of Faith*

recognize Him we must seek Him out, yet reveals God sufficiently that we can find Him if we choose to try.

This explains our mishna. The world was created in ten statements to give man reward for upholding it because only in a ten-statement world is this achievement accomplished by free choice, so that it merits reward.[4]

Upholding the world means cutting through the veils of finitude to connect all layers of creation back to their infinite Maker, the Source from which they derive existence.[5] This is the achievement of *yiḥud Hashem* we have been speaking about, where we understand the world as a created reality. Only with this understanding of the world is our recognition of the existence of God an organic consequence of our vision of reality. This, however, requires that we actively "uphold the world." We have the choice of passively accepting the immediate and superficial appearance of reality as an independently existing physical entity. Or we can choose to probe more deeply to reveal the different aspects of existence as facets of or stages in a process of creation.

The correspondence between ten statements actualizing ten facets of a created world and ten plagues that forced recognition of the Creator, suggests that the Egyptians failed the "ten-layer-test." Presumably they had come to view each aspect of reality as possessing existence independent of the transcendent Creator, and this view blocked them from recognizing God. The Jews, who as slaves of the Egyptians were exposed to their corrupt views, had also come to see the world in this manner. The ten plagues were then visited on Egypt to correct our understanding of the ten facets of reality. But we need to develop more background before this can become clear.

**CONNECTING TO GOD THROUGH CREATING**

In truth, we still have not explained the specific number ten. The mishna from Avot gives us only two alternatives when it asks why God created the world in ten statements instead of one. In the context of the mishna, "ten statements" is synonymous with "multiple statements." When the

---

4. See Ramḥal, *Daat Tevunot,* chapter 40.
5. Ramḥal, *Mesillat Yesharim,* chapter 1.

mishna answers "in order to give us free will" it means to say that multiple layers of existence are required to provide steps through which the Creator's existence can be uncovered. A single statement would have created a world without process, one in which the Creator was either already revealed or hidden without any path to His discovery. We are still left with the question: why specifically ten?

The ten statements through which God created finite existence constitute the ten stages through which any creator travels in the process of bringing something into being, from the ineffable inspiration to create to the actual formation and release of the creation as an independent object.

We also move through these stages when we create. This parallel is not a matter of "anthropomorphizing" God; rather, God created us in His image,[6] and specifically in the image of God as Creator.[7] It is because we are created in the image of God the Creator that we can recognize God's creation of the world, as we perceive our own process of creating mirrored in His.

It also means that when we create we *emulate* the Creator. Emulation produces a connection that goes beyond recognition.[8] This is because we are changed through our actions. By doing specific acts we become the kind of person who does those actions.[9] For example, by building we become a builder, and not merely in name; we are transformed by the experience of building. We are forced to look at the world as a builder would, weighing possibilities in a certain way, determining priorities, and making decisions. We then excite within ourselves the enthusiasm and energy required of a builder to build. We begin the project, work through the process, and experience the frustrations, thrills, and satisfaction that are unique to building. We think like a builder, feel like a builder, and act like a builder. In short, we experience the world as a builder experiences the world.

---

6. Gen. 1:26.
7. Rabbi Hayim of Volozhin, *Nefesh HaHayim* 1:2–3.
8. The Creator Himself goes through these stages *in order* that we may have a process to emulate. See, for example, *Mekhilta, Parashat BaHodesh HaShlishi* 7 regarding Shabbat.
9. *Sefer HaHinukh*, mitzva 16.

*Part 2: The Character of Faith*

Every builder feels a commonality and shared understanding with other builders. True, someone who builds a house and someone who builds an eighty-story skyscraper have not built the same thing – the accomplishment of one is only a pale shadow of the accomplishment of the other. Still, the builder of the house will understand the builder of the skyscraper in a way that someone who has never built cannot.[10] This is also true when we emulate the Creator by engaging in an act of creation. Though our creation can only be a distant echo of His, it is still sufficient to give us an affinity with God, taking us beyond mere recognition.[11]

We were created to connect to God, we connect to God through emulation, and we emulate God through creating. Thus, the ability to create and all that goes into it structures and defines our humanity.[12] This is the deeper meaning of our being created in the image of God the Creator. The fact that today we live in a society that does not understand the self in this way or foster this structure of personality goes a long way toward explaining our difficulties with *emuna*.

### THE MITZVOT OF THE EXODUS

The relevance of all this to the Exodus is made clear by the mitzvot which we were given as we departed from Egypt. Before the tenth plague the Jewish people were given their first two commands as a nation: to sanctify Rosh Hodesh (the New Moon) and to offer the Passover sacrifice.[13] Completion of the Passover sacrifice brought the completion of the plagues: when we finished eating it, the firstborn died. Rosh Hodesh

---

10. Emulation as a way of connecting to God is discussed extensively in *The Choice to Be*, chapter 6.
11. When we talk of emulating God we are not referring to God Himself, to the necessary (uncaused), unitary Being that creates reality from nothing. God Himself is totally beyond the comprehension of any creation. Rather, we refer to the aspect of the Creator which He revealed through His act of creation, i.e., His trait of *malkhut* (Rabbi Hayim of Volozhin, *Nefesh HaHayim* 2:2). This aspect was revealed specifically to be recognized and emulated; see Rabbi Chaim Friedlander, note 2 to Ramhal, *Da'at Tevunot*, 2nd edition (Bnei Brak: Rabbi Chaim Friedlander, 1975).
12. For that matter, it defines and structures all of reality since existence was only created to provide a medium through which man can connect to God.
13. Ex. 12:1–12. The midrash adds a third: circumcision.

was a prerequisite to the sacrifice, as it set the date for when it was to be offered.

The Passover sacrifice, as our first act of worship, initiated the Jewish people into the service of God – an intrinsic part of the *emuna* these plagues were structured to impart.[14] More precisely, an unusual feature of this sacrifice is the frequent references to unity and the number one. The sacrificial lamb had to be one year old; it had to be roasted, not boiled, so that it would not fall apart; it had to be roasted whole, with no bones broken; and it had to be eaten by one group together in one place. The commentaries explain that this is because through this sacrifice we specifically acknowledged that God is One.[15] It was the sacrificial equivalent of the *Shema*, an enactment of *yiḥud Hashem*. Thus through this mitzva we became active participants in achieving the purpose of the plagues – recognition of the unitary Creator.

But what about the mitzva of Rosh Ḥodesh? Beyond setting the date for the sacrifice, did it have its own connection to the intent of the plagues? We will have an opportunity to discuss this mitzva in greater depth later.[16] But briefly, the waxing and waning of the light of the sun conveyed to the world by the moon symbolizes the changing amount of God's revelation that man conveys to the world. The extent to which we block God's light or let it through depends on our free choice. Thus Rosh Ḥodesh commemorates man's free will and is the mitzva equivalent of the world being created in ten statements to give us reward. With free will the prerequisite to meaningful action, Rosh Ḥodesh preceded offering the Passover sacrifice.

We celebrate specifically the moment of the new moon – Rosh Ḥodesh – because it represents the point when we manage to stop our slide away from God, during which we brought less and less of His light to the world. The new moon marks the moment we turn the corner to begin bringing more and more of it to the world. The new moon

---

14. See chapter 1 and introduction to part 2, note 1, that according to Ramban servitude to God the King is an aspect of *emuna*, while according to Rambam it is an aspect of *yiḥud Hashem*.
15. Maharal, *Gevurot Hashem*, chapter 60. This is also synonymous with accepting God's kingship. See Rambam, *Sefer HaMitzvot, mitzvat aseh* 2.
16. See the discussion of *tiferet* in chapter 15.

*Part 2: The Character of Faith*

represents the use of our free will to do *teshuva*, to repent. Hence the emphasis in the Rosh Hodesh prayers on the sin-offering that is brought on Rosh Hodesh.

Repentance does not mean merely saying I am sorry for a wrong action. It is a determination that who I am now, who I have become, could not have done the prohibited act. It is the ultimate exercise of free will;[17] through repentance we choose self. It is our most profound act of self-creation. Thus Rosh Hodesh signifies and celebrates our becoming *creators*. This is the very identity through which we emulate God the Creator and become sensitive to His acts of creation reflected in our world, through which we recognize Him.

Our next step is to identify and examine the ten stages intrinsic to the act of creation. We will then be able to identify how they are reflected in the world around us.

---

17. Thus Rambam places his discussion of free will in his section on the laws of repentance: *Mishneh Torah, Hilkhot Teshuva* 5:7.

*Chapter 13*

# The Ten Stages of Creation

The ten stages of creation are connected in kabbalistic literature to the ten *sefirot*, the ten aspects of emanations of the Divine. There are many different understandings, facets, and applications of the *sefirot*, and we must, of course, select among these understandings for our purpose here. The reader will not need a background in Kabbala to understand the following exposition, which is based not on kabbalistic texts directly but on the work of authors such as Maharal, who for centuries have been translating these ideas into more mainstream intellectual formulations, allowing a broader community to understand them and integrate them into our way of looking at the world. But though this chapter requires no esoteric knowledge, it does require sustained concentration.

First, we should understand these stages of creation as *we* experience them. This is the first step toward learning to see them reflected in our world, thereby understanding it as a creation and so recognizing the Creator. Though we often move through these stages without thinking and one stage can imperceptibly merge into another, all are always present.

The ten stages can be broken down into three categories: the intellectual formulation of what is to be created and how, the emotional preparation to act, and the actual physical creation of the desired object in the world as a separate entity. Our experience of these stages may be outlined as follows:

I. The intellectual formation of the goal of creation
   1. (*Keter*) An indeterminate inspiration to create. This is an expression of our deepest *ratzon* (will/desire) and essential self, our desire to become actualized.
   2. (*Hokhma*) A general formulation of the goal of our act of creation.
   3. (*Bina*) Development of a specific and concrete idea of what we must create and how we must create it.

II. Emotional/internal preparation to actually create
   4. (*Hesed*) An overwhelming, internally generated desire to come out of ourselves and act on our inspiration to create or give.
   5. (*Gevura*) A reining-in of that desire so that we do not lose control of the creative process in a manner that would smother our intended creation (think of an overprotective mother).
   6. (*Tiferet*) Achieving a harmony between the desire to express and the need to contain that desire, resulting in a measured intent appropriate to the specific thing we wish to create.

III. Active, physical creation
   7. (*Netzah*) To overcome the inertial restraints to action, we apply forceful physical expression into the world to actually create something outside ourselves.
   8. (*Hod*) Having succeeded in initiating action, we contain that forcefulness so that we do not overwhelm or destroy what we are creating.
   9. (*Yesod*) We apply force in a measured fashion that produces the specific object we originally intended.
   10. (*Malkhut*) We release our creation to exist as an independent entity so that we can use or relate to that creation. This is the attainment of our original goal.

## THE TEN STATEMENTS OF CREATION

Next we need to understand how these same stages of creation are manifest in God's act of creation. This will facilitate our recognition of His acts of creation in our world as they mirror stages familiar to us.

In God's act of creation, each of the ten *sefirot* is actualized through a statement and its associated creation.[1] The intellectual stages manifest themselves in the most basic structures of existence, culminating in the creation of distinct otherness to God. The emotional stages, which prepare for the actions that create man (the goal of creation), are manifest in preparing a place for man. They form a world in which man can develop himself and thus achieve his purpose. The stages of physical action create actual facets of man's personality and man himself.

1. (*Keter*) Corresponds to *"Bereshit"* (In the beginning of...).[2] This hints at a statement that actualized the first stage of creation – God's *ratzon* (inspiration/desire/will) to create. *Ratzon* is prior to the articulation of even a general concept of what to create. This statement, therefore, does not speak of any specific creation. In fact, we do not even hear the creative statement; it is only *understood* from the verse that it was spoken. We do not know what was said; all we hear is "in the beginning of," which implies chronology and the introduction of time. In addition to time, this stage is made manifest through a creation without definition – utterly formless physical matter that stymies any attempt at description.[3] It is the creation of otherness to God which is not yet something.[4] *Ratzon* expresses essence, and

---

1. There is a dispute between the Talmud and the Zohar as to what the ten statements are. Here we use the scheme of the Talmud. For one explanation of the argument see Rabbi Tzadok HaKohen, *Pri Tzaddik, Vayikra, ot* 7.
2. Rashi, Gen. 1:1.
3. Ibid.
4. According to Reish Lakish man's *neshama* (soul) was created at this point (otherness) but presumably was not yet articulated or individualized to be a distinguishable someone (*Tanḥuma, Tazria* 1 and Leviticus Rabba 14:1). According to Elazar ben Padat, the human soul was not created until day six. He would understand that the potential for the *neshama* was created at this point but did not become an actuality until the sixth day.

we cannot relate to God in His Essence. We can only move toward appreciating Him by realizing successively more subtle levels of what God is not: He is not this, He is even more than that; He is not even this, He is even more than that.[5] So also God's pure *ratzon* is manifest in a creation that we can only relate to through negation – we can only describe what it is not, for it is not yet "something." But just as empty space is the prerequisite for fullness and holds the possibility of fullness, so this nothingness already contains the potential for any and all of existence. This first statement, hinted to by "Bereshit," results in what is effectively the evening before the morning of existence, the creation of potential that will draw after itself the actual.

2. (*Ḥokhma*) "Let there be light." This statement actualized the second stage of creation, setting its general goal, which is relationship between God and His creation. This was manifest through light, a non-physical light of wisdom that revealed the truth of that which it illuminated – the truth that all things play a role in connecting man to God.[6] This actualized the relationship with God because all relationships, including that with God, are founded on understanding. This light brought some understanding of God, or rather of our world, which is the medium through which we come to our understanding of God.[7]

3. (*Bina*) "Let there be a heaven in the midst of the waters and let it divide between the waters." This actualized the third stage of creation, the formulation of a defined vision of what would be created. Out of the infinite possible expressions of God's general desire to create (*ḥokhma*), *bina* determines the specific goal, or at least the direction in which the goal will lie. While still an intellectual trait, the particularity of *bina* breaks it off from the higher

---

5. Ramchal, *Daat Tevunot*, 34–38.
6. Genesis Rabba 12:6.
7. See Rambam, *Moreh Nevukhim* I:34. In *Mishneh Torah, Hilkhot Yesodei HaTorah* 2:2 Rambam identifies understanding creation as the path to loving God.

trait of *hokhma*,[8] which is undifferentiated, all-encompassing, unitary, and potential rather than actual. The break between *hokhma* and *bina* became manifest in the appearance of a reality that was split off from God and the metaphysical realm. This was a significant advance toward the specific goal of creation, as a realm was formed that was sufficiently distinct from God to allow relationship, as opposed to the situation before this statement when creation was effectively still an extension of God. This statement separated the boundless oceans of physical existence[9] from higher planes of reality but also, paralleling this, hints at the articulation of man's soul as something distinct from God and therefore already longing to return.[10]

4. (*Hesed*) "Let the waters under heaven gather into one place and dry land appear." This statement corresponds to the first stage of emotional preparation for action – *hesed* (kindness), the desire to create/give. Man, the true goal of creation, is not yet taking form; that must wait until the expression of *netzah*, which is a desire to give *to someone*, and therefore initiates the process of actually creating man, the receiver of God's giving. *Hesed*, however, is an internally grounded desire to give, rather than an externally directed desire to give *to* a specific receiver. Because *hesed* begins the emotional *preparation* to act, it is manifest in *preparation* for the creation of man, the making of his environment. Dry land provides a place within which a creature capable of developing himself – man with his intellect and free choice – can interact

---

8. See Maharal's statement that the acquisition of language – through which ideas become articulated and specific – causes the loss of Torah, which is connected to a level where understanding is above particular expression, retaining infinite possible specific expressions (*hokhma*). *Hiddushei Aggadot* IV, 159; see note 23.
9. See Job 11:9. The numerical value of *yam* (sea) is 50, corresponding to the 50 gates of *bina*.
10. See Rabbenu Bahya on Lev. 2:13. According to Leviticus Rabba 14:1, Reish Lakish held that man's *neshama* began to be formed on the first day (see note 4). Presumably, as creation developed with each passing day, so did man. The actualization of *bina* would then be expected to bring sufficient definition to the *neshama* for it to experience full distinction from God.

with his environment, transform it, and in the process grow and create himself in relationship with God.[11]

5. (*Gevura*) "Let the earth bring forth grasses that create seeds and fruit trees bearing fruit." The particular way in which trees came forth from the earth made *gevura* manifest in the world by restricting creation to a natural order. Structure was imposed on God's creation in the form of cause and effect, and this same structuring would eventually channel God's giving through the system of reward and punishment. With the world ordered by laws, it appeared to operate independently of any oversight. God's outpouring of *ḥesed* in the previous stage was constrained, so that when man was created he would not be led by his surroundings to an immediate and automatic recognition of the Creator continuously guiding the workings of physical reality.[12] *Gevura* formed the world as a place where man would need to strive to find God; it gave motivation and purpose to man's efforts by constraining God's giving to a system of reward and punishment.

6. (*Tiferet*) "Let there be lights in the heavens to distinguish between day and night...." The formation of the sun and moon actualized the balance between the desire to give and the need to contain that desire, which was necessary for successful creation. A finely calibrated relationship between the sun as source light and the moon as its reflector develops out of this statement, whereby the sun gives the moon the light that it needs without overwhelming its ability to convey that light in its own way. This provided a symbol and paradigm for the parallel relationship between God and man. We will discuss this in more detail later.[13]

7. (*Netzaḥ*) "Let the waters swarm with living things...." This statement began the stages that express traits of physical action and resulted in the first creation of life: birds and fish, including

---

11. Genesis Rabba 5:1.
12. See chapter 15 for a discussion of Rashi, Gen. 1:12.
13. See chapter 15.

the leviathans.[14] These mighty creatures embodied all that God desired to connect with in His creation,[15] so they made manifest God's overwhelming desire to give or connect to an other distinct from Himself (in contrast to *ḥesed*, which is a desire to go beyond oneself without any specific target for the giving). The overwhelming desire to connect that produced the leviathans was evident in the leviathans' own overwhelming desire for connection, which required the neutering of the male and the killing of the female to protect creation from them.[16] Otherwise, their uncurbed energy would have destroyed the world, either by compelling connection to God and overwhelming man's free choice, or else, once this desire was mixed with selfishness, by bringing about inappropriate and destructive connections.[17] We will see later, that through this trait God gave the Torah to the Jews, forming them into His *bat zug* (mate) in creation. We already discussed how that giving overwhelmed the Jews (they felt as if a mountain were held over their heads) and that the Jews responded with an overwhelming desire to connect back to God (their souls flew back to God, requiring that they be revived).[18]

8. (*Hod*) "Let the earth bring forth living creatures, animals…." Among the animals created by this statement was the serpent that enticed Chava.[19] Its successful effort to undermine Chava's appreciation of God's omnipotence actualized God's restraint of His overwhelming expression into and connection to the world. As the embodiment of evil, the serpent's motto is *"ani ve'afsi od"* (I exist and there is nothing else).[20] When evil's intense focus on

---

14. Gen. 1:20–21.
15. See, for example, Maharal, *Be'er HaGola*, Beer 4.
16. Bava Batra 74b.
17. See the Vilna Gaon, *Perush Tzafra DeTzniuta*, chapter 1, and Rashi, Gen. 1:21, from Bava Batra 74b. Some hold that the containment happened immediately, while others hold that it occurred after the sin of Adam (Rabbi Tzadok HaKohen, *Likutei Amarim* 16).
18. See chapter 4 and chapter 6, note 19.
19. Genesis Rabba 7:5.
20. Is. 47:8, 10; Zeph. 2:15.

its own existence was infused into man, it curbed our desire to connect back to God. So whereas *netzaḥ* expressed God's desire to connect to creation, resulting in a creation that desired to connect back to Him, *hod* restrained both aspects of *netzaḥ*. The actualization of *hod* reduced man's sense of God's overwhelming greatness, allowing man to experience his autonomous individuality and requiring him to exercise his free will to choose to connect to God.

9. (*Yesod*) "Let us make man." Man was the creature God ultimately intended when He began the process of creation, a being that is truly capable of relationship with God. Man is the only entity with both a divine soul and an earthly body, allowing him to bind the Creator to physical reality through his person, connecting the whole of creation back to God.[21]

10. (*Malkhut*) "Behold I have given you all the grasses... and all the trees with fruit...." In this statement God gave man control over his sustenance, the ability on some level to exist from himself within the context of physical reality. This was the release of man, granting him independence within the limitations of being a creation. It also introduced the possibility of confusing physical independence with existential independence. This enabled the full scope of choice over man's relationship with God and allowed man to emulate God's kingship by determining himself. If he does, he fully actualizes his *tzelem Elokim* (his capacity to choose) and so achieves both the greatest expression of God into the world and creation's deepest connection with Him.[22]

This process of creation is not one in which each succeeding stage supersedes and absorbs its predecessor. Rather, each adds a new

---

21. See Rashi, Gen. 2:7.
22. This statement completes the *active* part of creation. Shabbat was still to follow. Shabbat represents the realm of reward, which is the aspect of God's relationship with man in which man receives rather than being responsible for the relationship. For reasons that go beyond the scope of this book, the Sages give several different versions of how to divide up the ten statements of creation. We have been using the talmudic version (see note 1 to this chapter), but none include Shabbat.

layer, with the previous ones remaining as distinct facets of existence. They support and affect the whole like so many layers of paint on an oil painting, adding color and tone to the final work. For example, God's intention to create for the purpose of giving to man, which launches the project, remains a vitalizing force even at the end of the process, when man is finally granted his independence.[23]

Moreover, each statement not only brings something new into being but also continues to sustain that aspect of creation until the end of time.[24] And not only the thing specified by the statement, but all things that are relevant to that aspect of creation depend upon that statement for their existence. For example, the tenth statement gave man control over plants and thus made him responsible for his sustenance. For all of time, the existence of anything affording man this ability emanates from this tenth statement. One example is the Nile in Egypt, which is the source of that country's sustenance. A fully integrated vision of existence as a creation would identify each facet of reality with one of these ten statements.[25]

Taken together, these different layers constitute existence. Understood correctly, they form a path that leads back to their source, the infinite Creator. This requires that we recognize them as manifestations of God's creative traits, which we can do because we share these same traits and so are familiar with them. But we will only recognize their reflection in creation if we have purified them in ourselves.

---

23. In a similar vein, any profound spiritual insight cannot be fully captured in words, for words are a thing of this world and spiritual ideas are larger than this world. Still the insight must be verbalized if it is to be shared with others. But the idea will only retain its power if connection is maintained to the aspect of the idea that defies articulation even at the very moment that it is being given concrete expression in speech.
24. Ps. 119:89.
25. Rabbi Hayim of Volozhin in *Nefesh HaḤayim* 1:2 points out that the verb *oseh* (making) in Ps. 136:7 ("To the One who is making the great luminaries") is in the present tense and not the past. This indicates that God continually creates/sustains existence. This is accomplished through the continuing influence of the ten statements. The Psalmist states: "Forever Your statements are established in the heavens" (Ps. 119:89). See, for example, Rabbi Tzadok HaKohen, *Pri Tzaddik, Tetzave, ot* 10, in the name of the Baal Shem Tov.

*Part 2: The Character of Faith*

What does it mean to purify them? Character traits arise from the merging of our spiritual essence, our *neshama* or *tzelem Elokim* (image of God), with our physical being, our bodies. A purified trait is one which the *neshama* defines, with the physical component acting as the *neshama*'s medium of expression. An unpurified trait, on the other hand, is one where the body is driving the trait, co-opting the consciousness arising from the *neshama* to feed the body's physical desires.

### EMUNA AND OUR CREATIVE TRAITS

We can now match the traits of creation as a person experiences them with the facets of creation that actualize God's parallel stages of creation. With that we can form a picture of how a person of purified character would become aware of the world as a creation through experiencing his own traits of creation. For our example we will look at an idealized case of a person's first creative act, one through which he first emerges into true individuality and comes to know himself.

1. (*Keter*) As my will/desire to create/give stirs, I begin to awaken to my self becoming distinct from Him Who *is* existence and the source of all existence. My growing awareness of my still-amorphous otherness to God makes me aware of a context to my emerging existence, creation, which at this point is as unformed in my mind as my own selfhood. This is the awareness of time.

2. (*Hokhma*) As I begin to formulate my intention of what to create, I move increasingly toward individual awareness and I understand that all things are a means or opportunity for man to connect back to God – that this is their meaning, purpose, and only reality. Similarly, my effort to create is meant to connect me to God.

3. (*Bina*) As my thoughts become more concrete and I clarify my specific intent – what it is that I desire to create – I become aware of myself as a fully distinct individual. I strive to understand myself and my project in the context of the larger truth that everything exists only to allow relationship with God, to counter the extent to which my emerging selfhood disconnects me from Him.

## The Ten Stages of Creation

4. (*Ḥesed*) The increasing integration of my spiritual self, my *neshama*, with my individuality of being and body results in a powerful desire to go beyond the confines of myself and be expressed in the world through my act of creation/giving. I see this trait mirrored in the existence of the world, making me acutely aware that the world is the result of an act of creation from the *ḥesed* of the Creator.

5. (*Gevura*) I react to this powerful desire to give by containing myself so as not to lose control of the creative process. I see this containment mirrored in the precise order and functioning of the natural world within the structure set by God. The world's causal organization conditions me to understand that all actions have defined consequences and, by extension, that even though God's creation was motivated by *ḥesed*, our relationship is mediated by reward and punishment.

6. (*Tiferet*) In final preparation to act, I achieve equilibrium between my desire to be expressed and my need to contain myself, and this prepares me to create in a way that will not overwhelm that which I am creating. At the same time I become aware that though God is absolutely omnipotent and all that I am and have to give comes from Him, He still leaves space for human action, leaving me responsible to act in the world as His representative. I see this relationship mirrored in comparable relationships throughout creation, notably in the relationship between the sun and the moon.

7. (*Netzaḥ*) The continuing integration of the *neshama* with my body leads me to an overwhelming need to actually express myself into the world by bringing my specific creation into existence so that I can connect to something outside myself. This leads to a forceful initiation of action to create and connect. I become sensitized to the fact that existence is a tribute to God's overpowering desire to connect to His world and that His creation, which includes me, mirrors that in its own desire and capacity to connect to Him.

*Part 2: The Character of Faith*

8. (*Hod*) The forcefulness of my initial action threatens to destroy what I am creating; so I pull back into my self, which I experience as isolated individuality. The sense of inadequacy characterizing this form of awareness, along with the emptiness I see mirrored in the world around me because of my sense of personal limitation, drives me to reach beyond myself to the Creator. I also recognize that the narrow boundaries of physical existence. as they appear to me, do not define the limits of reality; they only exist to challenge me to reach beyond them to the expansive basis of existence.

9. (*Yesod*) By means of Torah and mitzvot, my body becomes the vessel through which my *neshama* is expressed. By integrating my *tzelem Elokim* (image of God) with my physical being, I become aware of the fullness of my humanity and bind God to His creation through my person. I achieve an inner balance between my need to express myself and the constraints of physical reality, so that I can act appropriately to achieve my specific creative intent.

10. (*Malkhut*) I choose to release my creation and give it the gift of independent being. Through this choice I determine and create my self as a giver, emulating the initiative and creativity of the Creator, resonating with Him and conveying the deepest aspect of His image to the world (the ability to choose, initiate, and create). I am capable of choosing only because this aspect of God is the core of my being, which I actualize in the act of choosing. I experience the act of choice, which is the full creation of self, as the ultimate merging with and return to God, achieving the purpose of creation.

Earlier generations were more spiritually attuned and aware of themselves as creations and creators. Their experience of self and reality was structured by the traits of creation. Their process in achieving the immediate and integrated faith we are describing was more intuitive and unconscious than what we go through today, when we experience self and reality so differently.

## The Ten Stages of Creation

But this does not mean that if we could once again filter reality through these aspects of character structured in this way, we would automatically achieve faith *in God*. As we said earlier, just as these layers can provide us with a path to faith and an opportunity for all aspects of our personality to support faith, each layer can also block our awareness of God when interpreted through an impure character. Each can be misinterpreted in a manner that reinforces a sense of independent physical existence or even leads to actual idolatry, where we identify it with a force that is ultimately just a projection of ourselves. In short, each facet can function either as clothing of God, selectively revealing Him as clothes do, or as a curtain that obscures Him.

At the time of Adam, when the Creator was clearly revealed in the world, the dependence of every facet of existence upon God was clearly visible. But beginning with the sin of Adam and continuing with Cain's murder of Abel, the idolatry of Enosh, the wantonness of the generation of the flood, the pridefulness of the generation of the tower, etc., man's self-centeredness intensified.[26] The rising egotism that lay at the core of each of these transgressions distorted the various character traits through which we experience reality. It placed our awareness of self at the center of our consciousness and made it increasingly difficult to recognize God as the true Source of all the different facets of existence.[27] Each of

---

26. Genesis Rabba 19:7. The midrash mentions seven levels, yet we are discussing ten plagues. According to Ramban (*Ḥiddushei HaRamban, Shemot* 10:1), the last three plagues were not punishments. This was because they dealt with levels which man had no ability to directly corrupt at that point in history, because those traits were abstract and it was a time when abstraction had not yet become an integral part of human awareness. See Rav Gedalia Schorr, *Or Gedalyahu, Bo*. The lessons of the last three plagues became more relevant later in history.
27. It is important to note that the terms "egotism," "self," and "self-contained" as used here are not meant in a decisive sense. Rather, they are to be understood relative to a full and defining awareness of our dependence upon the transcendent God. When we are talking about the Garden of Eden or Egypt or any time up until the destruction of the First Temple, some form of abiding awareness of God or gods was a given for everyone. Human consciousness was experienced as an extension of some greater being, and individuality was experienced in the context of one's people. Ramban's statement, quoted at the beginning of the book, that the purpose of the miraculous Exodus was to counter, among others, those who denied the existence of God, should not be taken to imply that there was anyone who denied the existence

*Part 2: The Character of Faith*

the layers of existence became a veil opaque to any transcendent basis. The world came to appear as a self-contained and self-sustained reality (or its idolatrous equivalent).

Recovery from this initial slide away from God began with Abraham's recognition of God's existence. Isaac, Jacob, and individuals that followed them built upon Abraham's discovery.[28] Each developed a unique relationship with God based on the character trait he refined in himself and that came to define him.[29] Simultaneously, however, the Jews multiplied, changing from a small family to a people and finding themselves in Egypt. While a select few individuals were creating the basis for what would eventually become our national relationship with God, their accomplishments were lost on the expanding Jewish population. Exile and bondage in Egypt were casting their shadow over the Jewish spirit. So apart from these few remarkable individuals, awareness of the Creator as the source of existence was lost to us and the world soon after we entered Egypt.

### TEN PLAGUES TO PURIFY THE TEN TRAITS

In order to wake us from this sleep, ten plagues were brought upon Egypt. Ten traits of character had become corrupted, so that the ten facets of creation were viewed as independently existing arenas of reality and their transcendent root was hidden. Ten plagues arrived to reveal the Creator

---

of gods. This was discussed in the first half of this book. When applied to these early generations, "egotism" and "self" and any other related terms should be understood as referring to a consciousness centered more in our humanity than in God or, in the case of Egypt, in the Egyptian people. The term "egotism" and the like are primarily intended to contrast with the selflessness that lies at the basis of true worship, which can only be directed toward the transcendent, unitary Creator. Idolatry (polytheism) is worship of aspects of personality that have been alienated from the self and projected outward. Although in the worship of the Creator we also find something within us that is associated with the Creator – the *tzelem Elokim* or *neshama* – that is the root of our self which is *ḥelek Eloka mimaal*, a part of God from above which is in us, rather than a part of us that we alienated and designated as divine.

28. Genesis Rabba 19:7.
29. This underlies the concept of the *ushpizin* on Sukkot, when we identify with specific individuals who achieved greatness of faith through focus on a specific one of these creative traits.

as the source of each facet, peeling back the obscuring veils and healing the corrupted character traits through which we were misunderstanding each of these layers.

With this introduction in mind, we can look at the plagues individually. In relation to each plague we will aim to understand (a) to which statement of creation and associated facet of creation it was directed; (b) what character trait was actualized through the statement and how through that trait's purified form we understand its associated creation in a manner that contributes to our *emuna*; (c) how that creation would be misunderstood when viewed through an impure version of the trait; and (d) how the plague healed the trait, correcting that misunderstanding.

This approach to the plagues will provide a vision of how studying and internalizing the Exodus can bring a level of *emuna* that far surpasses anything we can reach through our own private contemplation. For if each trait of our character contributes to our conceiving the world as a created reality, our *emuna* grows organically from our awareness of self and world (*yiḥud Hashem*), as opposed to the modern experience of faith as one more item plastered onto the collage of our consciousness.

This chapter has already introduced a great deal of material on these traits, and there is a lot more to come as we examine each one individually. It can get confusing and it will be easy to lose the larger picture in the mass of details. So I have created a chart that gives a snapshot of the whole enterprise. You might consider consulting this chart as you read through the coming chapters, you will find it easier to retain a sense for how each trait and the perspective it should foster fits into the larger whole of our perception of reality as a creation. The chart is too extensive to fit legibly on a book page so I have made it available as a download at http://nevey.org/downloads.html.

*Chapter 14*

# The First Plagues

Understanding the plagues is challenging for a number of reasons. They came to uncover God's traits of creation, which had become obscured through our impure character and misinterpretation of the various facets of existence. Moreover, as noted earlier, recognizing these traits of creation would no longer be intuitive to us even if our character were clean, because we do not define ourselves as creators and our personalities are not structured around creating. This obviously complicates our efforts to understand how the plagues clarify these traits.

There is another factor adding to the confusion about the plagues. The traits through which God creates unfold in the order dictated by the process of creation. This is something that we understand, so their sequence is easy enough to follow. But each additional statement of creation applied a new layer of physical existence over the face of God, embedding us ever more deeply in finite, physical reality and leaving us further from God. To achieve full *emuna*, our path back to God must begin from our distant starting point and move step-by-step through all the intervening layers. So we must encounter the creative stages in the order opposite to that of creation.[1]

---

1. Many sources link the plagues, the statements, and the traits (*sefirot*). See, for example, Rabbi Tzadok HaKohen, *Pri Tzaddik, Bo* 2 (based on the Zohar); *Pri Tzaddik, Vayera* 1,

*Part 2: The Character of Faith*

The plagues were therefore directed at the statements of creation in this same reverse order, with the first plague directed at the tenth trait, the second at the ninth trait and so on.

### MALKHUT AND THE PLAGUE OF BLOOD

In the ten stages of creation, *malkhut* was actualized through the statement "Behold I have given you all the grasses...and all the trees with fruit...." In this statement God gave man control over his sustenance – the ability on some level to exist from himself.

Giving man dominion over the plants was an expression of God's creative trait of *malkhut* (kingship). This final creative trait is called kingship because a king can only be a king if he rules a people – an entity separate from himself.[2] This corresponds to the last stage of any creative act, which is to release the created object so that it can exist independently of its creator, allowing its creator to relate to it. Control of sustenance effectively separated man from God by making man self-sufficient within the context of creation.

We said that separation is a prerequisite of relationship. Paradoxically, man's separation from God also provides the actual *basis* for this relationship. Emulation is our deepest mode of union with the Divine, and man's independent control of his sustenance gives him sovereignty through which he can emulate the sovereignty of God and thus achieve connection.[3]

The fact that this facet of creation allows emulation highlights another reason why the final act of creation is called kingship. A creator not only creates something he can relate to or use, but also wants to see

---

and *Pri Tzaddik, Pesaḥ Sheni* 3. Maharal, however, differs with this approach. Though he agrees that the plagues are associated with the statements, he understands the plagues to follow an order dictated by their relative intensity rather than simply inverting the order of the statements. The Ari *z"l* has an entirely different way of associating the plagues and statements. In this book we will follow the approach of Rabbi Tzadok, which is the most straightforward and easiest to comprehend.

2. Without a people the title "king" is nonsensical; *Pirkei DeRabbi Eliezer* 3.
3. Ramḥal, *Derekh Hashem* 1:2:3. We spoke about how by becoming creators we emulate God. Kingship is a way of creating, since the king, by choosing how he rules, determines himself and the structure of his world. God's kingship is more fundamental; for He not only determines the structure of His kingdom but creates it from nothing.

himself expressed through his act of creation. This means that his creation must resemble him, and this resemblance in turn allows for connection through emulation, which is the deepest connection. Just as God is a king in His act of creation, He wants His creation to reflect or express His kingliness. Therefore He creates something that is itself a king.

With control over his sustenance, man gained physical independence, and this made it possible for him to confuse his independence with total autonomy from God, removing all constraints on his free will. Physical sovereignty therefore provided the context in which man became fully responsible for determining and creating himself through his choices – the deepest sovereignty and emulation of God. When an individual decisively takes charge of himself in this way, he experiences a powerful sense of significance, weightiness, and wholeness of being. This sense of independent being, with the capability that fosters it, is the distinct facet of creation called *malkhut*, the final facet that allows creation to achieve the emulation and resonance that is its purpose.

Man's challenge is to remain fully aware of his utter dependence on his Creator in the midst of his independence, whether independence is defined as physical self-sustenance or the exercise of free choice. In either case the sense of being complete unto one's self awakens the temptation to think "I need nothing and no one, therefore I am totally free." For this reason the Torah requires us to bless God for our food after we eat and are satisfied. At that moment we feel complete, as if we did not need anything from outside ourselves to exist, so there is danger that we will think we do not need God.[4]

A paradigm for the delicate balance required for this relationship of dependence/independence is presented by the sun and the moon (whose creation in God's sixth statement established the possibility for man's relationship with God). The moon rules over the night by determining, through its waxing and waning, how much light enters the world. The sun does not control the amount of light that the moon conveys to

---

4. Deut. 8:7–18. Similarly, the offering of the Omer is the antidote to the sense of autonomy that comes from growing our own crops. See Leviticus Rabba 28:1–3.

the world; this is under the dominion of the moon. Yet all the light with which the moon rules is derived entirely from the sun.[5]

King David serves as our archetype for this connection to God. By ruling his world and his people decisively, he personified God's quality of kingship. But his authority never obscured David's sense of his dependence upon God. In fact, by humbling himself toward God and His commandments, he ruled as God would rule, acting as a representative and conduit for God's authority. It was God's kingship that flowed through David; by ruling, David was connected to his Creator like a branch to its root.[6]

On a deeper level, the ability to choose (*malkhut*) is a divine quality. We are only able to choose because of the spark of the Creator within us, our *tzelem Elokim*. We actualize this godliness within us in the act of choice. So David, who was the very picture of independent authority as he determined his rule, was in those moments actually exhibiting his deepest connection to God. In his acts of choice he was an echo of God's *malkhut*.

This quality of kingship is not only found in those rare individuals who hold the political position of king. As much as David himself personified this trait, he was a paradigm for each of us to experience this connection through our own personal kingship. Every human being experiences this quality of sovereignty whenever he chooses. He is determining through his free will who he is (effectively creating himself) and, by extension, he is determining his vision of the world, allowing him to resonate with God the Creator.

Egypt mistook this independence-within-the-created-context for total independence, cutting God out of the picture. Egypt understood itself to be self-sustaining without any need of a transcendent Source. In fact, it had lost recognition of the transcendent God's existence entirely.[7] The great source and symbol of Egypt's self-sufficiency was the Nile, which

---

5. The metaphor is not perfect because the moon's "choice" to convey or not convey the light of the sun is something separate from the actual light it is "choosing" to convey, whereas in the case of man the "light" that he is receiving from God includes the actual ability to choose.
6. See Ramḥal, *Derekh Hashem* 1:2:3.
7. Ex. 5:2.

provided all the water needed for agriculture on a regular and reliable basis. The Nile was worshipped as a god.[8] But this, like idolatry generally, was a projection of an inner quality that had been externalized and deified. It was actually an indirect worship of self.[9] This was made clear in Pharaoh, the god-king of Egypt. He was identified with the Nile, and the annual inundation was understood to be his responsibility. Pharaoh saw himself as its embodiment: "The Nile is mine and I have made it." Since Pharaoh was the personification and projection of all Egyptians, in worshipping the Nile Egyptians were worshipping themselves.[10]

Turning the Nile to blood thus shattered the Egyptians' sense of control and self-reliance. On a practical level the Nile was immediately neutralized as a provider, so that Egypt's survival was threatened. But even more destabilizing was the clear revelation that an alien power existed that was greater than the Nile and generally threatened the control and independence of Egypt. The Nile was turned specifically to blood because blood is man's liquid of life, whereas water is outside us and from God. Egypt claimed that man sustained himself through the Nile, with the Nile a projection of man. God simply let the world reflect this corrupt understanding. If the Nile is an expression of man, then blood should flow through it, not water.

We have already mentioned that the plagues, whether they appeared in the precinct of the Jews in Goshen or not, did not affect the Jews.[11] The midrash tells us that the waters of Egypt remained water for the Jews even though they were blood for the Egyptians. This extended to the case where an Egyptian and a Jew were both drinking from the

---

8. Actually, it was primarily the inundation of the Nile that was worshipped. The god associated with the inundation was closely tied to Pharaoh. Redford, *Ancient Gods Speak*, 336.
9. See Genesis Rabba 69:3.
10. Ezek. 29:3. Genesis Rabba 5:14 notes that declaring the Nile a god did not preclude Pharaoh from claiming to own and to have created the Nile. This is not to say that an average Egyptian did not have the sense of being controlled by something higher than himself. But because this "something higher" was identified with Pharaoh, and an ordinary Egyptian would have perceived Pharaoh as an idealization of himself, ultimately he and the god were one.
11. See chapter 11.

same glass – the Egyptian drank blood and the Jew water.[12] Since the Torah tells us that the fish in the Nile died, it is clear that while the water remained water for the Jews, it *actually* became blood for all other creatures; the transformation into blood was not an illusion. How are we to understand this?

As we have explained, the point of these plagues was not merely to punish the Egyptians but to reveal deeper truths about the nature of reality. The Zohar, based on a verse from Isaiah, teaches that every plague was a blow to Egypt and simultaneously a *healing* for the Jews.[13] While a plague was striking the Egyptians, the Jews were gaining clarity about the true nature of reality and escaping the illusory understanding of Egypt.

As we saw, God actualized His trait of *malkhut* during creation in the form of a statement granting man control of his sustenance. From that moment on this statement sustained the aspects of creation pertaining to sustenance.[14] In Egypt it was actualized through the Nile, which was Egypt's mode of sustenance. The purpose of the independence granted by this statement was to allow man to emulate God and so connect to Him; but the Egyptians had mistaken this independence for true autonomy and used it to separate themselves from God.

In general God allows man to function within the framework of his fanciful realities, in order to give him an opportunity to reach a deeper truth and repent.[15] This had been the situation in Egypt until the time of the Exodus. But when the plagues came, that changed. The first plague was a consequence of God's actualizing His *malkhut* in Egypt in a manner that *only* allowed for its true understanding. That meant recognizing the Nile as a source that allowed man to sustain himself in order to emulate God.

For the Jews, who were able to grasp this, the Nile remained water; it continued to be supported by God's *malkhut* as a source of sustenance. But for the Egyptians it was a different story. Their worldview

---

12. Tanḥuma, Vaera 13; Tana Debei Eliyahu Rabba 7:6.
13. Zohar II 36a, based on Is. 19:22: "And the Lord shall smite Mitzrayim, He shall smite and heal."
14. Ps. 119:89: "Eternally, Hashem, Your word is established in heaven," meaning that the word of God, which creates, continues eternally to sustain what it creates.
15. Rabbi Moshe Cordovero, *Tomer Devora*, perek 1.

## The First Plagues

and self-understanding were wedded to the notion that the Nile was an expression of Pharaoh. The new clarity revealing the true role of the Nile contradicted their very identity. They could not be themselves and relate to this deeper awareness. But during the plague the truth of *malkhut* was the only way to relate to actualizations of *malkhut*. Since the Egyptians could not do this, the Nile for them ceased to be an expression of *malkhut*, a source of sustenance. Instead, the Nile mirrored to the Egyptians their delusion. For them, the Nile was blood, the liquid of man rather than the life-sustaining fluid provided by God.[16]

This is somewhat similar to two people viewing the same scene from two different angles where each sees different facets of one thing. In this case, however, rather than viewing the Nile from different angles, the Jews and Egyptians were experiencing it from different realities. For the Jews the Nile was water from God, gifted from Him with the power to sustain. For the Egyptians it was an alienated aspect of independent self – blood outside the body, no longer sustaining life.[17]

Each of the plagues can be understood in a similar manner: God revealed a trait unambiguously, in a creation which could only express that trait in its intended manner. This contradicted the Egyptians' worldview and self understanding on an existential level, so that they could not change their way of relating to it. Therefore, instead of actualizing the trait for the Egyptians, that creation reflected their illusory reality, which resulted in a plague. The Jews, on the other hand, were pushed to

---

16. *Zohar* II 36a states (roughly translated): "The powers above simultaneously possess both judgment and mercy in equal measure." It is explicit in the Haggada and commentaries with regard to the striking-down of the firstborn that the plague was a consequence of God revealing Himself (Rabbi Tzadok HaKohen, *Maḥshavot Ḥarutz, ot* 4). Some commentaries also state that the plague of darkness was the result of God revealing His light (see, for example, Kalonymus Kalman Epstein, *Meor veShemesh, Bo*, "ve'al"). These commentaries thus understand the Zohar's "judgment and mercy in equal measure" to mean that the plagues on the Egyptians and the elevation of the Jews were equally consequences of God's revelation. How people experienced it depended upon their ability to connect to the revelation.

17. The fish died because in Egypt the Egyptians determined the reality that was actualized. The Jews were able to experience the Nile as water because they were in the process of being decoupled from Egypt and the Egyptians and moved to a different engagement with reality. This is the deeper truth of the Exodus.

*Part 2: The Character of Faith*

connect to the deeper vision being revealed, integrating themselves ever more consistently with the concept of themselves as servants of God existing for the sake of their relationship with Him. Each plague was a blow to the Egyptians and a healing for the Jews.[18] This happened ten times until all facets of existence were revealed to be instruments for relationship with God, fully freeing the Jews while utterly destroying Egypt.

We might compare the Jewish people and the Egyptian people to two different kinds of trees. Both trees have a trunk with nine branches, and both have ten roots with each root feeding one of the branches or the trunk. The Jewish tree is native to Israel where, though the soil is dry, there is an aquifer of sweet clean water deep underneath the earth. All ten of the roots of the Jewish tree naturally grow all the way down to take their nourishment from the aquifer.

The Egyptian tree is native to Egypt, where the soil is moist from the inundation of the Nile. The deeper the soil, the more water available. The ten roots of the Egyptian tree each grow to different depths, because different branches need different amounts of water. But even though Egypt also has a clear aquifer at its depths, the deepest root of its tree, the one feeding the trunk, stops short of the aquifer because it, too, is sated with dampness from the soil. Unfortunately, though the water in the soil is easy to reach, it is not clean water, so the trunk and all the branches of the Egyptian tree are misshapen.

When the Jewish tree was first planted in Egypt, it grew its ten roots all the way to the aquifer. But it was so much easier to draw water from the soil that eventually the Jewish tree began drawing its nourishment from the soil instead of the aquifer. Each root developed the ability to draw from the shallowest depth that would sate the needs of its branch, while the full length of all the roots, the part that reached to the aquifer, became dormant. Because the Jewish tree was drawing unclean water from the soil, it became misshapen like the Egyptian tree.

But then a great drought occurred, and the Nile did not overflow its banks. The soil began to dry out, with the desiccation reaching to ever deeper and deeper levels. As each layer became dry, the branch of the Egyptian tree fed by the root drawing its water from that layer

---

18. See note 16.

withered. But the same branch on the Jewish tree was instead able to reactivate the long dormant length of its root and begin to draw water from the aquifer. Instead of withering, now that it was sustained by the clean water of the aquifer, it recovered its originally beauty. This process continued until the Egyptian tree in its entirety died while the Jewish tree in its entirety recovered its original splendor.

In this metaphor drawing nourishment from the aquifer represents recognizing that the transcendent, unitary God is the Source of existence both for the trunk and for all nine branches. Drawing nourishment from the soil represents attributing existence to a physical, idolatrous intermediary. Because of the forefathers, the Jews by nature attributed existence to the transcendent Creator; all their roots reached to the aquifer. But through their enslavement to Egypt they came to share Egypt's idolatrous view – their roots started drawing their nourishment from the soil, which, like idolatry, is more immediate and easier to reach.[19] To bring the Jews back to clarity and free them from Egypt, God sequentially revealed that each facet of reality derived its existence only from Him. Each new revelation blocked the attribution of the associated facet to an idolatrous source (the ground feeding that root dried up). For the Jews this reawakened the dormant part of the root and it returned to drinking from the aquifer (we once again recognized the Creator as the source of that facet of existence). The Egyptians, who could not accept the transcendent Creator as the Source, lacked the deeper root. They could not switch from their now-bankrupt idolatry and could only watch as the branch fed by that root withered and died. For the Egyptians that facet of existence ceased to play its role in creation, and they experienced a plague.

## YESOD AND THE PLAGUE OF FROGS

The ninth statement of Creation – "Let us make man" – actualized the trait of *yesod*. Man was the creature God originally intended when He began the process of creation, a being truly capable of relationship with God. Man is the only entity with both a divine soul and an earthly body,

---

19. Maharal, *Gur Aryeh*, Bereshit 18:4.

allowing him to bind the Creator to physical reality and, through his person, to connect the whole of creation back to God.

*Yesod* balances the expression of the overwhelming drive to create with the need to hold that force in check, allowing precise formation of the object intended to achieve creation's goal. This was man before he was granted sovereignty over his sustenance and became an independent being with a fully activated free will. At this stage of *yesod* man combines an inner spark of Godliness with external physical being.

God formed man by infusing His breath – the most internal facet He brings to creation – into a material vessel for containing and actualizing it in the physical world. *Yesod*'s balance showed itself in the discretion with which God blew in the soul. Rather than overwhelming man, the soul was infused in a manner that allowed the body to contain it and man to experience both dimensions of his being. By integrating these two aspects of himself through his actions, thoughts, and speech, man becomes the bridge between the Creator and that physical creation. Man's ability to stand between these two realms and unite them in his person is a distinct facet of creation and forms a step in the path of achieving fully integrated *emuna*. (It is not the final step, as the emulation enabled by *malkhut* brings God more fully into the self and into physical reality.)

Because *yesod* combines a divine spark with a physical body, man is by nature sandwiched between the internal and the external aspects of experience. Our challenge is to maintain our connection to and awareness of the full spiritual depths of our inner world while functioning amid the alluring distractions of physical reality which draw our center toward superficial, physically based aspects of inner experience. The person in history who most fully actualized this trait was Joseph, who remained conscious of his inner connection to God no matter how enticing or dark his surroundings became.

Today we are overwhelmed by our awareness of external reality. Our inner awareness is less conscious and sharp than in the past, our reach less deep. We have only a fleeting sense that there is more to us than what our immediate awareness makes available. In earlier times, however, we were in touch with our personality as it dissolved into ever deeper and more inclusive levels of spirit, disappearing into layers emanating

## The First Plagues

directly from God.[20] But even though the internal places available to us today are relatively shallow, they still connect us to our spiritual core.

Man's individual consciousness arises from his spiritual root, his *neshama*, which extends down from the Creator and makes contact with his physical body. The *neshama* itself is aware of its higher Source and is drawn toward that Source. But once the *neshama* awakens individual self-consciousness in us, we also become aware of crude desires deep in the physically based subconscious. So while man necessarily experiences himself as a meeting between clearly articulated, material reality and an inner world that is ineffable, he does not have to identify that ineffable inner core with the elevating inner self which is consciousness of his *neshama*. Instead he can identify it with his physical desires, which also provide an inner life. Since man only understands the nature of reality with reference to his own experience of being, such a mistake leads to profound misunderstandings of the world.

The Egyptians followed this second path, shunting their awareness of inner depth toward immediate, selfish desires rather than seeking the more subtle spiritual greatness of the *neshama*. They corrupted their humanity by locating it between consciousness and man's physical subconscious emanating up from below, rather than actualizing the *tzelem Elokim* within them and connecting their consciousness upwards toward God.[21] As these subterranean forces became identified as the source of Egyptian personality, they became identified as the basis of existence itself, with the Egyptians worshipping idolatrous projections of these physical energies.[22] Through their long servitude in Egypt, the Jews had been influenced to follow the Egyptians in identifying with these aspects of their humanity.

Egypt's distortion of man's true nature was made manifest through the plague of the frogs. God actualized His trait of *yesod*, which was responsible for the integration of man with his *neshama*. For the

---

20. We have already had several occasions to mention the change in man's awareness that was ushered in as abstract thought came to dominant man's cognition.
21. Leviticus Rabba 23:7.
22. The Egyptian world was thus folded in on itself, a presumed self-sustaining reality cut off from any true transcendent connection. This misunderstanding was in harmony with their corruption of the trait of *malkhut*, which we discussed before.

*Part 2: The Character of Faith*

Jews, this resulted in a powerful surge in our awareness of our *neshama*, anchoring our personality, transforming our sense of self, and leaving no room for an illusory vision of man's nature. For the Egyptians, however, this recognition would have contradicted their very identity. They could not switch without a complete loss of self. So instead they were stuck with their false identification. But because truth was being revealed in relation to this facet of existence, they were forced to confront the reality of their illusory vision. This came in the form of frogs.

Frogs connect land, the arena in which we develop our consciousness, to their home in the murky depths of the Nile, the place "under the land."[23] Thus they can represent Egypt's corrupt view of man as a connector of external awareness of the land with an internal awareness that wells up from depths of subconscious physical desires. The midrash emphasizes the directionality of the frogs coming up from below.[24]

This plague saw frogs go everywhere: the houses, the bedrooms, the slave quarters, the ovens, the mixing-troughs.[25] All the capacities that make man uniquely human were blocked. The frogs got in the way of food preparation, which represents man's creative capacity.[26] The Egyptians' ability to procreate was also destroyed by the frogs: the midrash tells us the frogs castrated the Egyptians.[27]

This was not a mere *dis*placement by frogs, it was a *re*placement by frogs. The midrash states that the worst part of this plague was the

---

23. In the cosmologies of the ancient Near East it was held that beneath the earth was water, on which the world of land floated like an island. This was the case in Mesopotamia (Bottero, *Religion in Ancient Mesopotamia*, 77–81) and in Egypt (Wilson, *The Intellectual Adventure of Ancient Man*, 45). The Egyptians, who almost never saw rain, believed that the source of the Nile was an ocean that was under the earth which flowed upward through caverns (ibid., 38). The idea that beneath the earth is water is also found in Torah (Ex. 20:4).
24. Exodus Rabba 10:3.
25. Ex. 7:28.
26. When we prepare food we prepare that which sustains us. The distinction between the festivals, when we are allowed to prepare food, and Shabbat, when cooking is forbidden, is that the festivals celebrate man's efforts to create relationship with God through free will, whereas Shabbat is a celebration of our passive reception of relationship.
27. Exodus Rabba 15:27.

noise the frogs made. The frogs entered the bodies of the Egyptians, and when the Egyptians tried to speak the sound of croaking was heard instead.[28] Speech expresses *yesod* and defines our unique humanity, for it integrates the physical with the spiritual. We gained the ability to speak in the moment when man was formed by the divine soul combining with the physical body.[29] The fact that during this plague the Egyptians croaked when they tried to speak indicates that their corrupt understanding of man had effectively made their nature indistinguishable from that of frogs.

This plague made manifest the destruction of true humanity that Egypt had wrought by her identification of the source of man's inner life with physical desires. If man's inner root connects him back to nothing but himself, then the basis of true human speech is lost and we become indistinguishable from croaking frogs.

The depth to which the frogs nullified Egyptian humanity is made clear in the midrash discussing the castration of the Egyptians.[30] The language of the midrash is startling: "The coinage of your gods has been abolished, so yours cannot continue." A king mints coins because he determines the form of his society. Just as he impresses the image of his personality on his kingdom, he gives form to the currency with which the kingdom functions by pressing his image on the coins. When a king is defeated and replaced, his currency is annulled. The invalidation of any coin with the king's image on it mirrors the king's loss of the ability to put his stamp on his society.

Man's ability to procreate is here compared to minting a coin. The soul gives specific form to the material of our being. Conceiving a child involves passing our soul or form on to the child; it is like minting a coin in our image. But just as the king needs authority to mint coins, so we need authority to impress our form on the world. We gain that authority from God, the source of our soul, in Whose image we are made and Whose image we pass on.

---

28. Ibid. 10:6.
29. Gen. 2:7 with the Targum Onkelos.
30. Exodus Rabba 15:27.

*Part 2: The Character of Faith*

By choosing their physical inclinations as their defining inner experience, the Egyptians identified these energies as the basis of reality and externalized them as gods. But though the Egyptians formed their gods by extrapolating from themselves, they understood themselves to have authority in the world as extensions of their gods, in whose image they experienced themselves as being created. When the frogs demonstrated that our physical inclinations are not the source of our humanity, the gods which the Egyptians understood themselves as representing were shown to be false. Egypt's rule was therefore without foundation, for they represented no higher authority; thus they lost the legitimacy to "mint coins," to procreate in their image. The form they were trying to impress on the coins, the image the Egyptians found in themselves and were passing on through procreation, had lost significance. With no meaningful image to impart to their offspring, they lost the ability to procreate.

Through the plague of frogs God actualized His trait of *yesod* unambiguously. This trait unites God with physical reality, which is actualized in the existence of man insofar as man embodies this joint entity; this is man's definition and the only basis for his existence. This identity was accentuated in the Jews. But the Egyptians understood and experienced man as something else. During the plague their fantasy version of *yesod* ceased to be sustained, and the Egyptians were faced instead with the reality of their illusion.

The plague of the frogs clarified that man, who by nature bridges two realities, exists to bind the divinity of God to the world. Genuine experience of self integrates our transcendent spiritual core with our physical being. This experience of integration allows another facet of reality to reveal its divine source and another trait of our personality, *yesod*, to contribute to full, integrated *emuna*.

**HOD AND THE PLAGUE OF LICE**

The divine trait of *hod* was actualized through the statement "Let the earth bring forth living creatures, animals…." *Hod* is usually translated as "splendor" but is also related to the word *hodaa*, meaning "admit." *Hod* scales back the intensity of God's revelation so that man experiences his individuality, giving him the space to choose his relationship with

God rather than it being forced upon man by the compelling presence of the Creator. In a sense God admits to the existence of man, which gives man the opportunity to admit to the existence of God.[31]

This scaling-back was accomplished by the creation of animals, specifically the serpent, which gave material expression to evil (*ra*) or, more precisely, to separation.[32] The serpent radically altered the nature of God's revelation in creation. The way the serpent tempted Eve reveals the specific nature of the change. The serpent told Eve that God had forbidden them to eat from the Tree of Knowledge because God Himself had eaten from it to create the world. God was jealous and did not want man eating the same tree and becoming a creator in his own right.[33] According to the slander of the snake, God suffered from feelings of inadequacy. But the more potent poison of the snake's claim was the implication that something existed outside of God upon which He was dependent, namely the tree from which He needed to eat in order to create. The snake drastically constricted our perception of God in the world,[34] thus actualizing the trait of *hod* in creation.

The reduction in our experience of God's revelation introduced by *hod* leaves our awareness of God sufficiently clouded that we are able to perceive ourselves as "outside of God." We lack an intrinsic sense of attachment to and dependence upon Him; we experience ourselves as isolated individuals.

This sounds similar to the corrupt interpretation of kingship (*malkhut*) which we described in relation to the tenth statement of creation. But there is a very important difference. In corrupt *malkhut* we experience ourselves as our own source; our elevated sense of personal greatness arising from our capacity of free choice displaces our connection to God. In the case of *hod*, it is the diminishing of the greatness of God in our eyes, the shrinking of our horizons, our lack of connection

---

31. I understood this interpretation from a lecture of Rav Moshe Shapiro.
32. See Ps. 2:9 where the word *tero'em* means "you shall shatter them."
33. Rashi, Gen. 3:5.
34. *Hod*, which is actualized through the snake's statement about the tree, is related to the trait of *gevura* which became manifest in the creation of the tree itself. We will discuss the similarity and differences between these two traits later.

*Part 2: The Character of Faith*

and our aloneness that produces our attribution of existential primacy to our own individual existence.[35]

Though *hod* does not give us the sense of greatness experienced through making a choice that we find in *malkhut*, the free choice of *malkhut* is only meaningful when it is made while faced by two potential options. The isolated individuality resulting from *hod* provides a coherent alternate vision of a reality constructed around man to oppose to the vision of absolute dependence upon God.

The proper response to this experience of isolation is to follow the lead of the Creator by turning the energy of holding-back upon ourselves. Just as God restricted His revelation to allow for some level of independence in man (God acknowledging man), man must hold his ego in check to recognize that this independence exists only within a context of dependence (man must acknowledge God).

All the distortions introduced by the serpent result from blocking our direct awareness of having a Source, allowing us to take our own existence as a given. But the reality is that we cannot sustain our own being. We are capable of discerning that our existence is utterly contingent, that the diminished reality experienced through *hod* cannot be the complete picture because it is neither adequate nor viable.[36] We are, in fact, no more than a revelation of God, existing through and for His will. Awareness of the dependency of existence upon God is what is called *yirat Hashem* (fear of God). *Yirat Hashem* is the compliment to *hod* that enables us to meet the challenge of the snake. The individual who personified this *yirat Hashem* and the trait with which is its associated, *hod*, was Aaron.[37]

Aaron lacked the closeness to God that brought his brother Moses unparalleled levels of prophetic clarity – that is, he experienced the world

---

35. Thus the corruption of kingship leads to a sense of personal greatness and eventually self-deification, as expressed in the phrase *asa atzmo elohut* ("he made himself god"), a phrase the Sages apply frequently to corrupt kings (for example Exodus Rabba 10:6, where it is applied to Pharaoh). This is in contrast to the corruption of *hod*, which leads to the in significance of others, as expressed in the phrase *ani ve'afsi od* ("I exist and there is no other") (Is. 47:8, 10; Zeph. 2:15).
36. As Abraham concluded. See chapter 9.
37. See Leviticus Rabba 26:6.

through the limiting trait of *hod*. But Aaron's relative distance from God only sharpened his awareness of the precariousness of being and led him to focus on bringing the creation back to the Creator. For this purpose he was appointed High Priest. Rather than accepting individual isolation as definitive of reality, he recognized it as a challenge to overcome.

Aaron was a "lover of peace and pursuer of peace."[38] He sought to overcome the divisions among men which result from our sense of individual isolation and limit our experience of greatness. In his capacity as High Priest, this was part of his effort to connect the nation with God, since national unity is a prerequisite to actualizing our relationship with God. Aaron also "brought (the Jews) close to Torah,"[39] working to bridge the gap between man and God.[40] Aaron set the example of what we are supposed to do with our sense of isolation: to freely choose our relationship with God, to actively admit to God's existence and kingship, and to strive to overcome our distance from Him.

But obviously, this experience of isolation presents an opportunity to deny the existence of God. This was the option taken by the Egyptians, who followed the lead of the serpent. Instead of turning the energy of restriction characteristic of *hod* upon themselves to restrain their egos and recognize existence outside themselves, they turned it outwards to shrink God and make more space for themselves. Pharaoh, the personification of all Egyptians, was perceived as associated with the sun, the greatest of the Egyptian gods. The syncretization of Pharaoh

---

38. Avot 1:12.
39. Ibid.
40. The Torah of Aaron is also affected by his trait of *hod*. Aaron's isolation from God made what God wants from us much less clear. Since Aaron's *hod* precluded prophecy, he used his intellect to derive what was hidden from what he did know of God's will. He was the first person recorded in the Written Torah to discover a halakha through logic in the absence of prophecy (Lev. 10:19 with Rashi; see Rabbi Gedalia Shorr, *Or Gedalyahu, Parashat Shemini, likutim* 2). This identifies him and his dominant character trait of *hod* as the root of *Torah shebe'al peh* (the Oral Torah), which enables us to continue our communication with God even when we are distant from Him and no longer have prophecy. See Rabbi Tzadok HaKohen, *Pri Tzaddik, Ḥanukka* 1–3; *Pri Tzaddik, Lag BaOmer, ot* 1.

with the sun god meant that the sun god could not be transcendent, nor could he even encompass all of physical existence.[41]

The plague of lice came to reveal the existence of something greater than what was allowed by this Egyptian vision. God turned dust into lice, and the Egyptian magicians admitted: "*Etzba Elokim hi*" (This is the finger of God).[42] The Egyptians were forced to realize that their assumption of their own omnipotence, based on their perception that nothing greater than themselves could exist, was false. How was this realization forced upon them by the lice?

In the first two plagues of blood and frogs, the Egyptians were able to mimic through magic the miracles performed by Moses.[43] The imitation may have been pathetic (perhaps turning a glass of water to blood as they gazed at the mighty Nile flowing red before them), but attributing Moses' abilities to magic was a comfort. Moses might be unusually powerful, but he still fit into a familiar mold. The lice, however, changed that.

As we mentioned in chapter 11, magic is based on the illusion that objects are separable from God and that man can therefore control them. The particles of dust that were turned into lice are so insignificant in their own right that we cannot relate to them as distinct objects. They are null and void before the vastness of creation, so that only a being Who encompasses the entirety of existence can manipulate them magically.[44] The plague of lice proved the existence of the all-encompassing God, something the Egyptians viewing reality through an impure trait of *hod* found inconceivable.

In response to the Egyptian misappropriation of *hod*, God actualized His true expression of the trait. For the Jews, this led to an accentuated awareness of our individuality, but also of its limitations, that we cannot sustain our own existence. Rather, there must be a greater, transcendent Source. This became overwhelmingly manifest in the

---

41. From the dawn of kingship in Egypt, the sun god had been the overriding deity. But according to Egyptian mythology, even this deity had to battle forces of evil, and to enlist the help of other gods, when traveling through the underworld at night.
42. Ex. 8:15.
43. Ibid. 7:22, 8:3.
44. See Exodus Rabba 10:7; Rashi, Ex. 8:15; and Maharal, *Gur Aryeh*, Shemot 8:15.

*The First Plagues*

omnipresent lice that had once been dust. The commentaries emphasize that all the dust of Egypt turned to lice, even in the Jewish region of Goshen.[45] But the lice did not attack the Jews; instead they formed the ground on which the Jews walked, a reminder of God's all-encompassing power. Only the Egyptians, whose very identity ran counter to the acceptance of this transcendent Source, were attacked by the lice.

We understand why dust was the thing that was transformed; the minuteness of the dust particles was essential to what the plague was demonstrating. But why specifically lice?[46]

Lice do not merely bite people; they colonize them. By denying that reality had a source greater than themselves, the Egyptians equated themselves with the Creator (this was precisely the slander of the snake). Effectively, they were taking responsibility for our world, the ground on which we tread (we will explain in our discussion of the trait of *ḥesed* that dry ground is the creation that most directly reveals the Creator). Just as Pharaoh had declared "I am the Nile,"[47] in effect Egypt was claiming "Pharaoh is the ground." When the ground turned to lice the true Creator was revealed. For the Jews the lice remained ground, but ground that was obviously of divine origin. The Egyptians, who could not accept this, were shown the truth of what it looks like for man to be the ground of existence: instead of their standing on the lice, the lice colonized them.

The transformation of dust to lice made it compellingly clear to the Egyptian magicians that Moses was representing a Being that encompassed all of reality – something far beyond the reach of humanity. The human experience of autonomy, which was the basis of the Egyptian illusion of omnipotence, did not really imply independent existence

---

45. Rambam, *Perush HaMishnayot*, Avot 5:4.
46. The midrashim focus on the small size of the dust particles; they also note that dust was affected "measure for measure," because the Egyptians had forced the Jews to clean the dust of Egypt (*Tana Debei Eliyahu Rabba* 7:8; Exodus Rabba 10:7). But they say little about the lice other than that there were fourteen varieties of lice. The commentaries give a kabbalistic explanation for this number fourteen (*Tana Debei Eliyahu Rabba* 7:8 with the commentary *Tosefot Ben Yeḥiel*), which is beyond our scope, but I was not able to find a source that discussed why the dust turned specifically to lice.
47. Ezek. 29:3.

as the Egyptians had supposed. It was revealed that the experience of autonomy was actually only a prerequisite for free choice. Rather than constituting an alternative reality, the paltriness of existence experienced in individual isolation was meant to drive man toward God. The perceived alternative to relationship with God was seen to be nothing more than a means to that relationship. The plague of lice returned another of our character traits, *hod*, to the task of recognizing the Creator.

## NETZAḤ AND THE PLAGUE OF WILD ANIMALS

God's creative trait of *netzaḥ* became actualized through the statement "Let the waters swarm with living things and birds flying over the land...," which filled the sea and the sky with life. *Netzaḥ* is usually translated as "eternity," but it shares its root with "overpower." The trait of *netzaḥ* initiates actual physical creation, when after all the stages of internal preparation, a creator breaks out of himself into the world around him. This trait bears similarity to the trait of *ḥesed*/kindness (to be discussed in the next chapter), which initiates emotional preparation after the completion of the intellectual basis for the creative act. They differ in that *ḥesed*, though it may motivate action, is in and of itself an emotional desire to give; whereas *netzaḥ* is intrinsically a trait of action. Also, while *ḥesed* is a desire to go beyond one's self in giving, *netzaḥ* is a desire to give *to* – there is a specific recipient in mind.

In God's creation *netzaḥ* begins the formation of the recipient. Thus among the creations that came into being through *netzaḥ* were the leviathans, mighty creatures that embodied all that God desires to connect to in creation.[48] This necessarily included, in some form, man insofar as he is able to internalize and actualize Torah; through Torah man is the *bat zug* (mate) of God, consumed by desire to connect to God and existing to express and actualize Him in physical reality.

*Netzaḥ*, as the first of the active traits, requires extraordinary force to get over the hump of transitioning from internal preparation to actual physical creation. This is much greater than the energy required to continue physical creation once started. So this breakthrough into action carries enough power to send the creation hurtling toward completion

---

48. Gen. 1:21, Maharal, *Beer HaGola*, Beer 4.

before its time, threatening disaster. Thus *netzaḥ* is followed by *hod*, the restraining trait we just spoke about.

This overwhelming character of *netzaḥ* was represented by the power of the leviathans. Unchecked, they threatened to destroy the world. The Talmud states that in order to prevent this, God neutered the male leviathan and salted the female away for the end of history, when it will be eaten by the righteous.[49] What is the Talmud conveying with this imagery? What exactly was the threat these creatures represented?

Eating in Torah literature is seen as an act which brings completion.[50] When I am hungry – that is, lacking in a physical sense – I eat to satisfaction, completing the lack. But eating is used in Torah to refer to completion on all levels, not just the physical.[51] The end of history is the time when the world will transition to a higher state. Eating at the end of history means coming to the completion needed to make that transition. This means attaining complete clarity about God within the limitations of physical existence as a preparation for ultimate connection to the Creator. The world was created to give man the opportunity to merit this achievement, but the leviathans threatened to short-circuit that process and bring the end before its appropriate time. They embodied an unbridled desire for connection to God which was capable of forcing full relationship with Him instantly, overriding man's ability to make choices in the matter. In keeping with the trait of *netzaḥ* to which the seventh statement gave expression, the leviathans were too much and had to be scaled back.[52]

*Netzaḥ*, then, involves an almost irresistible drive toward connection and completion. In man *netzaḥ* shows itself as an overpowering desire to connect to others. In its purity it expresses a desire to connect

---

49. Bava Batra 74b.
50. Maharal, *Netivot Olam, Netiv HaAvoda* 1.
51. *Gur Aryeh, Bereshit* 1:21. See also *The Choice to Be*, chapter 2.
52. According to Rabbi Tzadok HaKohen (*Likutei Amarim* 16), the need to scale back the leviathan only came after the sin of Adam. But most commentaries hold that the leviathan threatened creation from the beginning. See the Vilna Gaon, *Perush Tzafra DeTzniusa*, chapter 1.

*Part 2: The Character of Faith*

to God, or to connect to others in a manner that achieves completion and manifests God in creation.[53]

From God's side this desire for connection is associated with the giving of Torah, the medium of His connection to creation.[54] The giving of Torah has this overwhelming side to it. When it was given to the world, it came with a clarity that compelled its acceptance, as we said earlier.[55] From our side, we wanted closeness so badly that our souls flew to God and we had to be brought back to individual life.[56]

The person who personified this trait of *netzaḥ* most purely was Moses, the conduit of this very powerful giving of Torah. What allowed Moses to exhibit *netzaḥ* with such purity and give Torah was his humility. Torah passed through him unaltered by Moses' personal interests because his ego didn't get in the way. This is characteristic of *netzaḥ* – where there is no selfishness, it drives us relentlessly to connect with God or to serve as His instrument.

When the self mixes in, however, this compulsion is felt in a corrupted form. It is still experienced as overwhelming desire for connection, but in a form that isolates it from any aspect of giving or larger unifying context. The most powerful expression of a corrupted *netzaḥ* is a desire for inappropriate physical relations where the potential for sanctity and expression of the unitary Creator is lost.

Egypt is held up by the Torah as the paradigm of a people awash in sexual impropriety.[57] The epitome of uncontrolled physical energy is the frenzied horse attacking wildly in all directions in the heat of battle.[58] Egypt is strongly associated with the energy of horses.[59]

---

53. Before Adam's sin mixed it with selfishness, the consummation of physical relations was a purely sanctified act, a way of achieving completion and bringing God's presence to the world. See Rabbi Tzadok HaKohen, *Likutei Amarim* 16.
54. See Rav Yitzchak Isaac Chaver, *Beurei Aggadot Afikei Yam*, Bava Batra 75, for the connection of the leviathan to Torah and Moses.
55. Shabbat 88a (discussed in chapter 4).
56. Shabbat 88b.
57. Lev. 18:3 with Rashi and *Gur Aryeh*. See also Leviticus Rabba 23:7. See also Maharal, *Gevurot Hashem*, chapters 4 and 11.
58. Jer. 8:6.
59. Deut. 17:16, Ezek. 23:19–20. See also Ramḥal, *Mesillat Yesharim*, chapter 2.

## The First Plagues

This immersion in physical desire was a direct extension of the Egyptian perception of the nature of humanity. As we explained in our discussion of the plague of the frogs, the Egyptians identified their awareness of their physical desires as the internal focus that defined their humanity. With the trait of *netzaḥ* our focus is not awareness but rather the compulsiveness of these inclinations. We feel ourselves driven to connect beyond ourselves; this is a basic component of human personality. But what is the true nature of this drive? Egyptians had embraced the random, selfish expression of *netzaḥ*, defining the compulsion of existence as selfish desire.

In the fourth plague God actualized true *netzaḥ* – the compulsion to connect to God – in the world, leaving no room for its false expression of base selfish desires. The Egyptians, who could not commit to this aspect of internal compulsion, were forced to confront the truth of their connection to *netzaḥ*. This came in the form of wild animals, the embodiment in nature of these same powerful, undirected energies. Wild animals roamed freely through Egypt, preying on the Egyptians. As in the earlier plagues, the Egyptians were confronted with the implications of the way they related to reality. They were shown what the world would look like if their interpretation of *netzaḥ* were true.[60]

God's actualization of purified *netzaḥ* left no room in the Jewish psyche for the misdirected forms of this desire. This was externally manifest in the exodus of all wild animals from Goshen.[61] The uncontrolled energy of these creatures no longer had any place with the Jews; they were being drawn to the Egyptians, who resonated with the wild energies coursing through these animals.[62] The desire of the Jews to connect beyond themselves became focused exclusively on connection to God or on bringing God into the world through connections to others.

---

60. For the connection between wild animals and physical inclinations, see for example Genesis Rabba 84:19, cited in Rashi, Gen. 37:33.
61. See Malbim, Ex. 8:19.
62. The process of the Exodus was one of separating the Jews from Egypt and all it represented. The draining of wild animals from Goshen to Egypt proper is reminiscent of the process we undergo on Yom Kippur when one goat can enter the *Kodesh Kedoshim* in its purity only because its sins are transferred to the goat sent to *Azazel*.

*Part 2: The Character of Faith*

The plague of the wild animals actualized the true nature of this basic component of man's inner world – his inclination to connect beyond himself. Another trait of man was revealed to be a vehicle of relationship with the Creator.

*Chapter 15*

# The Middle Plagues

When we explained the ten traits, we mentioned that they are divided into several groups. The three earliest traits to be expressed are involved in the intellectual conceptualization of what we are creating, the next three are concerned with emotional preparation for the act of creation, while the final traits power the physical acts of creation. In God's creation all traits become manifest through the creation of some facet of existence. The intellectual traits structure reality, the emotional traits structure our environment, and the traits of action create life and man.

There is a shared pattern that characterizes the relationships among the traits in each group (at least for those involved in emotional preparation and those involved in physical expression).[1] The first trait in each group is a facet through which the creator forcefully emerges from himself. The second is a facet where the creator needs to contain himself to allow space for his creation. The third is a facet that harmonizes and

---

1. When the process of creation is viewed starting from a later stage (i.e., after the initial awakening of as-yet-undefined *ratzon* [will]), *keter* is not included; instead, *daat* is added after *bina*. In this formulation, the intellectual traits also parallel the pattern found in the emotional and physical traits, but this formulation is not relevant to our discussion.

*Part 2: The Character of Faith*

synthesizes the two, allowing for a balance between creator and creation. The group of traits involved in physical action then has a fourth trait which releases the creation to independence and uniqueness, thus completing creation.

So as we move from the fourth plague to the fifth one (moving, as always, in the reverse order to that through which the traits express themselves in an act of creation) we make the transition from the first trait to express itself in the category of action to the last trait to express itself in the category of emotional preparation to act. We therefore expect the upcoming traits to show parallels to traits we have already discussed.[2] They will differ, however, in that the next set of traits we examine will be more internal and the creations that actualize them more fundamental. Rather than initiating life and the elements of man himself, these creations give form to the world in which man operates. Since we learn about God's relationship with creation from the world, the three plagues in this category repudiated basic confusions about God's unitary control over existence as well as dispelling the illusion of a self-sustaining physical reality.

### TIFERET AND THE PLAGUE OF PESTILENCE

The sixth trait of creation, *tiferet*, was actualized through the statement "Let there be lights in the heavens to distinguish between day and night…," which created the sun and the moon. The word *tiferet* is usually translated as "splendor" or some equivalent term. *Tiferet* is a blend or balance between the trait of *ḥesed* ("kindness" or "giving") and *gevura* ("strength" or "containment"). We will have a chance to consider these two traits in detail soon. But in order to give context to our present topic, I will anticipate part of that future discussion.

We will learn that through the trait of *ḥesed* we discover the existence of the Creator, while through the trait of *gevura* we create ourselves as servants of the Creator. Through *tiferet*, which balances them, we discover that the process of self-creation is actually a process of revealing the Creator who is the basis of our existence. In other words:

---

2. See Genesis Rabba 84:6.

## The Middle Plagues

*ḥesed* – God exists; *gevura* – I exist; *tiferet* – my "I" is an actualization of the Creator (*tzelem Elokim*).

How does the creation of the sun and the moon reflect this trait of *tiferet*? The act of creation that brought these two lights into existence is unique in that it took place through a process. The verses associated with this statement are:

> And God said, "Let there be lights in the firmament of the heaven to divide between the day and the night; and they will be for signs, and for seasons, and for days, and for years. And they will be for lights in the firmament of the heaven to give light upon the earth." And it was so. And God made the two great lights: the great light as ruler of the day, and the lesser light as ruler of the night and the stars.[3]

The Sages note a contradiction in the last verse. First we are told that God made "two great lights." Then we are told that He made, "the great light as ruler of the day, and the lesser light as ruler of the night." They explain that originally the sun and the moon were made equal in size – "two great lights." But the moon complained: "Two kings cannot share one crown!" God responded to the moon's complaint with the command "Make yourself small!" Thus we were left with "the great light as ruler of the day, and the lesser light as ruler of the night."[4]

The sun and moon were both created to be rulers. They are rulers because they determine: they determine the structure of time through variations in the light they bring to the world. The sun was made to be the "ruler of the day" and the moon was made to be the "ruler of the night."

Since to rule is to determine, there cannot be two kings for one crown. One will have to defer to the other, compromising his kingship. In the original creation the sun and moon were equal in size, so that the moon reflected all of the light of the sun and appeared to be the same

---

3. Gen. 1:14–16.
4. Ḥullin 60b. A chapter in *The Choice to Be* (103–16) is devoted to this difficult aggada. Here our discussion will be more concise, confined to those aspects relevant to our present topic.

size. Under such circumstances any stretch of time that the moon structured by means of its light was actually determined by the sun, because whatever light the sun produced the moon conveyed automatically. So although the moon *appeared* to play the role of a ruler, as it structured time, in actuality it did not rule because the light by which it structured time was entirely determined by another, the sun.

The moon "complained," i.e., the Sages gave voice to the view on creation seen from the isolated perspective of the moon. The moon's problem was that it embodied a contradiction. It was given the role of a ruler but did not rule. So God instructed the moon to make itself small. Since this change unlocked the amount of the moon's light from that of the sun, it allowed the moon to wax and wane.[5] This answered the moon's complaint, because from then onward the moon did determine something. Though the sun established how much light was available, the moon determined how much of that light would be conveyed.

This scenario works out the delicate balance between a source and what we can call its primary conveyor and representative. The sun is the source of light. The moon receives light from the sun and is responsible for conveying that light to the world as a representative of the sun. In the original creation, when the moon reflected all the sun's light, it represented the sun in the sense that it appeared as bright as the sun. But on a more internal level the moon did not resemble the sun at all, for the sun is a source and determiner while the moon did not determine anything. This led to the moon's complaint, which was addressed by shrinking the moon, initiating its waxing and waning, thereby giving the moon its own responsibility – that of determining how much light reaches the world. It is not a source in the same sense as the sun. That is not possible; the moon cannot produce light. At least, however, it ruled.

But this solution generated a new problem. In the continuation of the aggada the moon then "complained" that it was evident from the original creation, when the sun and moon were the same size, that the moon's rightful due was equal glory with the sun. That was lost when

---

5. We will better understand the link between the shrinking of the moon and its waxing and waning when we explain the parallel between the moon's situation and that of man. See note 10.

the moon was shrunk.[6] The moon gained its appropriate ability to rule only at the cost of its proper glory. According to the aggada, God resolved this issue by instituting a sin offering on Rosh Ḥodesh, the day of the new moon.[7]

Before trying to understand how this answered the moon, we should note the significance of the fact that this second complaint could not be resolved without the participation of man at some point in the future. Man will bring an offering on Rosh Ḥodesh, the day that marks the renewed waxing of the moon, when this day is recognized by the Jewish people. Thus the tension between the sun and the moon has implications for man. This makes sense, because man plays the same role of primary conveyor to God that the moon plays to the sun. In addition to the sun and the moon, what is being created by the sixth statement of creation is the relationship that will eventually become the one governing the relationship between God and man.

Where do we find the tension inherent in the creation of the sun and the moon on day four reflected in the creation of man on day six? When man was first created – before Adam sinned – man was a perfect conveyor of the glory of God. The midrash goes so far as to say that the angels bowed to Adam, confusing him with God.[8] The full glory of God was seen through man because it passed through him unhindered, without attenuation by his ego. But this also meant that the necessity of obedience was so clear to man that it was virtually automatic. Adam had only the faintest shadow of ego, because he had only the faintest shadow of choice.

Under these circumstances man could not be God's true representative, even though the glory of God was revealed through him. For essential to God's relationship to creation is that He is the determiner, the "King" of creation. Man appeared in the role of king to the world, representing the *rule* of God. But he could not represent *God*. For man was not himself a ruler – he did not determine anything; he almost

---

6. Ḥullin 60b.
7. See Maharal, *Gur Aryeh, Bamidbar* 28:15.
8. Genesis Rabba 8:10.

*Part 2: The Character of Faith*

automatically conveyed the determinations of God. Man, like the moon before it shrank, was a living contradiction.

Man responded by, "making himself small."[9] He sinned, darkening his clarity about the necessity of obedience and thereby enhancing the meaningfulness of his choices. He became like a waxing and waning moon, determining for himself how much of God's glory he would convey. He had become a king in his own right, able to represent God on another level. But the full glory of God no longer shone through him; for even when Adam chose to fully express God, his ego now buffered the representation. The Talmud expresses this by telling us that after the sin Adam was shrunk from his original height that reached to the heavens down to one hundred cubits.[10]

Adam's diminution was redressed by man's ability to bring a sin offering – that is, to repent. Repentance is a decision whereby a person fully determines who he is. With every meaningful choice – every choice that has moral implications – a person affects who he is.[11] If I choose to give money to charity rather than order a second round of dessert in a restaurant, I make myself into a more giving person. This personal development is the whole point of making choices. Repentance is the ultimate choice, because the choice itself is about who I am; it is a complete revolution and determination of self.

Through repentance, who I am is of my own making; in effect, I come from myself. This is the greatest resemblance to God that is possible. For God's essential characteristic is the necessity of His being. He *is* by virtue and by necessity of *His* nature; He is from Himself. We cannot share this quality, at least not to this extent. But when who we are comes from us in the sense of coming from our own choice, we

---

9. Ramḥal, *Daat Tevunot*, ot 72.
10. Ḥagiga 12a, Sanhedrin 100a with Rashi, and *Yalkut Shimoni, Devarim* 4:827. The metaphorical extension of the relationship between the sun and the moon to the relationship between God and man makes clear why the waxing and waning of the moon was dependent upon shrinking it. Man can only make meaningful choices about how much of the glory of God to convey into the world when his overall clarity, and thus the overall extent to which he can convey God's glory, is reduced.
11. *Sefer HaḤinukh*, mitzva 16.

## The Middle Plagues

approach this quality to the highest degree possible for created beings.[12] A sin offering – representing the ability to repent – remedies the loss of man's apparent resemblance to God, because he now resembles God on a much more essential level.

Man's repentance is specifically associated with Rosh Ḥodesh, the New Moon, because they parallel each other. The moment man repents and chooses to convey God's light rather than block it, he resembles the moon on Rosh Ḥodesh when it turns the corner, beginning to convey more light of the sun rather than less.

On one level man's ability to choose – the essence of repentance – is more pertinent to the tenth and final statement of creation, which gives man actual *malkhut* in emulation of God. On the other hand, the tenth statement refers to a choice of action; whereas here we are interested in repentance as an internal determination of self, making it relevant to this sixth statement.

In any case this statement creates the possibility of choice by establishing balance in our relation to God's revelation. On the one hand we have an obligation to attain awareness of the complete omnipotence of God, particularly during the recitation of the *Shema*. When we pronounce the word *eḥad* in the *Shema*, the declaration that God is One, we are paralyzed by our clear perception of God's singular control and greatness. On the other hand we are obligated to act, to make the world over into a place that reflects its Creator and allows for His worship. In order to take personal initiative, we must recognize that our choices and actions are significant, that we make a difference. It is difficult to imagine how we can do so while cognizant of the complete control of God, so these two perspectives seem contradictory. Yet both facets of service are required for a full relationship with God. The ability to achieve a synthesis of the two is demonstrated by the moon, which determines the light it conveys to the world, while the light it conveys originates in the sun.

Because man is identified with the moon, and his role is to convey God's light and to represent Him, the Jewish calendar is lunar. Man has light – true understanding and insight – which he only achieves through supreme effort. But it is not his own. Its source is in God. Understanding

---
12. Ramḥal, *Derekh Hashem* 1:2:1–2.

*Part 2: The Character of Faith*

is not something man creates; rather, he discovers it within himself.[13] Although through his sin man turned accessing that understanding into a challenging responsibility, the source of that understanding remains with God.[14] The fact that we can achieve this without being overwhelmed by God's revelation, is a consequence of the balance created through this sixth statement of creation.

The individual who most fully personified this trait was Jacob. As we mentioned earlier, *tiferet* integrates the traits of *ḥesed* and *gevura*. Jacob combined the *ḥesed* that characterized his grandfather Abraham with the *gevura* that characterized his father Isaac. Abraham's *ḥesed* enabled him to derive overwhelming awareness of the Creator from the existence of physical reality. Isaac's *gevura* allowed him to earn his own existence by strict obedience to the standards established by God, achieving a this-worldly emulation of God's necessity of being.

Jacob put Abraham and Isaac together. He understood that Isaac's project of self-creation was actually an uncovering of the Godliness discovered by Abraham, filtered through us in the form of *tzelem Elokim* (image of God). Jacob thereby combined Abraham's overwhelming awareness of God's omnipotence with Isaac's understanding of the need to act in order to achieve greatness.

---

13. We are not talking here about scientific knowledge of the structure of nature, which is gained through external observation. We are talking about Torah, the wisdom to understand reality and the self as a medium and opportunity to connect to the Creator. This comes from within (see Nidda 30b). In the dialogues *Meno* and *Phaedo*, Plato develops the idea that all learning regarding the forms is really a process of anamnesis (recollection).
14. Rabbi Tzadok HaKohen writes that the innovations of the Oral Torah actually come through a hidden form of prophecy. He specifically compares the insights of the Oral Torah to the light of the moon which, though it appears to come from the moon, actually originates in the sun (*Pri Tzaddik I, Ḥanukka* 4). This connection between man and his Divine Source is reminiscent of the creation of the ninth statement (*yesod*), which gives us the sense of self as a complete integration of our divine spark with our physical being. There, however, the focus is on the actual creation of physically and spiritually integrated man. This sixth statement is concerned with a more fundamental creation: the template for the proper balance and integration between these two dimensions, which will later take on expression in the actual creation of man.

We see Jacob's affinity with Isaac as the ultimate doer from his time spent in the darkness of exile, where God was most hidden.[15] Even there, without any support from his environment, he was able to serve God. He was the ultimate initiator, with his choice to serve coming completely from him. He resembled God in the sense of coming from himself to the highest degree possible. God actually called Jacob *"el"* (lord), which is one of God's own names.[16] The Sages understand this to mean that God declared Jacob to be *elohim betahtonim* (lord in the lower realm), resembling God who is Lord in the upper realm.[17]

We see Jacob's affinity with Abraham from what happened to him as he left the land of Israel on his way to exile. He lay down to sleep with his head on a pile of rocks and dreamed that God was standing upon him – imagery the Sages use to express the idea that he was the vehicle that conveyed God into physical reality.[18] The midrash derives from verses in the Torah that the rocks under his head fused into a single stone.[19] Whether this was a dream or an actual occurrence in the physical world, it indicated that the world was unified by direct connection to God, its unitary Source, through the person of Jacob. In his sleep Jacob was the conduit to the world of "Hashem *Ehad*," that aspect of God which utterly nullifies us before His omnipotence.[20]

The combination of these two qualities in Jacob is seen in his institution of Maariv, the evening prayer.[21] Maariv comes at night, when reality is hidden and so is God, its creator. Jacob chose to act in the apparent absence of God. But his action was to pray, to request God's intervention.[22] Jacob brought light to a darkened world, but the light he brought was the light of God. Like the moon, Jacob personified *tiferet*.

---

15. Rashi, Gen. 46:29.
16. Megilla 18a.
17. Maharal, *Gur Aryeh, Bereshit* 33:20.
18. Genesis Rabba 82:6.
19. Hullin 91b.
20. Maharal, *Gur Aryeh, Bereshit* 28:11.
21. Berakhot 26b.
22. Jacob created specifically the evening prayer, Maariv, which is voluntary (Berakhot 27b), whereas the morning and afternoon prayers created by Abraham and Isaac are obligatory.

*Part 2: The Character of Faith*

Because of its spiritual height, *tiferet* is susceptible to the most extreme perversion. The greatness of this trait is dependent upon the humility to retain awareness that the light we convey does not originate in us. If we lose sight of that, we credit ourselves with determining aspects of creation that we really only convey, thus usurping God's mastery. We locate reality in ourselves, rather than recognizing that all existence emanates from God. In the extreme case we confuse ourselves with God – or, at least, see ourselves as also God. This confusion is endemic to Esau's descendants, as we saw in our discussion of Rome in the first half of the book;[23] in the Purim story Haman (a descendant of Esau) also suffers from this confusion.[24]

Egypt, too, was guilty of this perversion. In the paradigm of the sun and the moon, the sun is the source representing God and the moon is the conveyor representing man. While the Jewish people identify with the moon, the Egyptians identified with the sun. Man, personified in Pharaoh, was regarded as a god, the son of the sun god Ra.[25] The sun was syncretized with the Egyptian creator god.[26] So Egypt saw Pharaoh as a source of reality in tandem with the sun.

Here we need to distinguish the fifth plague, which will come to clarify the true nature of *tiferet*, from the first plague. The first plague also attacked Pharaoh's identification with a god. But in that case it was with the god of the Nile. For all its importance, the Nile was ultimately only the source of *sustenance*. Through Pharaoh's identification with the Nile he was seen as responsible for the bounty of Egypt, so that man appeared to sustain himself through an aspect of humanity alienated and made into a god. But here we are focusing on Pharaoh's identification with the sun, which was viewed not as the source of sustenance, but as the source of reality itself.[27] The idolatry of the sun and Pharaoh's

---

23. See chapter 7.
24. Megilla 10b.
25. This association goes as far back as the fourth dynasty (2500 BCE). See Redford, *Ancient Gods Speak*, 325.
26. Ibid., 242–43, 246.
27. However, we should bear in mind the limitations of the Egyptian concept of the creator. As we will explain later in this chapter, Egypt's creator was understood to operate within the pre-existing framework of the primordial waters.

identification with it was therefore a deeper corruption than Pharaoh's association with the Nile.[28]

Since it is through the trait of *tiferet* that proper balance is achieved between the conveyor of reality and its source, this Egyptian confusion was a corruption of the trait of *tiferet*. The fifth plague resulted from God's fully actualizing this trait, leaving no room for false expressions of *tiferet*. The transcendent God is the only source of reality, with man his representative and conduit. The Egyptians, who on some level attributed the source of existence to man and were incapable of moving away from that vision, lost connection to any source of existence. They should have died during this plague. As Moses told Pharaoh, the Egyptians were only spared in order to allow the full ten plagues to strike Egypt and reveal the totality of God's omnipotence.[29]

In this regard the plague of pestilence was like the plague of the firstborn, which also came to clarify that God is the sole source of existence. Like the plague of the firstborn, the plague of pestilence was applied directly by God without the intervention of Moses or Aaron.[30] But the plague of pestilence focused on man's role as representative and conduit of the Source of reality. Hence the relevance of the flocks, those dependent on man for their existence. Seeing themselves as the source of reality, the Egyptians would have understood the existence of their flocks as also coming from them. When their false vision lost all support, the flocks of the Egyptians lost their source of existence and died. This was no ordinary pestilence: all the Egyptians' animals died simultaneously and instantly as their existential support ceased.[31]

---

28. Multiple associations like this are confusing and contradictory to the Western mind but are common and acceptable in polytheistic systems. See, for example, Wilson, *The Intellectual Adventure of Ancient Man*, 46–47.
29. Rashi, Ex. 9:15.
30. Exodus Rabba 12:4.
31. See Malbim, Ex. 9:1. In Egypt, Moses' bringing a pestilence would have been understood as an assault on the sun and all it stood for, a co-opting of its power. The ancient world generally identified the god responsible for pestilence as a solar deity. In Egypt the deity immediately responsible for pestilence was Sekhmet, the daughter of the sun god Ra (Redford, *Ancient Gods Speak*, 17, 123). In the Mesopotamian tradition Nergal, the noontime sun with its destructive heat, was the god of war and brought pestilence. In Greek tradition too, a solar god was responsible for pestilence; see

*Part 2: The Character of Faith*

The actualization of God's trait of *tiferet* would have strengthened the awareness in the Jews of their proper dependence upon the transcendent Creator in the context of their role as conduits of God's strength. The text emphasizes the fact that while all the flocks of the Egyptians died, none of the Jews' animals did. The animals owned by the Jews went on living not because they were saved from the plague; they were never threatened by it. Rather, their continuing to live underscored our role as conduits of God's support to those dependent upon us.[32]

With this fifth plague another fundamental aspect of creation – man's *relationship* with transcendence – was revealed in its proper light. We play a role in creation; we convey existence into the world. But God is the singular source of that existence. This revelation allowed us to harness yet another trait of our personality in the development of complete and integrated *emuna*.

### GEVURA AND THE PLAGUE OF BOILS

The fifth trait of creation, *gevura*, was actualized in the world through the statement "Let the earth bring forth grasses that create seeds and fruit trees bearing fruit."[33] *Gevura* means strength. In the context of creation it is understood as the power to contain the boundlessness of existence into a structured whole which consists of specific, distinct entities that function systematically based on fixed rules. It also means strength in the sense of the power to force results based on those rules. We are aware of this trait in the world around us because of the consistent and predictable causal functioning of the natural order according to the laws of nature, which we will see was imposed on the world through the creation of the trees. But it is also reflected in Torah law and the concept of reward and punishment as direct consequences of our actions.

The mere fact of existence should overwhelm us with the awareness that it is the product of a transcendent Source, in the manner of

---

Book I of the *Iliad* where Apollo brings a plague. Apollo was a solar deity (see Jane Ellen Harrison, *Myths of Greece and Rome* [Garden City: Doubleday, Doran and Co., 1928], 35).
32. See Ramḥal, *Mesillat Yesharim,* chapter 1.
33. Gen. 1:11.

Abraham's discovery of the Creator. However, the expression of the trait of *gevura* blunts that awareness. The functioning of reality according to the unwavering dictates of laws that seem to be embedded in nature invites a view of the universe as functioning from itself and, by implication, perhaps even existing from itself. It weakens our sense of a Creator and, by obscuring God's ongoing oversight of reality's functioning, undermines our recognition of His singular and absolute control over creation. It challenges man to choose to recognize the Creator and His complete omnipotence rather than being compelled to accept it by the weight of experience.[34]

In the ancient world, before the flowering of Greek culture, the fact that the world was created was a given. However, the absolute omnipotence of the Creator was concealed, so that man could ascribe existence to an idolatrous source. Idolatry, of course, is deceptive, since the gods are part of physical reality; identifying any one of them as the source of creation still leaves existence a self-sustaining entity, bereft of any true basis or source.

But beginning with Greece and continuing in the modern world, even the fig leaf of idolatrous creation is removed; the laws of nature and causality, which express the trait of *gevura*, become the basis for denying the initial act of creation entirely. We view today's world as the product of yesterday's world plus natural causality and some time, yesterday's world as the product of the day before yesterday, and so on. For the most part, what differentiates people's views on origins is how far they have to continue the regression before they are satisfied that they know what they need to know about where the world has come from. This shortsightedness is made possible by the actualization of *gevura*.

*Gevura's* containment of reality and hiding of the Creator resembles the limiting effects of the trait of *hod* that we discussed. *Hod's* limitations, however, focus on man's internal experience; *hod* fosters a sense

---

34. In the times we live in, when *emuna* is foreign, our perception that the world functions exclusively through natural physical law removes any need for a Creator. In earlier ages, when man still understood himself as a worshipper, the concept of nature, by implying limitations on the a creator's oversight, would have led to an idolatrous understanding of the divine, but would not have called into question the existence of a creator.

*Part 2: The Character of Faith*

of self as isolated and autonomous, hiding God as the source of man's being. That autonomy can then extrapolated to the world. *Gevura* operates at an earlier and more fundamental level of the creative process. It structures the environment within which man operates in a manner that allows him to understand it as self-regulated and autonomous in its functioning. This can and in modern society does lead to our viewing existence itself as autonomous.

Although *gevura* allows us to understand creation as inevitable and undirected, when interpreted correctly – that is, when understood in the context of the Creator's oversight rather than obscuring that oversight – the orderliness *gevura* imposes inspires strict service to the Creator. Creation functions precisely. All facets do exactly what they were designed to do, playing their exact role without variation or hesitation. There are aspects of our service to God where we need to emulate this precision.

Man is unique, however, in having free choice. This gives him the ability to creatively develop beyond his original self and change in ways that make him more connected to God. This added dimension does not, however, alter the fact that there are set boundaries within which man must remain while he develops.[35] The precise structure and unequivocal functioning of nature inspire us to remain within our prescribed boundaries as we go about creating ourselves.

For example, I am not at liberty to define myself as a chicken, developing my ability to sit under a table and squawk. This is not a courageous affirmation of my individuality, but insanity. Likewise I am not at liberty to develop myself as an accomplished thief. Both options are precluded by God – just as a person is not created to choose to be a chicken, he is not created to choose to be a thief.[36] There are limits. We

---

35. Maharal, *Tiferet Yisrael*, chapter 4.
36. *Sifri, Haazinu* 1. Maharal writes (*Tiferet Yisrael*, chapter 4) that the unwavering path of the sun with its consequent 365-day structuring of time is the defining symbol of the fixed structure of laws of nature. The Sages associate the 365 Torah prohibitions with the days of the solar year (Makkot 23b), because these prohibitions are viewed as an extension of the laws of nature. This is Torah's version of moral philosophy's concept of natural law.

must develop our humanity, but we must remain within God's definition of humanity.

The trait of *gevura* is also referred to as *din* (judgment).[37] Judgment, like causality, is a set structure. It determines reward or punishment according to a defined system of consequences that are strictly determined. Judgment mediates the relationship between God and man; God gives to man according to his deeds. Though God creates the world in order to give, He determines what to give through reward and punishment. Therefore we earn what we get and own what we receive, which is a greater good. We were created to serve and get what we deserve.

A world of *gevura*, judgment, potentially allows us to earn our own existence, and this is the purpose of the trait. It is extremely rare, however, that a person fully deserves this level of reward.[38] One has to be willing to sacrifice himself in order to create or justify himself. The individual who fully did this was Isaac. He offered himself up at the *Akeda* (the binding of Isaac). This prefigured a life in which Isaac constantly sacrificed who he was for who he could become. We look to Isaac as the paradigm of how to sanctify *gevura*. He aggressively bent every aspect of his personality to conform to the will of God. Rather than accepting the self he was given he recreated himself, constantly validating his existence.

Correctly understood, this capability to own one's existence is recognized as occurring in the context of God's overarching kindness: God established the rules and assigned the rewards out of His desire to give, just as He created everything else. Our "self-ownership" is not based on some objective system of laws that stands outside of God. Even when we earn our existence we do so by God's grace; justifying our existence does not break our fundamental dependence upon Him.[39] God gives us the context within which we strive to earn our relationship with Him so that He can give to us in the greatest way, which is the defining goal of creation. *Gevura* only exists within a context created by

---

37. The word *mishpat* (law) can be applied both to laws and to measurements. Rashi, Lev. 19:35.
38. Rashi, Gen. 1:1 (based on Genesis Rabba 12:15).
39. I understood this from a lecture of Rav Moshe Shapiro.

*Part 2: The Character of Faith*

God's unbounded *ḥesed* and ultimately serves *ḥesed*; judgment is for the purpose of giving.[40]

But we can lose sight of this deeper context to judgment and mistake it for an independent, objective structure of law, such that if we earn our existence we exist out of a necessity independent of God.[41] This sense of necessity independent of God can lead us to confuse ourselves with God. Furthermore, the ability to earn one's existence easily morphs into an *assumption* of automatic or intrinsic necessity.

Esau, Isaac's son, was the epitome of someone who corrupted *gevura* in this way.[42] The name Esau is from the word *asui*, which means "already made" in the sense of already completed. At birth Esau had the hair of a much older person; he possessed mature physical development from the beginning, as if he were already complete.[43] And this anticipated Esau's susceptibility to a deeper sense of innate completion, the sense that his existence was objectively necessary without having to do anything to earn it. This sense of being complete unto himself led Esau to reject obligations of service.[44] He sold his firstborn status along with its right to priesthood for a bowl of lentils. Esau "ate, drank, got up, went, and despised…his firstborn status" – that is, his entitlement to the service of priesthood.[45]

How does all this connect to the fact that *gevura* was actualized through the creation of trees? In the statement "Let the earth bring forth grasses that create seeds and fruit trees bearing fruit…" God does not create directly but rather commands the ground to bring something into being. This is not a unique instance; both the water and the ground were later commanded to bring forth life. What *is* unusual about this statement is that the ground did not do exactly as instructed. God commanded

---

40. Ibid.
41. Here we see another parallel between *gevura* and *hod*.
42. This is in contrast to his descendant Haman, who we said earlier corrupts the trait of *tiferet*.
43. Rashi, Gen. 25:25.
44. See the discussion of *malkhut* at the beginning of chapter 14.
45. Gen. 25:34 with Rashi.

that the earth bring forth *"fruit trees* bearing fruit." Instead, it brought forth a *"tree* bearing fruit."[46]

The Sages explain God's command to create "fruit trees" that would bear fruit to mean trees whose trunks would themselves be edible and tasty just like the fruit of the tree. But instead the ground brought forth the kind of trees we are familiar with – tasteless wood capable of growing fruit, but not itself a fruit.[47]

This midrash is bewilderingly difficult![48] How can anything inanimate disobey the command of God? That requires free will! We must presume that the ground was incapable of fulfilling God's command. But why would God command one of His creations to do something it could not do? And why not create it so that it can?

God commands the ideal. Creation is designed to fall short of that ideal to leave space for man to complete creation through his freely willed acts. Since *gevura* is imposed to camouflage the Creator's role in creation, we can understand why the ideal and the actual diverge specifically with this trait. But what would have been ideal about "fruit trees," and what was the significance of the specific shortfall of creating "trees bearing fruit" instead?

Physical reality is a shadow of the spiritual realm. We gain insight into the structure and nature of the unseen spiritual realm by looking at the physical world. The relationship of a tree to its fruit echoes the relationship of a creator to his creation – more specifically it suggests to us the nature of the relationship between God and His creation. The functioning of the world is determined by this relationship and our participation in the relationship is significantly affected by our perception of the relationship. So the influence of the fruit/tree "metaphor" on our understanding of this relationship is critical.

In the world as we experience it, when we plant a fruit-bearing tree our goal or intention is the fruit. The fruit has everything we want; it is the edible part and contains seeds that hold the potential to make more fruit (by way of a tree). In our world an orange tree is merely the

---

46. Gen. 1:12.
47. Genesis Rabba 5:9.
48. This midrash is discussed in *The Choice to Be*, chapter 16.

means to the orange. Had the earth produced a "fruit tree" bearing fruit, however, our primary interest would have been the tree itself – it would have had everything the fruit has and would also have been the source of the fruit. The fruit would only have been important as a means to new trees.

In the relationship between Creator and creation suggested by God's command, the Creator (our tree and source) is everything; we (His fruit) exist only to bring God into the new realm of physical reality. In the ground's actual creation the priorities are reversed. The succulent fruit (representing creation, man) is what we desire. The tree (representing the Creator) is only a means for making new fruit. The Creator, rather than being understood as the basis of existence taking on expression through His creation, is reduced to a means to the creation of man.

Maharal explains that because the ground, which is part of creation, was the one making the tree, it was not able to give priority to the tree, which represents the Creator. It could only favor its own kind, the part representing creation, the fruit.[49] In reality, then, God caused the shortfall in His creation by commanding the ground to bring forth the tree rather than doing it Himself. That the tree, representing the Creator, is being brought forth by the ground, representing creation, is also confusing.

What conclusions we draw from the metaphor of the tree and fruit about the relationship between Creator and creation, depends on what is or is perceived to be the determiner of events. In the version commanded by God – a "fruit tree" bearing fruit – the tree was to be the mover, producing fruit so that the fruit could produce new trees. Since the tree represents the Creator, this would imply that events are driven by divine oversight. In the ground's world of "trees" bearing fruit, the fruit is the goal and is therefore seen as the motivator and the true mover of events (even though, of course, the first fruit was created by the first tree).[50] Since the fruit signifies the creation rather than the Creator, by implication natural causality rather than divine oversight determines events. This confusion was made particularly acute by the fact that the

---

49. Maharal, *Gur Aryeh*, Bereshit 1:11.
50. When Aristotle discusses causality, one of the four forms of cause is purpose.

## The Middle Plagues

ground (creation), which made the first tree, determined the nature of things by "disobeying" God.

God is the ultimate determiner of all these events, for He is the One Who commanded the ground to be the source of the tree. Here God actualized His trait of *gevura* to mask His role in creation. But we do not see this from our vantage in creation; all we see is the ground shaping our world. It is this very sense that creation drives events – what we call natural causality – that allows for the illusion that reality is self-driven, functioning independent of any outside influence or manipulation. The creation of trees bearing fruit threw a blanket over existence, obscuring the Creator.

The Egyptians allowed the obscurity of the transcendent Creator to define their world view. In their eyes, there was no fully omnipotent, transcendent Creator. Though the Egyptians believed that their gods ran things, the gods were projections of the Egyptians. Ultimately, then, creation was driving events. This was reinforced by the strong Egyptian belief in *maat* – a structure of reality that existed independent of the gods and to which they were subordinate – as well as in magic, which allowed man to compel the gods.[51]

The Egyptians misunderstood the significance and role of containment and structure – of *gevura* – in existence. The sixth plague, boils, came to undo this misunderstanding and free the Jews from its influence. Through this plague God fully actualized His trait of true *gevura*.

To make manifest the true nature of *gevura*, Moses and Aaron were instructed to stand before Pharaoh, each taking two handfuls of ash. As we explained in chapter 11, all four handfuls were then placed in Moses' two hands. Moses next threw the ash skyward, and it covered the entire land of Egypt. When two hands held four handfuls, the small was shown to be able to contain the large. When these two handfuls then covered all of Egypt, the small was seen to fill the large.[52] This demonstrated that the structuring of physical creation does not define reality but only hides a more expansive level of God's complete freedom. God

---

51. See Redford, *Ancient Gods Speak*, xi. The Talmud (Sanhedrin 67b) sees magic as particularly obstructive of recognition of divine oversight.
52. Exodus Rabba 11:5.

is not determined by containment. He contains and controls it, He is its author.

God's *gevura* was manifest specifically through the ash of a furnace because fire and its products are associated with *gevura*. *Gevura* constricts the boundlessness of God into the limited and distinct particulars of reality. Fire reflects this, as it breaks composites down to their individual components. But because the Egyptians could not relate to the *gevura* of the Creator, this ash of *gevura* burned them and they erupted in boils.[53] *Gevura*, which is responsible for the specific definition and contours of the creation man (the centerpiece and purpose of creation), destroyed the uniquely human shape of the Egyptians. The ash caused boils to rise on their skin, expanding the individuals beyond their boundaries and destroying their form.

Furthermore, these boils were a version of *tzaraat*,[54] the biblical disease that was caused by specific transgressions and character flaws.[55] This disease was symptomatic of an individual whose personality was improperly skewed toward the trait of *gevura*,[56] one who was internally separated from others, contained within himself in a way that made him selfish and generally corrupted his relationships with people. While *tzaraat* erupted on people who did not give of themselves or their possessions,[57] it is primarily associated with those who speak slander.[58] The commentaries explain that a person speaks slander when he is so contained in himself that he lacks any sense of shared humanity with others – his trait of *gevura* lacks balance.[59] Since the Egyptians could not connect to God's control of *gevura* and freedom from limitation, they were defined by the limitations of this world and contracted boils of *tzaraat*.

The actualization of God's trait of *gevura* brought the Jews to a sharpened awareness of both the boundedness of creation and God's

---

53. Ramban, Ex. 9:9.
54. *Yalkut Shemot* 9:184, *Meshekh Hokhma*, Ex. 9:11.
55. Arakhin 16a, Leviticus Rabba 16:1.
56. Leviticus Rabba 15:2.
57. Ibid. 17:2.
58. Ibid. 16:2–7.
59. Maharal, *Or Ḥadash*, 130–31.

## The Middle Plagues

complete freedom from those boundaries. The strict order of nature was shown to be an instrument of God's will to demonstrate our obligation to remain within the confines of God's definition of humanity and of right and wrong, even as we exercise our free will to create our unique individual self. The appearance of the Egyptians covered in boils made clear that we exceed those boundaries at the price of losing our humanity.

Rather than obscuring God's existence or showing His limitations, the strict order of nature was seen to be a calculated act of creation. This facet of reality gave its own testimony to the omnipotence of the transcendent Creator, inspiring us to harness another character trait toward integrated *emuna*.

### ḤESED AND THE PLAGUE OF HAIL

The trait of *ḥesed* (kindness, giving) was actualized by the statement "Let the waters under heaven gather into one place and dry land appear." In the process of creation, *ḥesed* is the fourth trait to be expressed. Following the intellectual stages of development which we will discuss in the next chapter, *ḥesed* is the first stage of emotional preparation for action, which is the desire to come out from one's self, to give. Because *ḥesed* is the beginning of a new category of traits, the dry ground to which it gave rise is a momentous advance over the previous creations. For example *bina*, the intellectual trait immediately preceding *ḥesed*, divides the upper and lower waters, separating off a realm where God is immediate from a realm where God is distant. This is a fundamental distinction, but the ocean that results is boundless and unstructured. Its featureless expanse is incomprehensible; it is essentially matter without form. *Ḥesed*, on the other hand, reveals land: concrete, divisible, definable. So the actualization of *ḥesed* brings the beginning of fully physical creation.

The emotional traits of the creative process do not correspond to actions. Rather, they are *preparations* to act. So in God's creation they are manifest as *preparation* for man, who is the goal of the process. This preparation is the formation of man's environment, which is dry land. Since *ḥesed* is the first of the emotional traits, it is actualized in the emergence of that environment (whereas *gevura* will give it structure). Land is man's environment because it provides a place within which a creature capable of developing himself – man with his intellect and

*Part 2: The Character of Faith*

free choice – can interact with his environment, transform it, and in the process grow and create himself in relationship with God. A world of water, on the other hand, does not allow one to build. In fact, water breaks down structure.[60] The appearance of ground is, in a sense, the beginning of the creation of man, because it is the necessary prerequisite for his becoming what he was created to become.[61]

Our own trait of *ḥesed*, our desire to give, sensitizes us to God's giving which we see reflected in the existence of a world made to our needs. This would make the Creator obvious to us were it not for the overlay of *gevura* that hides Him behind a veil of natural functioning.[62] Our challenge is to engage our *ḥesed* to the point that we can penetrate that veil.

But *ḥesed* is more than just generic kindness. When the Creator "gave" creation it was not out of concern for the needs of others. There were no others. It was not a reaction to something external to God. It was entirely prompted by God's internal desire to give. This is a defining quality of the distinct trait of *ḥesed* – it initiates. It is an uncaused cause. Only having this level of *ḥesed* and seeing it reflected back to us in creation leads us to the real Creator, the true initiator of existence about Whom one cannot ask, "But who created him?" Abraham personifies this trait, which enabled him to leap beyond the idolatry of his generation to discover the transcendent Source of existence, as we discussed in chapter 9.

But in order to discover this *transcendent* Creator, the true initiator of existence, our *ḥesed* needs to be pure. *Ḥesed* becomes impure when it is mixed with an ulterior motive, so that instead of causing it is

---

60. Maharal, *Gevurot Hashem*, chapter 14.
61. I understood this from a lecture of Rav Moshe Shapiro. See Rosh HaShana 31a; Maharal, *Ḥiddushei Aggadot* II (his commentary on Kiddushin 13a); Maharal, *Gevurot Hashem*, chapter 40. This point will become important when we explain the *kolot* (thunder) that accompanied the plague of hail.
62. *Ḥesed*, like *netzaḥ*, is a transition trait. Transitioning from the intellectual traits to the emotional ones requires overcoming inertia to break into a new aspect of being. In God's creation this meant that *ḥesed* had a power that threatened to bring creation to its conclusion before its time – it made the Creator too obvious – so that the trait of *gevura* had to follow and scale back the level of revelation.

## The Middle Plagues

itself caused. If we look at the world through the lens of impure *ḥesed*, we can only see this impure *ḥesed* reflected back to us. This leads us to imagine a creator who acts out of need for something outside himself. Such a creator operates in a context larger than himself and is at best an intermediary. The worship of such a creator is idolatrous.

The seventh plague, hail, came to undo Egypt's idolatrous misinterpretation of this facet of creation. Egypt was a place where the search for the creator was mediated by an impure trait of *ḥesed*, so that it could not lead to the true Initiator. The most ancient of the Egyptian creation mythologies,[63] show the dry ground emerging from primal waters, as does the Torah. But whereas the Torah viewed this step as an advanced stage in the creation process, for Egypt the emergence of ground was the beginning. Egyptian mythology had the creator god himself emerging from these waters after the land appeared.[64] Thus their creator god existed within a context external to himself, a context not created and therefore necessarily eternally existing. These mythologies, then, were primitive versions of the theory of *kadmut* (the belief that physical reality has always been), which was held by Aristotle.[65]

The Big Bang theory is a modern version of *kadmut*, though if we are lazy thinkers we may assume that it corroborates the *"Bereshit"* of the Torah by confirming that there was a beginning. True, this is closer than the Greek view to *Bereshit*, since the Greeks held that the nature of physical reality is unchanging, that it always was and always will be the way it is now. The Big Bang at least recognizes that there has been a profound shift in the way physical reality functions, that there is a beginning to the universe *as we know it*. But as scientists, Big Bang theorists presume that the universe as we know it emerged out of a prior state of *physical* reality and that there must be a physical explanation for why and how that transition occurred, regardless of whether we can ever figure it out or not. Likewise the Egyptians understood there was a beginning

---

63. I.e., the Heliopolitan and Hermopolitan traditions, as opposed to the Memphite theology whose origin was contemporaneous with the First Temple or even later. Redford, *Ancient Gods Speak*, 241.
64. Ibid., 246–48
65. Rav Pinchas Eliyahu Horovitz, *Sefer HaBrit* 1:20:19, states that the plague of hail was designed to counter *kadmut*.

to things as they are now but assumed that that beginning arose from a prior this-worldly state.

The Torah vision is completely different. When Torah records land emerging from the waters, God stands completely outside of this process. And though the land that emerged at this stage is the creation that awakens us to the existence of a Creator, it is not the initial stage of creation. Rather, it is a later development, a consequence of the fourth statement.

To correct the Egyptian misunderstanding, God actualized His trait of ḥesed in a manner that could only be engaged in its pure form. The Egyptians, who could not relate to this trait in its purity, were cut off from that which was actualized through its expression – dry land. We will see how in a moment.

We might have expected the seventh plague to return the waters to their original place, bringing a flood to Egypt. This was not possible, however, because of the covenant with Noah.[66] Water would eventually be part of Egypt's suffering, but not until the splitting of the sea.[67] And even then the Egyptians ran into the water to drown; no flood was ever brought upon Egypt.[68] Instead the seventh plague overwhelmed the land with hail, with a different form of water.

Moreover, although Pharaoh was only warned about hail, when the plague came it included fire and *kolot*, which is generally translated as "thunder." When Pharaoh called on Moses to end the plague he begged that not only the hail stop, but also the *kolot* that accompanied it.[69] In fact, he mentioned the *kolot* first! What was the significance of the *kolot* in this plague?

We associate the sound of *kolot* with something significant coming into being or being actualized. For this reason shofars are blown when a king is inaugurated. This is also the reason there were *kolot* when the Torah was given, for at that time the kingship of God became

---

66. Gen. 9:8–11.
67. The midrash informs us that events at the sea were tied to the fourth statement of creation. See Exodus Rabba 21:6.
68. Sota 11a.
69. Ex. 9:28.

actualized.[70] Through God's trait of *ḥesed* creation becomes physically actualized for the first time. Perhaps this is why the clarification of this trait was accompanied by *kolot*.

We have said that each plague on Egypt clarified God's role in creation to the Jews. They would have experienced these *kolot* as marking the actualization of something by the Creator. We stated earlier that the dry ground that emerged through God's *ḥesed* was the beginning of the creation of man. It is the existence of man that makes God a king. So the plague of hail that clarifies God's trait of *ḥesed* actualized His kingship on a new level. Thus the commentaries connect the *kolot* of this plague to the *kolot* heard at Mount Sinai.[71]

There was even an aspect of this plague that was exclusively for the benefit of the Jews. Pharaoh was not warned that the hail would have fire in it, yet we are told that when the hail came that it contained fire.[72] We do not hear of any additional destruction coming upon the Egyptians as a result of this fire, and when Pharaoh begs Moses to end the plague he does not mention the fire. It appears that the fire in the hail was only perceived by the Jews.[73] What was the significance of this fire?

*Ḥesed*, the transition trait from the intellectual to the emotional traits, brings into being the first truly physical reality. The combination of fire and water is not possible in this physical world.[74] The ability to make peace between these mutually exclusive elements demonstrated that this plague, and by extension the creation of dry land associated with it, originated from a place beyond our world and our comprehension. It made clear to the Jews that the source of their world, the dry land which was their place in creation, was utterly transcendent. The Egyptians, who did not even recognize the existence of this transcendent

---

70. Maharal, *Tiferet Yisrael*, chapter 30.
71. Yaakov ben Asher, Baal HaTurim, Ex. 9:29. Man is the beginning of God's kingship because, as we said in the previous chapter, a king can only be a king if he has a people to rule.
72. Ex. 9:24.
73. Rabbi Tzadok HaKohen, *Pri Tzaddik*, Bo 3.
74. Exodus Rabba 12:4 on the words *"nes betokh nes."*

*Part 2: The Character of Faith*

realm,[75] could not perceive the fire and were therefore oblivious to this aspect of the plague.

But what was the effect of the *kolot* on the Egyptians? Anyone who has been in the middle of a thunder clap – when you stand under the spot where the thunder originates – knows the terror of that experience. It is not like hearing a scary noise that comes from a distance, where the natural response is to run the other way. When you are under a thunderclap the noise comes from everywhere – there is nowhere to run. It is the experience of losing *makom* (place). In fact, the Egyptians would have understood the *kolot* as threatening the return of Noah's flood, the complete loss of place.[76]

Ultimately, when God's trait of *ḥesed* gave man dry ground, it gave him place, the possibility of being. It was precisely this that the plague of hail with its thunder took away from the Egyptians. Their physical reality during the plague was one of being crowded in and confined to the inside of their homes along with their animals.[77] Their internal reality was the terror of the thunder. The plague came to demonstrate that without the utterly selfless *ḥesed* that can only come from the transcendent Creator – that Being who is complete, is all, and requires nothing – there cannot be place.

The primary point of this plague was to establish the *transcendence* of the true Creator of reality. This is the ultimate realization that we need to have about God. In this regard, the plague of the hail presaged the final plague, the killing of the firstborn. The similarity should not surprise us. Both the Torah and the Midrash identify the hail as the first of the group of plagues that ended with the killing of the firstborn.[78] Thus the hail is tied to the last plague,[79] but there are also important differences.

---

75. See the following chapter.
76. The *kolot* were the same as the *kolot* at Mount Sinai (note 80). When the nations of the world, people who could not connect to the actualization of God's kingship, heard the *kolot* of Mount Sinai, they thought that a flood was coming (Zevaḥim 116a). The Egyptians, who could not connect to the actualization of God's kingship that was occurring during this plague, would also have heard the *kolot* as announcing a flood, that is, a loss of place.
77. Ex. 9:19.
78. Ex. 9:14, with Rashi; Exodus Rabba 5:6.
79. See Ex. 9:14 with Rashi and *Gur Aryeh*.

# The Middle Plagues

The hail was directed at clarifying the trait of *ḥesed*. With the trait of *ḥesed* we extrapolate from physical existence to a Source wholly distinct from that existence that must have "given" or created it. Because the true initiation of creation must have been absolutely selfless and without need, we conclude that there is a transcendent Source. Our engagement of physical reality leads us to *derive* a transcendent Source. But through the plague that took the firstborn, we will encounter transcendence *directly*, recognizing reality's emergence into being from the transcendent Creator through His destruction of the root of creation. The hail clarified that God gives us physical "place," whereas the killing of the firstborn demonstrated that God is our existential "place."

The existence of the physical context in which we live and grow – dry ground – resonates with our trait of *ḥesed* to awaken our recognition of the selfless giving of the transcendent Creator. Though consistent physical laws mask this to an extent, purity was returned to our trait of *ḥesed* during the plague of hail so that we could see through it to once again discern the hand of the Creator in the existence of His creation.

*Chapter 16*

# The Final Plagues

The last three plagues correct misunderstandings related to the intellectual traits of creation: *keter* (the inspiration to create), *ḥokhma* (the determination of the overall goal of creation), and *bina* (the detailed understanding of the goal and a plan of how to achieve it). All three operate in the abstract, separate from the realms of emotion and physical expression. We already mentioned that the general cognition of peoples of the ancient Near East lacked pure abstraction; ideas were inseparable from concrete expressions. Therefore, though corruptions of these intellectual traits were implicit in Egypt's distorted understanding of reality, Egyptians could not corrupt them directly.

In fact, a careful reading of Exodus reveals that the Egyptians did not even know that these abstract traits existed. After each of the first five plagues Pharaoh hardened his heart against letting the Jews leave. After the sixth plague, however, the text states that "God strengthened Pharaoh's heart" so that he would not listen to Moses' demand to release the Jews.[1] By this sixth plague Pharaoh was too traumatized to stand on his own against the continuing onslaught. Left to himself, he would have allowed the Jews to leave. But his readiness to give in was not a consequence

---

1. Ex. 9:12.

*Part 2: The Character of Faith*

of recognition of God. Rather, it was to avoid further suffering. Had the Jews left before all ten plagues occurred, the process of revealing God would have been cut short. So God supported Pharaoh, giving him the strength to continue his resistance. In all the subsequent plagues we also find that God supported Pharaoh's intransigence with one exception: Pharaoh defied God on his own after the seventh plague of hail.[2]

The commentaries explain that this was because Pharaoh thought after the hail that the plagues were over.[3] Egypt had suffered seven plagues directed at the seven facets of character and their expressions in creation. In Pharaoh's mind there was nothing left to attack because Egypt knew of no other character traits.[4] Moses' God had done His worst, and Egypt had survived. We can imagine his shock and distress when Moses showed up to warn of yet another plague. In fact, it was so disturbing that for the first time in the process, Pharaoh's ministers pressed him to acquiesce.[5]

The last three plagues, then, are less directed at correcting Egypt than at fully revealing God and His rule over all aspects of creation. The lessons of these last three plagues – how we connect to the Creator through the different facets of abstract thought – would not become directly relevant until Greece broke upon the world stage, introducing a culture that processed reality through abstract intellect.[6]

---

2. Ex. 9:35.
3. Rabbi Tzadok HaKohen, *Pri Tzaddik, Bo* 2. This understanding implies that in ancient times all peoples experienced the world through the traits we have been describing.
4. This understanding is perhaps corroborated by the fact that the creation myth of Egypt *begins* with a mound of earth emerging from the primordial waters. (Again, this holds for both of the most ancient mythical systems: Heliopolitan and Hermopolitan; Redford, *Ancient Gods Speak*, 246–48.) Egyptian temples had a raised area to simulate this mound. According to Torah, however, the emergence of land from water is related to the *fourth* statement of creation, the one associated with ḥesed that we discussed at the end of the previous chapter. Ḥesed is the first of the traits that *follow* the three abstract traits. According to Rabbi Tzadok HaKohen (passage cited in the previous note), for Egypt this would have been the first trait, the beginning of creation.
5. Ex. 10:7.
6. Torah taught for the future as well as its present. See Ravi Avraham Yitzchak HaKohen Kook, *Ein Ayah Berakhot* II, 103.

## BINA AND THE PLAGUE OF LOCUSTS

The trait of *bina* corresponds to the statement "Let there be a heaven in the midst of the waters and let it divide between the waters." This actualized the third stage of creation, the formulation of a defined vision of what would be created. *Bina* specifies a goal out of the many possible expressions of the general desire to create – that is, out of *hokhma*.

We will discuss *hokhma* in the next section. For now we will recall that the *hokhma* of God's creation is that He created in order to be expressed into physical reality. Full expression into creation involves engaging and being recognized by that which is created. So this is equivalent to each of the following statements: (1) creation is in order that man may truly recognize God, (2) creation is in order that God may have a relationship with man, and (3) creation is in order that God may give to man. From man's perspective, *hokhma* is the understanding that everything exists only in so far as it facilitates man's connection to God. This is the true identity of all things and their meaning.

*Bina* is from the root B-N-H which means "build." To build is to make a structure, intellectual or physical. An actual structure obviously includes all of its details. *Bina* builds from *hokhma*'s overall determination of the goal of creation to a detailed understanding of the precise nature of the goal and the process through which it can be achieved. In this sense *bina* actualizes the abstract potential contained in *hokhma*; the structured vision implicit in *hokhma* becomes a blueprint for realizing it.

While still an intellectual trait, *bina*'s particularity breaks it off from the higher trait of *hokhma*, which is more potential than actual, undefined, all-encompassing, and unitary in character.[7] *Bina*'s break with *hokhma* became manifest in the appearance of a reality that was

---

7. We spoke in chapter 15 about a pattern in the traits of physical creation that recurs in the traits of emotional preparation but is not followed exactly in the intellectual traits. See note 1 there. However, part of the pattern is repeated. In this regard *bina*, which restricts the myriad possibilities of *hokhma* to a specific expression, parallels *hod* and *gevura*. Just as *hod* and *gevura* follow and contain traits whose expansiveness threaten to bring premature connection to God, *bina* brings restriction to the expansive trait of *hokhma*, separating us off from directly experiencing unitary spirituality. *Bina*, however, restricts on a much more fundamental level of reality, articulating understanding and giving it individual perspective; whereas *gevura* contains physical

*Part 2: The Character of Faith*

split off from God and the metaphysical realm – the boundless oceans of physical existence hinting at the articulation of man's soul as something distinct from God and longing to return.[8] Before the separation of the waters introduced by *bina* creation was effectively still an extension of God. But with the separation of the waters a realm was formed that was sufficiently other to God to provide the necessary framework for the achievement of relationship – a significant advance toward the goal of creation.

On the human level, the actualization of *bina* occurs as we strive to define our own specific purpose, what it is that we uniquely have to create. With this we experience ourselves separating out from the larger reality into the limitations of distinct, human perspective. To retain connection to the higher realm we work out the world as a place for connection with the Divine, understanding how all elements of existence function together to facilitate our recognition of the transcendent Creator. We are driven to achieve this by the claustrophobia of finite understanding and our desire to recover the expansiveness of connection to the limitless Creator that we had before *bina* brought us to distinct awareness of our goal and our self. *Bina* sounds similar to our description of *hod*. The two are related, but *bina* as an intellectual trait forms our vision while *hod* qualifies existential experience.

The eighth plague – locusts – came to clarify the proper understanding of *bina*. What was the specific corruption of *bina* that needed to be corrected by the plague of the locusts?

*Bina* develops understanding by building from the premises it receives from *ḥokhma*. Obviously, if the *ḥokhma* is false, the resultant structure will be false. But in that case, though the *bina* produces a corrupt result the corruption lies with the *ḥokhma*. That *bina* is allotted its own plague means there is also a corrupt *bina* which will draw false conclusions even when the starting *ḥokhma* is true.

*Bina* works toward a vision that ultimately lies beyond human comprehension. After all, while trying to work out the specifics of

---

reality and *hod* introduces individual experience and identity. Like *hod* and *gevura*, *bina* affords its own intimate connection to God, but one that is less direct.

8. Rabbenu Baḥya on Lev. 2:13 based on Genesis Rabba 5:4.

# The Final Plagues

creation, its underlying motivation is to recover connection to the infinite spiritual realm. If understanding is not pursued with this in mind, serious distortions result. We see this corruption of *bina* clearly illustrated by Greece. Though the Greeks recognized a higher realm of reality (that is, on a certain level their *ḥokhma* was correct), they assumed that all of reality is comprehensible by human intelligence.

We explained earlier that this led the Greeks to conclude, even while recognizing a supreme Being, that He was bound by the rationality that man understands. This meant that although they recognized a higher realm, that realm was not truly separate; it was in effect a department of this world rather than transcendent. An example of the distortion this caused was Aristotle's assertion that the world had always existed, something we mentioned earlier. According to Aristotle's logic, it was irrational to posit God changing in the manner Aristotle thought necessary to allow an act of creation. Therefore, it could not have happened.

The Greeks' oblivion to the truly transcendent realm was evident after their conquest of the Jews and capture of the Second Temple. Though they made impure the oil of the Menora – the vessel representing human intellect harnessed to relationship with God – we have no record of their ever entering or even being cognizant of the Holy of Holies. This was the area of the temple that transcended the boundaries of physical existence, for it contained the ark which, with its staves, was larger than the space it occupied. Because the Greeks did not recognize the existence of a truly transcendent realm, it was as if the Holy of Holies did not exist for them. The Greeks denied, or at least distorted, the separation of the upper and lower waters introduced by the third statement of creation.

Any attempt to understand the world assumes that the world is comprehensible, that reality has some underlying unity that makes it coherent. The Greeks regarded the world as understandable and therefore having some such unity. But there is a difference between apparent unity and true unity. We can use a political model to illustrate the difference.

Modern democracy can achieve the appearance of social unity. But it is really coherence rather than unity, for it is based on manipulating the societal context in such a way that every individual's self-interest leads him in the same direction so that everyone works in concert. But if

*Part 2: The Character of Faith*

anything upsets the delicate balance so that self-interests cease to align, the apparent unity disintegrates. Democracy, then, is a surface unity. True unity on the political level only comes with legitimate kingship, when the king leads by actualizing his *tzelem Elokim*. In such a case the king's subjects follow because they recognize their deepest self in their leader.[9] This is a unity that arises from the essence of each individual. Such kingship, though very rare, is stable precisely because it is based on essential qualities that are unchanging rather than accidental ones that can pass.

So, too, the unity accessible to the human intellect is a superficial unity, because it cannot penetrate to the true essence of reality which lies beyond human comprehension. Intellect's vision will always be incomplete. Because humanly perceived unity cannot encompass all of existence, any integrated whole it creates will leave something out of the picture. That part will stand in opposition and eventually bring about the collapse of the partial whole.

Returning to our political example, when the Greeks applied their ideas about rationality to politics they ended up as an agglomeration of squabbling city states. Greece only achieved empire when the kings of Macedonia intervened, forcing them to put aside their democratic ideals to unite behind a larger cause. Kingship is ultimately based on the Divine right of kings, where the king rules as a representative of the transcendent, unitary Source. True unity lies only with God. Since God is One and He creates reality in His image, reality has unity. But it can only be realized through connection to God, its unitary Source. When everything locates its "place" in God, all individual facets of existence find their integral and integrated purpose and position in creation.[10]

Without a transcendent basis, unity is illusory. This was the case with Egypt. Though they recognized a creator, he was himself a part of

---

9. I understood this from a lecture of Rav Moshe Shapiro. Similarly, we recognize God as our King, for we are *tzelem Elokim* to His *Elokut*. The shofar on Rosh HaShana establishes God's kingship by evoking this connection.
10. With the exception of King David and those who genuinely followed his lead, kings do not fully represent God. This, however, does not contradict the idea that unity must come from connection to God because as we saw in chapter 7 when we discussed the Sages comparison of the empires to animals with one sign of *kashrut*, corrupt partial connection to God can be sufficient to unify.

## The Final Plagues

physical reality. Therefore their vision of reality had no transcendent core, and so it lacked true unity. This was made clear by the plague of locusts.

The plague of locusts was a consequence of God making manifest His trait of *bina*, that genuine understanding can only be built on a transcendent truth. We see this in its effect on the Jews. The locusts catalyzed in them an intense desire to break out of the limitations of physical existence – certainly out of the specific version of physical existence they experienced in Egypt – and an accentuation of the need to base their world and worldview on a transcendent Source. We see an indication of this when God says to Moses with regard to the plague of locusts:

> I have hardened (Pharaoh's) heart, and the heart of his servants, in order to place My signs in his midst; and that you may tell over in the ears of your son and grandson, how I have toyed with Egypt, and My signs that I have placed among them, that you may know that I am the Lord.[11]

In other words, the locusts will cause us to "tell over" the signs to our sons and grandsons when we recite the story of the Exodus on Passover. Rambam describes this mitzva as telling over specifically the "miracles and wonders" that were performed for our forefathers in Egypt.[12] In other words, the actualization of *bina* pushes us to talk on Passover night about how we departed from the limited, natural reality of Egypt and entered instead into the miraculous realm and rule of the transcendent Creator.

Furthermore, when Pharaoh was told of the coming plague of locusts, he responded by warning the Jews that they were headed for disaster in the desert. This prediction was based on his study of the stars.[13] In the ancient world astrology was the equivalent of mathematical modeling. It was the art of extrapolation based on the interaction of the natural forces at play as revealed by the stars. Since at the time of Pharaoh's prediction God was in the process of actualizing His trait of

---

11. Ex. 10:1–2.
12. *Hilkhot Ḥametz uMatza* 7:1.
13. Rashi, Ex. 10:10.

*Part 2: The Character of Faith*

*bina,* Moses could ignore Pharaoh. Through *bina* God was raising the Jews above subjugation to natural forces and attaching them to their transcendent Source, so Pharaoh's prediction was irrelevant. It became a concern only after the Jews built the Golden Calf, thrusting themselves back into the realm of nature.[14]

The Egyptians, however, were irrevocably committed to a vision based on an idolatrous "natural" unity. They could not connect to any understanding with a truly transcendent basis. When God fully expressed His *bina,* it crowded out all false imitations of unitary understanding. This left the Egyptians with anarchy, which expressed itself in locusts.

The locusts illustrated the chaos underlying the Egyptian vision. Just as reality can only achieve coherence through an underlying unity, so also perception. We are bombarded by an almost infinite amount of information in every instant. Think of the number of pixels on a computer screen. How do we process millions of bits of information simultaneously and constantly? We have underlying concepts that unify vast amounts of data into perceived objects or characteristics of objects. If our mind did not work that way, we would be so overloaded by information that it would break down and we would perceive reality as gray, featureless fuzz.

This was exactly what the Egyptians saw during the plague of locusts. At any given moment the Egyptians were looking at thousands of these creatures. Each had to be processed individually because there was no essential unity to bring them into a coherent whole. All the Egyptians saw was featureless gray.[15]

The locusts destroyed the wheat, which had escaped the hail.[16] Wheat both brings and exemplifies understanding. Because growing and processing wheat takes so many steps, its cultivation forces man to remake his world and, in the process, develop himself. According to one opinion, wheat was the tree of the knowledge of good and evil.[17] By

---

14. Ibid.
15. Ex. 10:5 with Rashi.
16. Ibid. 9:32 with Rashi.
17. Berakhot 40a.

eliminating wheat from Egypt, the locust *symbolized*[18] the elimination of understanding from the Egyptians, even while *actually* blocking the Egyptians' ability to see.

The locusts graphically demonstrated the poverty of false *bina*. Genuine coherence of understanding can only come through a unifying center that is transcendent. Reality is truly harmonized only through connecting everything back to its transcendent Source and understanding it in terms of the purpose given to it by the Creator. A vision produced by human intellect alone may hold together for a time, like a successful democracy. But eventually its limitations and contradictions will become manifest and bring about its collapse.

## ḤOKHMA AND THE PLAGUE OF DARKNESS

God's *ḥokhma* corresponds to the statement "Let there be light." The light created through this statement was not the light we are familiar with that gives us awareness of physical reality; it was a light that allowed us to understand things on their deepest level.[19] This actualized the trait of *ḥokhma*, "wisdom," because *ḥokhma* refers to the kernel of insight that becomes the basis upon which all understanding is developed. In creation that would be the general goal behind the creative act. In God's creation the goal was God's intention to express Himself into another realm – that is, to another – which we experience as God's desire to give to us through relationship so that we can recognize and value Him. Since relationship for human beings is based on understanding the other, the *ḥokhma* of creation was manifest in light that brings true understanding of things – that is, recognizing that everything in creation facilitates connection to God, which is our means of coming to know God.[20]

Insights not centered on knowing God, or not centered on knowing the world as a medium for encountering God whether directly or indirectly, may broaden our understanding in seemingly satisfying and

---

18. The Talmud says eating bread in the morning brings wisdom to the simpleton (Bava Metzia 107b). According to this, the devouring of the wheat was more than symbolic of eliminating wisdom.
19. Genesis Rabba 12:6, and see Rabbi Hayim of Volozhin, *Nefesh HaḤayim* 4:21.
20. Rambam, *Moreh Nevukhim* I:34.

*Part 2: The Character of Faith*

useful ways. But their light is ultimately darkness because they are based on a vision that is indifferent to God or a barrier blocking relationship with Him. Their underlying *ḥokhma* is false and leads away from the essential understanding of things, which is their purpose for existence and thus their true reality. Any understanding that grows from this false *ḥokhma* covers the deeper truth and is therefore darkness.

We have already said that the Egyptians did not have access to pure *ḥokhma* as a trait; that requires a capacity for abstraction which was lacking in the ancient world. But there was *ḥokhma* implicit in their worldview and actions – an essential concept that was the foundation of Egyptian understanding even if they could not articulate it as a distinct idea. And since it did not involve encountering existence as a means of connection to the *transcendent* Creator, their *ḥokhma* was false *ḥokhma*; the light of their knowledge obscured real light and therefore was actually darkness.

The plague of darkness was a consequence of God fully actualizing His trait of *ḥokhma*, which resulted in a great light of understanding filling Egypt.[21] Thus the Jews experienced a penetrating light during this plague.[22] But since this light illuminated everything in the context of its purpose in God's world, and the Egyptians could not accept God, they could not perceive this light. Since its brightness outshone any false light or understanding, the Egyptians were plunged into absolute darkness.

There is an opinion in the midrash that the darkness of this plague was from *Gehinnom*, "purgatory."[23] At first this sounds like a very different understanding. In actuality, however, it is only subtly different from the first opinion; for *Gehinnom* is part of the realm of truth. In *Gehinnom* we experience the unreality of any falseness that we pursued in life, its non-being. Experiencing the emptiness allows us to wholeheartedly reject it before moving to higher levels of existence. The opinion that the darkness came from *Gehinnom* understands that this plague exposed the Egyptians to the non-being of the false world they had constructed.[24]

---

21. See Kalonymus Kalman Epstein, *Meor veShemesh, Bo*, "ve'al."
22. Ibid., and see Ex. 10:22–23 with Rashi.
23. Exodus Rabba 14:2, in the name of Rebbi Nechemia.
24. Exodus Rabba 14:2.

## The Final Plagues

The midrash continues on and explains the appropriateness of a punishment of darkness. Just as an earthen barrel has an earthen cover, so the evildoers, whose actions are darkness, should be covered in darkness. In other words, the darkness the Egyptians experienced was a reflection of the darkness of their own lives.

Thus according to the first opinion the Egyptians were left with non-being. According to the second opinion they were flooded with non-being. According to everyone the darkness exposed the Egyptians to the non-being inherent in the foundations of their worldview.

Another midrash adds a very important insight into this plague. It asks how thick was the darkness facing the Egyptians. It strangely answers as thick as a dinar, which was a valuable gold coin.[25] When asking about the thickness of the darkness it is presumably asking how difficult it was to see through or, according to those opinions that it had some solidity to it, how viscous.[26] The thickness of a coin is a specific linear measurement and makes no sense in the context.

In rabbinic language a coin is synonymous with value, a gold dinar with very high value. With the darkness reflecting back to the Egyptians the falseness of their world the thickness of the darkness would have reflected the intensity with which they had felt or valued their world and its values. Our discussion of the plagues could leave us with the impression that they were experienced by the Egyptians as an intellectual deconstruction of their worldview. We forget that this vision grows out of a desire to create or give, which represents a person's desire or will to actualize themselves. This is the most powerful desire a person feels and is the basis of his will to live.

Ḥokhma may be a person's conceptual frame of understanding. But it is not born of passing curiosity. It is a consequence of a person's need to understand the vision that underlies his being in the world. Ḥokhma emerges from that desire, and the depth of the ḥokhma that a person reaches is tied to the intensity of their need or desire to know.[27] This plague repudiated the Egyptian attachment to reality on its deepest and

---

25. Ibid. 14:1.
26. Rashi, Ex. 10:21; Ramban, Ex. 10:23.
27. Rabbi Tzadok HaKohen, *Resisei Laila*, ot 43.

most intense level. After the plague of darkness, all that remained to the Egyptians was life. That would be taken away in the next and final plague.

### KETER AND THE DEATH OF THE FIRSTBORN

The trait of *keter* (crown) corresponds to the first statement of creation, which actualized God's *ratzon*, "desire" or "will" to create. All the other statements of creation are introduced by the Torah with the words "And God said...." The exception is this first statement, where God's "saying" is understood merely by inference from the first verse of the Torah, "*Bereshit* (In the beginning of God's creating)...."[28]

God's independence of and priority to creation is evident in this. Making a statement assumes an other to hear it or, at the very least, some concept of otherness into which it is said.[29] But before creation there was absolutely nothing but the oneness of God. Since the first statement brought otherness into being, the statement was not articulated in the text.

"*Bereshit*" implies chronology; thus, this first statement created time. Time is the most rarefied aspect of material existence, assuming only extension and movement. There was also a more physical creation associated with this trait. But since the *ratzon* of *keter* is prior to even a general concept of what to create, it was made manifest by a creation without definition – utterly formless physical matter that stymies any attempt at description.[30]

This is called *tohu*.[31] Rashi links the word to bewilderment, meaning we become bewildered and desolate when contemplating such a creation.[32] We are incapable of grasping it, because it is not yet in any sense "something." It is the creation of otherness to God which is not yet something. If this is what "was" as a result of the statement, then we get deeper appreciation of the "wasn'tness" of before creation.

---

28. Rosh HaShana 32a.
29. This is to be distinguished from the otherness we referred to as coming through the third statement when the lower waters were separated out from the upper waters. Then we were speaking about otherness in the sense of meaningful separation from God.
30. Ramban, Gen. 1:1.
31. Gen. 1:2.
32. Rashi, Gen. 1:2.

## The Final Plagues

We associate a crown with a king's lordship over his fellow men. But really by extending above his head it is his connection to God and so represents his servitude to God. It symbolizes lordship over others because this very subservience to God is the source of the king's authority to rule. In our earlier discussion of *tiferet* and *malkhut*, we saw that the king's service comes through representation and emulation of God's initiative and creativity, which is more of an assertion of individuality. But here we are talking about the crown, the root connection from which his authority and ability to rule emanate, which is a source of humility.

In the case of God, the trait of *keter* obviously cannot symbolize His connection to a higher authority. Rather, the divine trait of *keter* is God's root connection to His subjects, for there is no kingship (at least in the context of creation) without subjects. This corresponds to His initial intent to create, that is, to create others.

The starting point from which any act of creation begins, our default awareness before we are stirred to action, is of our transcendent Source, an awareness so overwhelming that we cannot be fully cognizant of our individuality. We experience *keter* in the initial stirring of a desire to create, give, or serve.[33] This is our *ratzon* to be actualized, the will or want that is the essence of our selfhood but before it is articulated as a specific intent or desire. As we awake to personal initiative and action we begin to become aware of ourselves emerging from God into individuality.

Today our ability to fully relate to *keter* is compromised, because our default awareness is not of God. Instead we tend to be empty or, more often, filled with distractions; it is only rarely that we connect with our true self. We still do experience a version of *keter*, but more as an awakening from sleep or obliviousness.

The final plague, which struck down the firstborn of Egypt, was to clarify this trait of *keter* and the initial act of creation associated with it. Though the Egyptians also believed that reality was created, they viewed

---

33. Our deepest awareness of self and God occurred when we heard the first two of the Ten Commandments, though then we experienced the self merging with God rather than emerging from God. Then, also, the experience was one of obligation, as we heard the first two commandments in that moment. We are supposed to experience this merging when we recite the *Shema*. See our discussion of *tiferet* in the previous chapter. See Deuteronomy Rabba 2:30.

*Part 2: The Character of Faith*

the creator as a part of physical reality. They lacked any concept of a transcendent, unitary, and necessary creator utterly removed from physical being. Though the Egyptians recognized that existence *as we know it* was created, they assumed that it merely advanced the state of a prior reality that had always been. Egyptian creation mythology viewed creation as emerging from primordial waters that existed before the creative process began.[34] The final plague came to repudiate this view and affirm God's absolute transcendence. God's name *Makom*, "Place," captures this. We call God "Place" because He is the place of creation. Creation is wholly contained within Him; it is not in any sense the place of God.[35]

This point was made by killing only the firstborn rather than annihilating all of Egypt. The firstborn are the beginning of the new generation, the root of their parents' creation. Before a couple has their first child they are just a couple. Their firstborn transforms them into parents, creators of their first-born creation. The rest of the children merely build on this reality.

The firstborn, therefore, personify the transition from creator and creation. In the Egyptian view creator and creation are linked because both are part of physical reality. When God actualized His trait of *keter*, which is the essence of God's "connection" to creation, the manner in which He is its source, He actualized His transcendence. That is, that there is *no* direct connection between Creator and creation. The Egyptians' essential identity was bound up with their idolatrous beliefs about the roots of existence, so they could not relate to this transcendence. With the revelation of *keter* the Egyptian firstborn lost their source of existence and died.

By killing the firstborn God was demonstrating not His power, but His location. Rather than destroying Egypt to show Himself as the most powerful force *in* creation, He revealed that He is *outside*

---

34. Both the Heliopolitan and Hermopolitan cosmologies, which reflect ancient Egyptian beliefs, begin with the primeval waters. The Memphite creation story, which is closer to the Torah in its approach, is of much later origin. It was composed while the 25th dynasty ruled Egypt, well after the building of the First Temple.
35. Genesis Rabba 68:9. To imagine an empty void that was filled by the Creator through His creation is heresy, for emptiness represents an advanced level of creation. Besides being space, it holds the potential to be filled.

creation, standing prior to the *reshit* (root) of humanity personified in the firstborn, able to snip it off at its root. Since man is the essence and purpose of creation, by cutting off the root of man God was cutting off the root of all of creation. God thus demonstrated both the complete dependence of all of creation upon Him and His complete independence of creation.

With each plague, as we have seen, the actualization of a divine trait not only dealt a blow to the Egyptians who were unable to connect to God but also reinforced the intrinsic connection to God that the Jews had inherited from their forefathers, thereby elevating them. God's actualization of trait after trait resonated with the Jews' true self and brought it out step-by-step from the distortions introduced by slavery to Egypt and their worldview.

The actualization of *keter* also brought an intrinsic elevation for the Jews. The revelation of creation's total dependence upon God for its existence awakened the existential fear of God that is the basis and backdrop of worship.[36] But because this came through the actualization of God's absolute transcendent detachment from creation, the Jews should have been cut off in the same manner as the Egyptians. After all, they were still a part of creation.[37] How could they as part of physical creation be connected to that which is utterly disconnected from physical existence? The Jews, too, should have lost their firstborn.[38]

For this reason, the Jews were commanded to act in order to escape this plague. But what could they do? How could they bridge the divide? The Jews had to cease being a part of creation and become a part of the Creator! Astonishingly, that is exactly what they did – by bringing the *korban Pesaḥ*, the Passover sacrifice, they became servants of God. True servants only exist to serve; they lose their autonomous identity and become mere extensions of their master. Through this offering the Jews were saved from the plague of the firstborn because they were no

---

36. See Rabbi Natan Sternhartz, *Likutei Halakhot*, Hilkhot Bekhor Behema Tehora 4.
37. Ex. 4:22.
38. The approach that follows is based on Maharal, *Gevurot Hashem*, chapter 60.

*Part 2: The Character of Faith*

longer part of the creation, separated off from their source of existence. They had become a part or extension of the Creator.[39]

The Passover sacrifice is the only offering that is called in the Torah by the name *avoda* (service).[40] For this was the Jewish people's first act of worship, through which we accepted God as our King and were inaugurated into His service.[41] Because the plague we were escaping was revealing God's transcendence, the Passover sacrifice was specifically directed at God's unity,[42] His unity being synonymous with complete transcendence from the physical realm of extension and division.

We have pointed out several times that recognizing God's unity is synonymous with accepting His kingship. So this sacrifice neatly wraps up the plagues and we understand why the killing of the first-born is their appropriate conclusion. The purpose of the plagues was to bring us to *emuna* through an appreciation of *yihud Hashem*. Here we see that this final plague brought us to an action through which we recognized *yihud Hashem* and accepted God's rule, which is synonymous with *emuna*.

**CONNECTING THE BEGINNING TO THE END**

Though the trait of *keter* involves the most profound recognition of dependence and self-nullification before God, we experience it as or through an awakening to serve/create, which ultimately leads to the most powerful exercise of individuality – an act of original creation! But as we pointed out in our discussion of *malkhut*, this creation is for the purpose of emulating and connecting to God. And as we express our individuality through our act of choice we merge back with the Creator, for He is the basis of our ability to choose, our *tzelem Elokim*.

*Keter*, the beginning of the process, thus connects to *malkhut*, the end of the process. This mirrors the double role of the crown on the

---

39. See Maharal's statement (*Tiferet Yisrael, perek* 16) that we must enter God's service so as not to be like an existence unto ourselves separate from God, something that cannot truly exist.
40. Ex. 12:25.
41. Ibid.
42. Ibid. The lamb offered had to be one year old. It was cooked as one whole, had to be eaten in its entirety in one house, etc. Recognizing unity is also synonymous with accepting kingship. See Rambam, *Sefer HaMitzvot, mitzvat aseh* 2.

head of a king. On one hand the crown represents the king's subservience to God, on the other hand it represents his preeminence over his subjects or, in the non-political sense, our preeminence over ourselves. These are two sides of one coin, for it is through subservience to God that we have both the authority and capability to rule. As we assert our individuality through an act of choice, we become most transparent to God as the basis of our being. In self-defining choice our "I" becomes "i."

**PUTTING IT ALL TOGETHER**

The plagues reveal how we can integrate *emuna* into the fabric of our awareness in such a way that it defines our experience of self and world. If we could succeed in absorbing the lessons of the plagues, our ongoing awareness would be suffused with consciousness of the presence of the Creator as we go about our daily life, which we would experience as continuous acts of creation done in the context of relationship with Him. Through these creative acts we would become aware of different aspects of ourselves and see these aspects mirrored around us in God's act of Creation. We described a version of what this would look like when we first introduced the traits in chapter 13. Having gone through the traits in detail it is now time to revisit this integrated vision.

(*Keter*) As my will/desire to create stirs, I become aware of myself in distinction to the transcendent Source of all being. (*Ḥokhma*) As my awareness of my desire grows, my self becomes increasingly distinct and I recognize that my desire is to create in emulation of my Creator as a way of existing in connection to Him. I understand that connection to the Creator or facilitating that connection is the defining purpose of all that exists and its only reality. (*Bina*) As I clarify specifically what I want to create, my individuality becomes defined, separating me from God. This creates a great yearning to reunite with Him through my act of creation. (*Ḥesed*) I feel an overwhelming desire to go beyond myself through my creative act. This sensitizes me to God's desire to create, which is evident in existence, reinforcing my desire to create in emulation of God. (*Gevura*) I become aware that I must contain my desire to go beyond myself in order to successfully create what I want to create. This makes me aware of the containment evident in creation, the precise structure and functioning of physical reality, which reinforces

*Part 2: The Character of Faith*

the need to be exacting in my act of creation. It also impresses upon me that I must remain within the boundaries that define me as a created being as I go about my project of creating. That every action in the world produces a reaction, suggests that my actions will be rewarded or punished and that I need to justify my existence through the merits of my actions. (*Tiferet*) As I achieve balance between my overwhelming desire to go beyond myself and my need to properly contain myself, I become aware that the self that I am expressing through my intended action is an actualization of the image of God within me. I must balance and integrate my sense of His omnipotence with my responsibility to act. I must choose my actions, but through those choices be His representative. I become aware of how this relationship, the goal of creation, echoes through creation reflecting back to me my responsibility, such as in the relationship between the sun and the moon and the proper relationship of parent to child. (*Netzaḥ*) I feel an overwhelming need to act in order to connect with something other to me through my creation. As I forcefully overcome my inertia and begin to create, I sense the Creator's awesome desire for connection to creation which powers the emergence of physical reality; and I as a part of the creation, in turn feel an overwhelming desire to connect back to the Creator through my act of creation. (*Hod*) As my act of creation begins I need to control my overwhelming desire to create so as not to destroy what I am creating. I become conscious and directed in my actions. This restraint accentuates my individual awareness. I sense the isolation that comes with a developing ego and the inadequacy of the vision of reality that is formulated from that ego perspective. This impels me all the more to create/serve in order to reconnect with God. My isolation also separates me from my fellows, and I recognize the need to join with them in recovering connection to God. He is the Creator of all so though I can have an individual relationship with God it must be in the context of the larger whole. (*Yesod*) As I balance the overwhelming desire to create with restraint and precisely make my intended creation in emulation of God, I sense my *tzelem Elokim* expressed in my actions so that I become a synthesis of my body and *neshama*, connecting God to His creation through my person. (*Malkhut*) By choosing to selflessly release my creation to exist independently of me (this point best understood in the context of "creating" children), I emulate God on the deepest level possible and feel a powerful sense of "I." But since this comes through fully actualizing my *tzelem Elokim* (my capacity to choose) I am transparent to the Godliness within me so that this "i" is a projection from God.[43]

---

43. The human capacity to become ego-less and transparent to our Godly basis was reached by Hillel at the height of his joy during the *Simḥat Beit HaShoeva* when he said (Sukka 53a): "If I am here, all is here, and if I am not here, who is here." See Rabbi Tzadok, *Maḥshavot Ḥarutz*, ot 8.

*Chapter 17*

# Externally and Internally Based *Emuna*

In the previous chapters we looked carefully at human character, trait by trait, and how it should be structured to reflect what we learn about reality from the Exodus. We sketched an outline of our perception of reality as viewed through these traits and how integral our awareness of the Creator is to that perception. This is a vision of the integrated *emuna* we spoke about when we began this half of the book. Yet if we ask ourselves how much closer we are to actually having *emuna* as a result of this investigation, the answer is "probably not much." What did we miss?

For all its power, this vision seems very far from us. Though aspects of this personality are recognizable, our overall experience of self has little resemblance to it. Our default consciousness is not the awareness of nullification before a higher source. We do not define our being around an effort to create, and when we do create we are not aware of ourselves traveling through stages that reflect God's creation of the world around us. We rarely even notice when we make decisions, let alone sense that our choosing joins us with God.

This is a modern problem. The peoples of the ancient Near East were spiritually aware, so that their personalities would naturally have

## Part 2: The Character of Faith

been structured as creators in emulation of their gods.[1] So the Jews who experienced the Exodus would have been primed to resonate with the plagues on an immediate and intuitive level, transforming their natural spirituality into integrated *emuna* in the transcendent Creator. But as we chronicled in the first half of this book, from that moment on our *emuna* has been under ever-increasing pressure. The gradual loss of spiritual focus over the last few millennia has led to a reorganization of human character such that we are no longer in a position to rapidly internalize this fully integrated *emuna*. Perhaps we need to engage in an aggressive effort to reform our character and recover some semblance of the creative personality from which this *emuna* more naturally arises.

The fact that we need to prepare ourselves to be able to internalize this *emuna* should not surprise us. The Jews in Egypt themselves did not gain *emuna* from the miracles of the plagues alone – and they experienced them directly! Whatever effect the plagues had on them, the first time the Torah recognizes the Jews as having attained *emuna* was only after they saw the miracle of the destruction of Egypt at the sea, almost a week after the final plague:

> And Israel saw Egypt dead on the shores of the sea. And Israel saw the great power (hand) that God sent against Egypt, and the people feared God and believed (*vaya'aminu*) in God and in Moses His servant.[2]

The miracles we witnessed at the sea were more powerful than the ones we saw in Egypt, as we will discuss momentarily. So it is possible that for all their greatness, the miracles of the plagues were simply not of sufficient magnitude to catalyze *emuna*. In other words, though the plagues were structured so as to reveal to us all that we needed to know to achieve full *emuna*, perhaps they were not intense enough to "bring the message home."

---

1. See note 3 to chapter 16, citing Rabbi Tzadok HaKohen, *Pri Tzaddik, Bo* 2, to the effect that all ancient peoples experienced reality through these same traits of creation.
2. Ex. 14:30–31.

But this is clearly not the full explanation. For though the Jews are credited with gaining *emuna* at the sea, that *emuna* was not permanent. That achievement had to await the miracles at Mount Sinai when the Jews received the Torah:

> And God said to Moses, "Behold, I will come to you in a thick cloud in order that the people should hear My speaking with you and also believe (*ya'aminu*) in you eternally."[3]

Again, though the miracle at the sea was great enough to break through a certain barrier to bring us to *emuna*, perhaps the problem was that it was still not enough to bring the kind of integration that would make that *emuna* eternal. The Sages, however, tell us a different story. The midrash makes clear that the revelation at Sinai was of similar magnitude to the revelation at the sea.[4] If there was a difference in the outcomes on the two occasions, that difference must be attributed to changes in us, in our ability to internalize the experience.

There was clearly something blocking the Jews from internalizing *emuna*. And as they journeyed from Egypt to the sea and then to Sinai, they underwent some process that allowed them to overcome it and gain *emuna* from the miracles they were experiencing. So though developments in our character over the past millennia may complicate our ability to internalize *emuna* from the plagues, these only strengthen a barrier that has faced us since the time of the Exodus. If we want to identify what we ourselves need to do to make the *emuna* we have been discussing a part of us, we need to understand what the Jews of the Exodus did on this journey and how we can reproduce it.

## THE SONG AT THE SEA

Considering what we have said the plagues revealed, it is puzzling that following the tenth plague the Jews were not credited with achieving *emuna*. They also should have been freed immediately from Egypt, since they only remained there in order to complete the demonstrations

---

3. Ex. 19:9.
4. *Yalkut Shimoni, Shemot* 15, *remez* 253.

## Part 2: The Character of Faith

needed to bring them to *emuna*. The death of the firstborn healed the last remaining trait through which we understand ourselves and our world and brought clarity about the absolute nature of God's transcendence. Yet there is no mention at that point of their gaining *emuna*. And even though, as a result of this plague, Pharaoh allowed the Jews to leave the cities and go to worship God in the desert,[5] they were not yet free. As soon as it became clear that the Jews were not returning to captivity, Pharaoh came in pursuit, bringing the entire Egyptian army with him.[6] When they caught up to the Jews at the shores of the sea, the Jews stood before the final gate of Egypt but were still within its borders.

Only when the sea split did the Jews cross out of Egypt. And though the split cut a path in the shape of a bow, returning them back to Egyptian soil,[7] the destruction of the Egyptian army ended any possibility of the Jews being returned to slavery. Though they did not fully outgrow their Egyptian-influenced mentality until they reached Mount Sinai,[8] the miracle at the sea broke the lock Egypt had on their minds and bodies. This came together with the Torah's first recognition that the Jews had reached a level of *emuna*. What happened there that took us beyond the achievements of the plagues?

The splitting of the sea brought the power of God's miracles to a new level. The plagues in Egypt were all local phenomena, confined to the boundaries of Egypt. The midrash goes so far as to say that border disputes with Egypt were resolved based on where the plagues struck and where their reach ended.[9] In contrast, the midrash teaches that when the sea split, all the water in the world also split.[10]

Water is one of the four elements of physical reality. Therefore, with this midrash the Sages were telling us that the miracle at the sea penetrated to the very foundations of reality. Thus even if the degree of transcendence being demonstrated by the miracle was no more than

---

5. Ex. 12:31.
6. Ex. 14:5–7.
7. Rambam on Avot 5:4.
8. Zohar II 83b; Rabbi Moses Cordovero, *Pardes Rimonim* 13:1; Rabbi Yehuda Arye Leib Alter, *Sfat Emet BeMidbar*, Shavuot 645.
9. Exodus Rabba 10:2.
10. Rashi, Ex. 14:21 from the *Mekhilta*.

in the last plague, it was revealed on a completely different scale, transforming our appreciation of God's omnipotence.

The greater penetration of reality by this miracle was paralleled by a deeper effect upon us. We see that the Jews were changed by this miracle to an unprecedented degree, because they sang in response to it.[11]

This is the first song recorded in the Torah.[12] It may appear to be nothing more than an expression of thanks, but a verse in the Song of Songs indicates otherwise. There, among God's other exhortations to leave Egypt, appear the words *et hazamir higia* (the time for song has arrived). This, the Vilna Gaon tells us, refers to the song by the sea.[13] That is, God told the Jews to leave Egypt *in order* to sing. Rather than a mere acknowledgement of their salvation, this verse indicates that the song was actually the purpose of their departure! What was the significance of this song?

## SPEECH AND HUMANITY

Song is a special form of speech. Speech – at least what Torah considers speech – is unique to man.[14] Torah designates as speech only a revelation in external reality of an infinite, spiritual understanding. Words of Torah and prayer are examples of speech.[15] Mere symbolic communications, such as "Pass the bananas," do not qualify; even animals can communicate on that level.

Speech is possible for man because he is formed through the fusion of a *neshama* with a body. Man's *neshama* affords spiritual understanding, while his body allows external expression. In fact, when God infused a soul into Adam's body, along with life came the ability to

---

11. Ex. 15:1.
12. The midrash states that the Jews also sang after the plague of the firstborn (*Mekhilta, Parashat Shira* 1; *Aggadat Bereshit* 60:1). But the song at the sea was clearly on a completely different plane, as it was recorded in the Torah and was sung by the entire nation together.
13. Commentary by the Vilna Gaon on Song of Songs 2:12.
14. Though angels also have speech and song, the role of their speech and song is different from ours. This point, however, is beyond the scope of our discussion. See, for example, Rabbi Tzadok HaKohen, *Sihat Malakhei Hasharet*, chapter 2.
15. I understood this from a lecture of Rav Moshe Shapiro.

*Part 2: The Character of Faith*

speak.[16] The Torah actually refers to man's speech as his life.[17] Speech is thus definitive of man.

The slavery of Egypt, by miring us in extreme physical labor, blocked our ability to actualize or even experience our *neshama*, robbing us of our humanity and our ability to truly speak. The Torah hints at this when it tells us that at the height of Egyptian oppression the Jews could no longer listen to Moses when he promised them salvation because of *kotzer ruaḥ*.[18] *Kotzer* means shortness, and *ruaḥ* means wind or breath. The simple meaning of these words is that they could not hear Moses from a shortness of breath, either from the exhaustion of heavy labor or from the anguish of hopelessness.[19] But *ruaḥ* is also the name of the middle component of the soul – our consciousness of self. This connects the higher spiritual aspect of the soul, the *neshama* (our sense of connection to a transcendent source), to the more physical aspect of the soul, the *nefesh* (our experience of physical drives).[20] Therefore we can also understand *kotzer ruaḥ* to mean that the Jews lost hope of salvation because they became isolated in their physical being, unable to connect with their deeper selves and conceive of another reality. Their *ruaḥ* had become too short to reach their *neshama*. Since true speech requires the synthesis of the *neshama* with our physical self, they lost the ability to speak in the Torah sense of the word, to give expression to their spiritual depth. In fact, *ruaḥ* is the aspect of soul responsible for speech, and it had become "short."[21]

The centrality of this loss to the exile in Egypt is seen from the fact that the name for the holiday commemorating deliverance from Egypt – Pesaḥ – breaks down into the words *pe saḥ*, which means "the mouth speaks."[22] The Exodus from Egypt freed our ability to speak and thereby to be fully human.

---

16. Gen. 2:7 with Targum Onkelos.
17. Ibid.
18. Ex. 6:9.
19. See Rashi, Ex. 6:9.
20. Rabbi Hayim of Volozhin, *Nefesh HaḤayim* 1:17.
21. Ibid., 1:14. The *ruaḥ* is also the location of our free will.
22. Rabbi Hayim Vital, *Pri Etz Ḥayim, Shaar Mikra Kodesh*, chapter 4.

## UNDERSTANDING SONG

In normal speech there is a balanced interaction between the *neshama* and the body, as we weigh out and consider each word before it is spoken. Song goes beyond that. Song is inspired. It pours forth. Thus the song at the sea was introduced by the words "*Az yashir*" (Then he *will* speak).[23] The commentaries take note of the unexpected future tense of the verse. The simple explanation of this is that the verse is not describing the moment when Moses began to sing but rather the moment before, when he felt the inspiration welling up within him that would soon break forth in song.[24]

In a song of this kind it is as if the body's ability to hold back the *neshama* and actualize it in controlled expression has broken down. Inspired, prophetic song like that which the Jews sang at the sea is governed by the *neshama*. It is contained only to the extent that thoughts are formulated into sentences. But even this limitation is compromised as the words come out as poetry rather than prose, with meaning bursting the boundaries of language.[25]

A human being is composed of a *neshama* and a body. Normally, the body dominates our experience and limits the expression of the *neshama*. At the moment of the song, however, the Jewish people as a nation touched a level of self that released the *neshama* from its limitations; for a moment they were a people overwhelmed by the *neshama*, with their bodies merely serving as the *neshama*'s medium of expression.

This portrayal echoes our earlier description of the purification of character accomplished by the plagues. Traits arise from the merging of the *neshama* with our physical bodies, and the plagues came to purify the traits so that the *neshama* rather than the body determined each trait. The song, however, marked the moment at which the Jews' personality *as a whole* became defined by their spiritual core. Rather than

---

23. Ex. 15:1.
24. Rashi, Ex. 15:1.
25. Extra spaces between words in the Torah scroll indicate a need for introspection due to the completion of an idea or the depth of the concept being conveyed (Rashi, Lev. 1:1 from the *Sifra*). Songs are written in the Torah in two narrow columns to give a great deal of additional space because of the poetic nature of the song. See Rabbi Gedalia Schorr, *Or Gedalyahu* I, *Vayeḥi*.

*Part 2: The Character of Faith*

purifying individual facets of character as was accomplished by plagues, the splitting of the sea purified the self as a whole. Whereas each plague had altered reality in a particular place, bringing change to a particular aspect of self, the miracle at the sea, which altered the whole of reality, was paralleled by a change in the totality of self.

The Haggada hints at this when it tells us that five times as many plagues struck the Egyptians at the sea as hit them in Egypt. The plagues were compared to fingers of God,[26] whereas at the sea God revealed His *yad hagedola* (His great hand).[27] Fingers are parts of the hand, while the hand is the total limb.[28]

The verse that tells us that the Jews saw God's "great hand" ends with the words "and they believed in God and in Moses His servant"[29] and is followed immediately by the song. It was not until they witnessed this miracle and were purified to the point that they were totally controlled by their *neshama* as evidenced by the song, that the Torah credits them with coming to *emuna*.[30]

With this the Torah teaches a deep truth, one that is central to our project. The internal component of genuine *emuna* is not an arbitrary thought or emotion. It is a consequence of the influence of our *neshama* on our consciousness. Our *neshama* emanates directly from God and is acutely aware of His existence. True *emuna* results when our *neshama* integrates with and influences our self. This in no way minimizes the importance of the miracles. They provide the external anchor or proof to our *emuna*, the objective component. But without the internal, subjective component, without the influence of the *neshama*, we cannot reach *emuna*.

Here it is important to make a distinction. We have spoken about the plagues being directed at our traits of character and we are now labeling those miracles as bringing externally grounded *emuna*. We have just opened a new discussion about an internal, *neshama*-based component

---

26. Ex. 8:15.
27. Ex. 14:31.
28. See Maharal, *Gevurot Hashem*, chapter 58.
29. Ex. 14:31.
30. That is, they came to the advanced belief catalyzed by the Exodus as opposed to the more basic belief the Jews had from the beginning of the process (see Ex. 4:31).

to our *emuna*. The actualization of this component also seems to occur through character development, whether through specific traits or the personality as a whole. What is the difference?

When we spoke about the plagues and their structuring of character, we were speaking about the traits as they influence our conceptual vision of reality. For example, we spoke earlier about *ḥesed* influencing a person to view reality through a lens of giving, thus priming him to accept a Creator. When we talk about the internal component we are speaking about character as a conduit for the *neshama* to our awareness. Rather than the structure of our vision we are interested in our sense for what is real. After the miracle of the sea broke the general hold of Egypt on our psyche, this essential internal dimension became more open to change and the focus of the process of coming to *emuna*.

We could question our conclusion that what happened at the sea was based on a new, internal component becoming operative. Perhaps the song and the *emuna* we achieved were driven entirely by the extreme power of the external miracle we witnessed. The commentaries say otherwise. They describe the outpouring of the *neshama* heard in the song not as being caused by the miracle but as happening parallel to it. Just as supernatural forces are abrogating physical law in the external world at the moment of the miracle, so the spiritual *neshama* is overwhelming the body at the moment of the miracle.[31] These are independent, parallel processes.

It was not until Mount Sinai, however, that this internal development to our *emuna* was firmly established. As we mentioned, the level of miracle the Jews experienced there was comparable to the miracle at the sea, yet the level of *emuna* attained was qualitatively higher – it was *l'olam*, "forever." Sinai therefore proved that achievements in *emuna* are a combination of a miraculous event, which allows us to draw a rational conclusion about the existence of God, and the internal preparation that enables the influence of the *neshama* to provide an internal, subjective basis to *emuna*. We turn now to the Jews' experience at Sinai to better

---

31. Rav Yitzhak Hutner, "Pesaḥ," in *Paḥad Yitzḥak* (Brooklyn: Gur Aryeh Institute for Advanced Jewish Scholarship, 1984), 64–68.

*Part 2: The Character of Faith*

understand the preparations we need to make to gain this internal confirmation of *emuna*.

## A NATION CONCEIVED

The experience of *emuna* at the sea was a tremendous leap. A new nation was conceived that was connected to their *neshama* and therefore to *emuna*. But it was not the final stop. The *emuna* the Jews reached at the sea remained actual only in the immediate aftermath of that miracle. They experienced the primacy of their *neshama* only for that time. They were not able to hold onto the experience because even though the essential lock of Egypt on the Jewish psyche was broken at the sea, remnants of Egyptian influence remained with them. These remnants continued to block full internalization of *emuna* until they reached Mount Sinai. Only when they heard the command "I am Hashem your God who took you out of Egypt..."[32] did their *emuna* become eternal.[33]

Since the level of revelation at the sea was comparable to that at Mount Sinai, it was a change in the Jews that enabled them to more fully internalize the experience. The high point of that development was reached in the days before the giving of the Torah when the Jews succeeded in dedicating themselves entirely to the service of God by declaring *naaseh venishma*, "We will do whatever we are commanded and strive to understand it as best we can."[34] What does this declaration tell us about who the Jews had become in the run-up to receiving the Torah and, therefore, who we must become to fully internalize *emuna*?

## NAASEH VENISHMA

The Sages consider the commitment expressed in this declaration of *naaseh venishma* to be one of the greatest achievements of human history. They write that it brought the Jews to a level comparable to that of

---

32. Ex. 20:2.
33. Ex. 19:9, quoted earlier in note 4. See also Rambam, *Mishneh Torah, Hilkhot Yesodei HaTorah* 8:1.
34. We see that this represents full preparation because it is only as a result of our declaration of *naaseh venishma* that *Tosafot* asked why God had to hold Mount Sinai over our heads when we actually received the Torah (*Tosafot*, Shabbat 88a).

*Externally and Internally Based Emuna*

angels.[35] What was this level? Obviously through *naaseh venishma* we accepted the obligation to serve God. That is clearly relevant to *emuna*. Though we have focused more on *emuna* as recognition of the Creator, it is important to understand that this is not limited to a passive sense of belonging and protection. As we have explained numerous times, genuine *emuna* includes an awareness of obligation.[36]

But *naaseh venishma* was not merely a declaration of blind obedience. The Jews had already said *naaseh*, "we will do," twice in the days leading up to *naaseh venishma*.[37] With *naaseh* they accepted obedience. In spite of this, they were not yet ready to achieve permanent *emuna*. And though *nishma*, "we will hear," added acceptance of all future commands, it also included a commitment to try to understand the meaning behind our actions.[38]

We see this confirmed by the Talmud's statement that the Jews received two crowns for this declaration: one for *naaseh* and one for *nishma*.[39] Crowns represent unique connections to God. Had *nishma* merely expanded the acceptance of obligation to include future obligations, the crown of *nishma* would have encompassed the connection of *naaseh* within it and there would only have been one crown. Rather, *nishma* adds the dimension of understanding.

Intellect is a distinguishing characteristic of our humanity, and actions without understanding lack full humanity. The role of intellect in right action was debated by a Sadducee and Rava, a great talmudic Sage. A Sadducee once saw Rava so engrossed in his learning that he was

---

35. Shabbat 88a.
36. Included in *emuna*, according to Ramban, is the recognition that the Creator is our King whom we need to serve (Ramban's gloss to *Sefer HaMitzvot, mitzvat aseh* 1 and *mitzvat lo taaseh* 5, with his citation of the *Mekhilta*). Rambam understands acceptance of God's kingship as a dimension of the expanded *emuna* of *yiḥud Hashem* (Rambam, *Sefer HaMitzvot, mitzvat aseh* 2). See also our discussion in chapter 2 of the *Sefer HaIkarim*'s three pillars of *emuna*, which include the belief that God commands us.
37. Ex. 19:8, 24:3.
38. Translation according to Maharal, *Tiferet Yisrael*, chapter 29. A number of commentaries (for example the Rashbam) translate the verse: "We will do what we have been commanded and we will do whatever we will be commanded."
39. Shabbat 88a.

*Part 2: The Character of Faith*

unaware that he was rocking back and forth with his feet on his hands, making his fingers bleed. The Sadducee saw in this as an expression of the same trait that led the Jews to say *naaseh venishma*. He cried out to Rava, "You impetuous people who put your mouth before your ears… You should have first heard what was commanded and then decided if you wanted to accept it! And you, Rava, continue in the same vein!"[40]

The Sadducees were a heretical group who were influenced by Greek ideas.[41] As we mentioned in the first half of this book, the Greeks saw intellect as man's greatest and defining capability. Based on this, the Sadducee criticized the Jews for accepting commands before first hearing and evaluating them with their intellect.

Rava retorted with the verse "The trust of the upright will lead them, while the twistedness of the treacherous will destroy them."[42] This was a very strong comeback, indicating that *naaseh venishma* touches on fundamental issues. Rava's point was that when a person judges a command before accepting it, even if he does decide to follow it he is not obeying or serving the one doing the commanding. Rather, his intellect is determining his actions. This is ideal according to the Greek worldview. The Greeks believed that human intellect penetrated to the very essence of reality, so that to follow one's intellect was to serve the highest cause. But the Jews recognize that there is a realm of reality that transcends our understanding, with God above any insight man can reach.

The highest ideal for Jews is to follow God's commands so that our actions give expression to this higher understanding. This only occurs when we do an action because God commanded it and not based on our own judgment. Only then is God the initiator of the action; only then do we become a conduit for God's will. Since we were created for this service, following our intellect instead amounts to rebellion.

Both the Sages and the Sadducees valued intellect, but they used it differently. Jews do not use intellect to determine the goal; that is up to God. Rather, we use our intellect to clarify what God wants from us and to try to understand the reason for it, so that we can bring our full

---

40. Ibid.
41. Rabbi Tzadok HaKohen, *Pri Tzaddik, Ḥanukka* 3.
42. Prov. 11:3.

self to our actions. In this way the involvement of our intellect does not compromise our service but rather augments it. The Jews' commitment to accept all commands that God would issue and to bring the fullness of their humanity to fulfilling those commandments meant the Jews were all in. *Naaseh venishma* was not a declaration of obedience; it was a full dedication of self. The Jews transformed themselves into God's instrument.

Thus the Sages compare them to angels for having made this declaration. The Hebrew term *malakh* (angel) literally means "agent."[43] A *malakh* is a force created to accomplish a specific task. That task is its being. When we said *"naaseh venishma,"* we identified ourselves as existing to accomplish the tasks assigned to us by God, and thus we resembled *malakhim*.

They could only make such a dedication genuinely if they understood themselves to be achieving self through it rather than losing self. This required that they locate their center of self in God rather than in their individuality, or at least in the manifestation of God within them, their *neshama*. This identification is what prepared them to completely integrate their *emuna* when they heard the statement *"Anokhi Hashem Elokekha"* (I am the Lord your God).[44] They got ready to completely integrate their *emuna* with their self by integrating their self with their *neshama*.[45]

This achievement was reflected in what happened when God revealed Himself on the mountain. The event as described in Exodus included smoke and lightning, thunder and shofar blasts – an overwhelming assault on the senses. The Torah characterizes the Jews' experience of it by saying they "saw the sounds [blasts]."[46]

Interpreting this bizarre verse requires us to understand the Torah's view and usage of human physical senses. Our sense of hearing allows us to connect to things that are beyond our immediate

---

43. Rashbatz, *Magen Avot*, chapter 2 (*Nevuot Moshe Rabbenu*).
44. Ex. 20:2.
45. On a deeper level, this quote from the Talmud is teaching that dedicated learning is a primary path to the commitment of *naaseh venishma*, and therefore to *emuna* in our day. But this is beyond the scope of our discussion.
46. Ex. 20:15.

environment – we can hear sounds that emanate from a place we cannot see. The reach of hearing is far, but the lack of a visual component weakens our confidence in the reality of the incident the sounds convey. For this reason a person cannot testify in court about events he only heard occurring. Sight, on the other hand, has a limited reach – we can only see what is immediately before us. But seeing is believing.[47]

Torah identifies spiritual experience with hearing. We are not commanded to "see" that God is One, we are commanded to "hear" that God is One.[48] This is because our experience is dominated by our physical being; the realm of spirit is not immediate and our sense of its reality is weak. Our physical awareness is much more powerful and real for us – effectively, we "see" it.

When God revealed Himself on Mount Sinai these priorities were reversed. The Jews "saw the sounds." Spiritual experience was their immediate reality, with physical experience a vague awareness.[49] This means that when God announced, "I am the Lord your God..." the Jews were pulled into occupying their *neshamot*; they were one with their *tzelem Elokim* (image of God), that aspect of our humanity that is immediately aware of God. This is what made the experience so powerful, resulting in *emuna* "forever." Rather than believing that God exists, they "were" that God exists. The reality of God's existence was one with the reality of their own existence.

At the sea they were still identified with their bodies, but their *neshama* overwhelmed them; at Mount Sinai they became one with their *neshama* and utterly identified with it. As well as coming to know God, the Jews came to know themselves on the deepest possible level. Their unique identity, their only true identity, was revealed to them. While at the sea the Jews were *conceived* as a nation, at Sinai, by gaining this unique identity, the Jews were *born* as that nation.[50] Since being integrated with one's *neshama* and having genuine *emuna* are synonymous, at Sinai we became a nation defined by our *emuna*.

---

47. The word for sight in Hebrew, *re'iya*, is related to the word for evidence, *raiya*.
48. Deut. 6:4.
49. Rabbi Hayim of Volozhin, *Nefesh HaḤayim* 3:11.
50. See Shabbat 88b and Rabbi Tzadok HaKohen, *Resisei Laila* 58.

## Externally and Internally Based Emuna

**THE BASIS OF *EMUNA***

Let's step back for a moment. Why did we need all this? We had experienced the ten plagues. We understood the implications of those miracles, how they establish that the world was created. What is all this talk of *emuna* coming from our *neshama*? Why do we need internalization and integration? All was proven; what more was needed?

We see that the witnessing of events in and of itself does not bring *emuna* – at least not in the long term. We need some inner awareness that testifies to and anchors the truth of those events. This is not to undermine the significance of experiencing miracles or recalling those experiences and all that we said about gaining *yihud Hashem* from studying the plagues. But though our justification for structuring our vision of reality around *emuna*, the external or rational component, is built on our historical experience in Egypt, our faith in that history and the conclusions we draw from that history need an ongoing inner foundation. That inner foundation was eternally established on Mount Sinai when the Jews became identified with their *neshamot*.

**CHARACTER DEVELOPMENT AND *SEFIRAT HAOMER***

Where does this leave us in our quest for *emuna*? The Jews that left Egypt had to develop themselves as they journeyed from Egypt to receiving the Torah on Mount Sinai. Helped along by the miracle at the sea, they were responsible for bringing themselves to the point where they could eventually declare *naaseh venishma*, fully dedicating themselves to the service of God by identifying themselves with the image of God within them.

Human personality is composed of traits, all of which arise from the merging of our *neshama* with our physical being. Purification of character is accomplished by accentuating the influence of the *neshama* on that combination so that it ultimately governs the expression of the trait, with our physical being providing its medium of expression. It was the Jews' work on this purification as they traveled from Egypt to Mount Sinai that brought them to this dedication and identification.

This purification is also our task if we want to prepare ourselves to internalize our engagement with the miracles of the Exodus to achieve integrated *emuna*. Not surprisingly, the Torah requires us to focus on just this during the period of time from the holiday of the Exodus, Passover, to the holiday of receiving the Torah, Shavuot. This is the mitzva of *Sefirat HaOmer* (the Counting of the Omer).[51]

Ostensibly, the obligation of *Sefirat HaOmer* is to count the days leading up to the receiving of the Torah, expressing our excitement and longing for its arrival. But the commentaries direct us to focus each day on a specific aspect of character. The traits are based on the seven traits of emotion and action, refracting each one through the lens of these same seven traits.[52] For example, *ḥesed* from the perspective of *gevura* would be different from *gevura* from the perspective of *ḥesed*. This gives a total of forty-nine traits to work on, a project we complete on the forty-ninth day after leaving Egypt, the day on which the Jews said *naaseh venishma*, with the next day the holiday of Shavuot.[53]

We begin the counting on the day after Passover. This day is distinguished by a unique offering brought at the Temple on that day – the Omer offering. Thus the name, *Sefirat HaOmer*, the counting of the Omer. It is as if we are being required to view each trait in the context of this offering. What was this offering and what was its significance?

The Omer offering was of the first fruit of the first crop of the season – barley. One *omer*, the quantity of food needed by a single individual for minimal subsistence for a day, was brought for the whole nation once a year on that day.[54] No grain could be eaten until it had "seen" an Omer offering. That is, after harvesting grain it could not be eaten until the Omer offering was brought even if it meant waiting a year to eat the grain.[55] Many midrashim praise this offering, as small in size as it is large in significance.

What is the significance of this offering? Some aspects seem obvious. It is a first-fruit offering. Giving the *reshit*, the first, the beginning, the essence of a crop to God is a way of connecting the whole crop to God. This particular barley, the first fruit of the nation's first ripening crop of the year is thus a way of connecting all of the nation's produce

---

51. Lev. 23:15–16.
52. Zohar III 97a.
53. Ex. 24:4 with Rashi and Ex. 24:7.
54. *Sefer HaḤinukh*, mitzva 302.
55. Ibid., mitzva 303.

to God. We need to sanctify it to God or say "thank you" on some level for our crops before we can eat them. That seems clear enough.

One of the things that is strange about this offering is its name. The word *omer* refers to a measure of grain. It is actually one of the most commonly used measurements of grain in the Torah; it is a tenth of an *ephah*.[56] However, it is called by the name "*omer*" in only three places: in connection with this offering,[57] with the agricultural leavings for the poor,[58] and with the manna in the desert. Each individual got exactly one *omer* of manna each day in the desert.[59] This last usage is the point of departure of a key midrash:

> The Holy One, blessed be He, said to Moses: Go and say to Israel: When I gave you the manna I gave an *omer* to each one of you… but now that you give Me the Omer I only get one *omer* from all of you. Moreover, it is not of wheat but of barley. Therefore Moses cautions Israel and tells them: bring the Omer.[60]

Through this offering we are connecting our crops to the manna. We have worked hard to grow our produce, worrying and sweating over it. This tends to awaken in a person a sense of ownership, it is mine because I made it.[61] We are not allowed to eat our crops until we connect them back to the manna: for all our efforts the grain is no different from the manna, that bread which fell to us from the heavens without any effort on our part, an obvious gift from God.

On the simplest level, had God not brought the rain or all the other natural phenomenon that we depend on for growing our crops, all of our efforts would be for naught. Our work is no more than a frosting on God's cake. This understanding is supported by numerous midrashim

---

56. Ex. 16:36. It is, for example, the amount of the grain offering that accompanied the *tamid* daily sacrifice.
57. Lev. 23:10.
58. Deut. 24:19.
59. Ex. 16:16.
60. Leviticus Rabba 28:3.
61. Deut. 8:17.

*Part 2: The Character of Faith*

that state explicitly that the Omer is a thank-offering to God for the rain and wind and dew.[62]

The Omer is meant to bring home to us that though we live and work in a physical world upon which we depend, it is a thin veneer over another dimension of existence which is essential and determines it. As we examine each trait of our character, we must refer back to the Omer to understand the trait in the same way. We must think, "This facet of my character has a spiritual root and a physical expression. Though the physical component looms large in my experience, I recognize that its spiritual root is primary and is the basis of its existence," and strive to actualize the trait with these priorities in mind.

Another level of this message is hidden in the name given to this offering – Omer. Why call it by its measurement? We do not call a sin offering a 50-pounder because of the weight of the goat we offer. We call it a sin offering because this describes what it is, its essence. Why don't we call the Omer the Dependence offering? It is true that the measurement is significant because this links it to the manna. But that in its own right raises a question. Why did we get only an *omer* of manna each day in the desert? If it is basic subsistence, doesn't that mean we were hungry all the time there? Why would we commemorate that?

This last question stems from our present spiritual state. We associate subsistence with hunger and misery because we look to food for more than mere nourishment. It is a key source of life's satisfaction for us; we depend on it for joy and happiness. A person needs to feel himself to be growing, adding, experiencing, in order to have a sense that his life is worthwhile. Bare survival is not enough for us. When we are defined by our physical dimension, we search for that satisfaction in physical experiences and distractions. However a person who is anchored in his spiritual dimension, defined by his *neshama*, seeks that satisfaction in spiritual expansion and experience. He *is* satisfied with a subsistence level of food because he relies on his food for nothing more than subsistence.[63] The fact that we each received an *omer* of manna in

---

62. Leviticus Rabba 28:1–3.
63. See the Vilna Gaon, *Perush al Kamma Aggadot* (Jerusalem: Keren Chokhma VeDaat, 1997), 105–6.

the desert was indicative of this focus. We specifically link our crop to the manna through this measure because we are interested in linking ourselves to this prioritization. As we work on our character, we need to have the manna and all it represents clearly before us.

It is upon this model that our project of character development depends. It is upon this character development that our *emuna* depends. It should not surprise us that achieving *emuna* requires hard work. The point we are adding is that as well as directing this work toward discovering God, it must be focused on preparing ourselves to internalize that recognition. We need the experience of miracles or the study of the miracles of the Exodus. But that study must be complemented by transforming ourselves into someone who can make the *emuna* a part of us.

**GROUNDED *EMUNA***

This returns us to the discussion that began this book, bringing us full circle. We spoke then about the objective *emuna* required by Rambam and Ramban and compared it to the subjective *emuna* that intuitively attracted me at the start of my involvement in Torah. We concluded then that though subjective *emuna* can help as an interim stop-gap, the mitzva of *emuna* requires an objective foundation – rational proof for Rambam and the miracles of the Exodus for Ramban. Subjective *emuna*, even a compelling *emuna* if it is compelling only to me, is not adequate because it cannot implicate anyone outside the individual, subjective self. This conclusion led to much of the rest of the book in which we investigated how to strengthen this objective *emuna* through study of the Exodus.

But what if my belief is personally compelling because I have access to the ground of existence itself? Since my *neshama* emanates directly from the Creator, I can potentially reach deep enough inside myself to reach God. In that case my awareness of His existence, though accessed through my subjective experience, would be objective – that is, would implicate everyone (even though I could not directly share its compulsion with anyone). I hinted to this possibility in the first chapter.[64] Is this potentially a substitute path to the mitzva?

---

64. See chapter 1, note 55.

*Part 2: The Character of Faith*

We have learned that this internal, subjective factor is in fact an essential component of our *emuna*. Torah did not credit us with having *emuna* until our *neshama* was coursing through us, bringing us to song. And only when our identity became permanently linked to our *neshama* did we achieve "permanent" *emuna*. But all this was not a substitute for the objective paths of Rambam and Ramban. These achievements of *emuna* at the sea and at Sinai were accompanied by miracles – there was an objective component. But this *neshama* awareness added a necessary inner grounding to these external experiences.

We instinctively discount subjective *emuna* because we associate its subjectivity with groundless fantasy, a fleeting feeling emerging from the stew of our thoughts, emotions, and wants. But because we have an inner connection that allows God's existence to well up to us from our *neshama*, subjective *emuna* has very real value. Because we cannot adequately distinguish grounded beliefs from the many fantasies that flood our minds, this subjective component cannot supplant the objective paths of Rambam and Ramban to become the sole basis of our *emuna*. But we have learned from our study that we do need it.

My early preference for a subjective rather than an objective basis for *emuna* was coming from an instinct for the value of this internal source of knowledge. The instinct is accurate, but as a *preference* over the objective approaches it is naïve. The inner path is a necessary component, but not a complete path.

But where did I, a college student who grew up in a non-religious household, get this instinct? The answer is at Sinai, which helps us answer an otherwise difficult question. The Torah teaches that at Sinai *emuna* was established in the Jews "forever." What does that mean? If we had really achieved *emuna* forever, there would be no need for this book!

"*Emuna* forever" means that *emuna* is integral to our essential self and our only possible identity. We can lose awareness of this level of self and the *emuna* that goes with it; but when that happens, our identity does not change. Rather, under such circumstances our true self is simply not actualized. But it is still there, as evidenced by its continuing influence on us.[65]

---

65. Song 5:2, Song of Songs Rabba 5:2.

When our *emuna* is not actual, it gets bottled up. We experience a certain inner disquiet and alienation, a sense that we are lost to ourselves.[66] Efforts to suppress it can lead to strange reactions such as the strident antisemitism we sometimes find in Jews, or extreme pleasure-seeking as an attempt to distract from its pull. Efforts to give it expression when Torah is not available in a satisfying form lead to the ubiquitous searches by so many Jews for alternate ideals and causes. And when Torah is available in an authentic form it can lead to Jews returning to their faith, as happened to me. The *emuna* is there, meaning the connection to a facet of self that gives a foundation to *emuna*. It just has to be tapped.[67]

Every human being has a place within himself where his individual self dissolves into the Creator. This is the locus of this "*emuna* confirmation." Conversion, joining the people of *emuna*, is possible for non-Jews because an individual can, with sufficient will, move the center of his personality to that point, in what we might call extreme *teshuva*. But because of what the Jews experienced at Mount Sinai, on a national level we are already defined by this point. Though we can fall away from actualizing this aspect of self, it remains the basis of our identity, so that we are inextricably bound to it. The Torah guides us to actualize it through developing our character. When we spoke at the beginning of the book about various approaches that can awaken subjective *emuna*, they were all either different ways of affecting character or inspirational adjuncts to the basic responsibility of personal development.

We can achieve *emuna*, certainly a level of *emuna*. It requires a combination of study of our historical experience of miracles along with working on our character so that we properly prioritize within ourselves our spiritual and physical dimensions and open ourselves to the influences arising from our core. The need for this internal component has never been greater than in our times, when the sanctity of humanity is under such vigorous attack. We need to experience that internal depth to know that we can be more than animals. In fact, we have reached the point where we need it to distinguish ourselves from inanimate matter!

---

66. Maharal, *Ḥiddushei Aggadot* IV, 41, and Rabbi Chaim Friedlander, *Sifsei Chaim, Moadim* 1, *mahadura murḥevet* (Bnei Brak, 1994), 4–5.
67. See Deut. 30:11–14 and the commentary of Ramban.

*Part 2: The Character of Faith*

Without connection to this deeper reality, *emuna* becomes impossible because it becomes inconceivable.

We are a direct emanation of the infinite and eternal, necessary Source of existence, Who is the basis, arbiter, and guardian of meaning and moral good. Without making this connection a living reality, we have no ground on which to stand as we battle the shallowness of materialism, fighting for our humanity and a basis for our *emuna*. Our *emuna* is in a Being that is real; our challenge is to make it real *to us*. That requires work, dedicated and difficult work. But there is no more valuable achievement, for our own value depends upon it.

*Appendix*

# The Passing of an Honest Man

On the 10th of Tevet, 5777 (January 7, 2017), the Jewish people lost Rav Moshe Shapiro. His funeral was attended by tens of thousands of mourners. In the Orthodox community such a number is not usually seen except for great legal authorities or the heads of prestigious academies. Rav Shapiro was neither. Rather, over the course of decades he gave classes in the philosophical aspects of Torah attended by hundreds of students each week. He showed generations of Orthodox Jewry what it means to think deeply about existence. Those who had heard him speak knew his death marked the passing of a unique source of insight and came to pay their respects.

Though Rav Moshe was focused completely in Torah and drew his inspiration from its deepest recesses, one did not need to be steeped in it to appreciate his public addresses. There were, of course, private classes that plumbed the subtleties of the Torah's most esoteric branches – they were reserved for advanced scholars. But the open lectures were directed at a broader audience. Soon after completing my degree in philosophy at Yale, though still very new to Torah study, I began attending them and was captivated. Many of the issues he grappled with echoed ones that had interested me in college and in ways that were as familiar as they were new. He would have been offended to have his thoughts

# Appendix

described as modern. But they certainly resonated with the most modern of thoughts.

This was because he was a genuinely honest person. The development of humanity, at least in the context of civilization, is universal; we are in it together. All who engage life honestly face a number of questions in common, and Rav Moshe was unfailingly honest. So many of the issues he worked on were ones with which any thinking person struggles, regardless of background. People flocked to hear him because he brought the weight of his genius and the guidance of thousands of years' worth of Torah tradition to his phrasing of the questions and the pursuit of their answers.

Though Torah is an ancient document, its guidance remains both profound and relevant because it conveys essential truths about humanity, which are unchanging. That said, deriving that guidance and presenting it in a way that speaks to us today is not a simple process. While the truths of Torah may not change, the ways we actualize them do. The unfolding of civilization forces us to experience ourselves from all the different vantages afforded by the halting evolution of human culture. Therefore the manner in which we face life's challenges is different in each generation. If we want relevant guidance from a timeless document like the Torah, we cannot merely mouth the understandings of it produced in the past. We must read the Torah in a way that is uniquely appropriate to our time in history.

That requires pressing the self that we genuinely are against the Torah, honestly asking the questions that bother us in the ways that they bother us. This takes a surprising level of integrity. Once one understands the millennia-old yet timeless standard to which the Torah holds us, there is a powerful temptation to be some fantasy of who we should be, want to be, or might have been in a different era as we engage it. Rav Moshe resisted that temptation – there was no shtick about him. He came to the Torah as himself, which gave his understanding a remarkable clarity and relevance that made him the broad and effective resource that he was for his generation.

## UNDERSTANDING MODERNITY IN ITS CONTEXT

When I arrived in Jerusalem to attend yeshiva and first encountered Rav Moshe, I was not a stranger to genius. In my time at Yale I had heard

Karsten Harries, a towering figure in the Graduate Department of Philosophy. From Professor Harries I learned that civilizations have certain underlying bases or insights upon which their outlooks are founded. The cultural history of each civilization is the process through which these underlying insights or premises work themselves out in an increasingly unadulterated form socially, intellectually, and artistically.

Building on the work of other modern philosophers, Professor Harries identified the defining characteristic of modernity as the awareness of perspective: that all outlooks, whether visual or intellectual, are determined by a point of view. This is an extraordinarily powerful and effective awareness. But, as Professor Harries pointed out, it undercuts our ability to see anything as sacred – a word that I was not comfortable with at the time but came to appreciate.

Once I began my studies in Jerusalem in earnest, it was Rav Shapiro's weekly classes that added the intellectual component I craved and made me feel most at home in Torah. I quickly picked up that the topic of cultural development I had studied under Professor Harries was a thread in Rav Shapiro's thinking also. From Rav Shapiro I learned that the Torah parallel to this concept of cultural evolution is that of the empires.[1] A number of nations conquered the centers of civilization and made civilization over in the image of their national cultures. These cultures were distinct from one another, each animated by a different primary character trait or inclination.

The Sages trace an organic development of civilization over historical time from its Near Eastern beginnings to the present. Four principal empires structure this process: Babylon and Persia, the culmination of Near Eastern civilization, were followed by Greece and Rome, the cultures of the West. The progression of traits characterizing these empires roughly parallels those dominating an individual as he matures from childhood through adulthood.[2]

The fact that the development of civilization is an organic process does not preclude abrupt transitions. After all, though a person is the same individual as he passes through his various stages of development,

---

1. See Dan. chapter 2, and Maharal, *Ner Mitzva*.
2. Maharal, *Ner Mitzva*, 10–11.

## Appendix

his parents may barely recognize him when he enters adolescence. When the Greeks took over the leadership of civilization, shifting its center from East to West, a significant break occurred. The Western vision of man and reality was very different from the one that characterized Near Eastern civilization. Whereas Aristotle defined man as the rational animal, the cultures that preceded Greece in the Near East understood man first and foremost as a worshipper and servant of the gods. The change from the Near Eastern vision of man as dependent upon a higher source and authority to the Greek emphasis on individual rationality actually parallels in important ways the transition to adolescence.

Academics identify the ascent of Greece with the advent of abstract thinking as the primary mode through which man interprets his surroundings.[3] In this they celebrate the change for what was gained, give the background story to Aristotle's identification of man with rationality, and reveal why we today, who process our world through reason, intuitively resonate with Aristotle's definition. The rabbis, however, describe this transition as an annulment of the inclination in man to worship idols.[4] Since this implied the passing of an intuitive sense of worship, the rabbis associate the transition with what was lost. In so doing they recognize an early root of the phenomenon Professor Harries associated with modernity – the loss of the sacred – and help us understand why the Near Eastern view of man is so foreign to us.

This rabbinic view highlights the yawning gap between today's spiritually barren experience of reality and the nature of man's experience in the past. As a consequence of this gap the entire direction and intent of the Torah, which emerged from the ancient Near East, is out of sync with present-day intuition. Torah is structured to develop us spiritually; it speaks to a side of our humanity which modern experience and culture ignore, demean, and anesthetize.

It is because of this that Rav Shapiro's existential honesty was so crucial. There is a distance that must be bridged between Torah's default assumptions about man and our actual starting point. To be genuinely

---

3. Frankfort, "The Emancipation of Thought from Myth," in Frankfort et al., *The Intellectual Adventure of Ancient Man*, 373.
4. Yoma 69b.

relevant we must relate to Torah from a stage prior to what was necessary in the past. Torah always gave direction to our spiritual cravings. Nowadays, however, it must also help us recognize and develop those cravings. Otherwise, our efforts at personal development are directed at a self that does not really exist; and our efforts to deepen our understanding of reality formulate a fantasy world rather than informing the reality that we actually occupy.

Rav Shapiro was acutely aware of this. He constantly reminded us of where we are at in relation to the teachings of Torah, translated concepts into a language that spoke to our reality, and guided us in how to get from where we actually are to where we need to go.

To fully appreciate Rav Shapiro's achievement and the challenge he faced, we need to understand more deeply our distance from the ancient civilizations of the East. What was this natural sense of worship that characterized them? Why did it pass and why did its passing coincide with the ascendance of abstract thought?

## WORSHIP AND ABSTRACT REASON IN CONFLICT

The specific location of self in the structure of personality is not fixed. We see, for example, that as individuals mature it moves. When our self first emerges in infancy it is integrated and identified with our physical needs and desires. When a child says, "I want a piece of chocolate," he is totally present in the desire. But as we develop, the focus of our self slowly shifts to higher aspects of personality. In adolescence, for example, we identify primarily with our sense of autonomous selfhood, and our need to assert individuality becomes paramount.

This shifting of self is also evident in humanity as a whole over historical time in the context of civilization. We already mentioned that the cultures of the different empires that dominated civilization were anchored in different character traits. This is equivalent to saying that self in each of these societies was located in a different aspect of personality. This affected both the conscious interests of the societies, the nature of their experience of selfhood, and the form of their understanding.

At the dawn of civilization our consciousness was enmeshed with our physical being and dominated by its influences. This firmly grounded our awareness in our material environment and blocked pure abstraction. Ideas were conceived in images – that is, together with their actual physical expression in specific form.[5] For example, though we could be aware of seven bushels of wheat being seven bushels, the abstract idea of the pure number seven would have been challenging to grasp. We processed our world through *dimyon* (imagination) rather than through *sekhel* (intellect).

Paradoxically, this physicality made us more "spiritual." Our physically based consciousness with its particular mode of comprehension was limited in its ability to understand, leaving the world on some level unknowable and awesome. And that consciousness also could not identify with something as ethereal as the self in a way that was fully defined. We therefore remained open to and integrated with deeper levels of consciousness that extended beyond our individuality and were rightly perceived as the root of self. Because of our need to remain connected to our source and its awesome and unknowable character, this fostered worship. That worship had a decidedly idolatrous slant because our inability to separate concepts from their concrete expressions meant that any forces we worshipped were perceived as existing through their physical actualization.

But with time, the role of abstraction grew in our conscious process. This increased the acuity of our understanding, making our perception of the world and awareness of self increasingly defined and demarcated. The world lost its sense of mystery and we came to experience ourselves as isolated, autonomous individuals and lost sight of the roots of personality that extend beyond individual awareness. Together, these eliminated the intuitive sense of man as an extension of something higher, undermining our instinct for worship; thus, as mentioned earlier, the inclination to worship idols disintegrated. This transition away from the worshipful self stretched roughly from the destruction of the First Temple to the rise of the Greek Empire.

The profound loss of the transcendent dimension from experience was partially masked by the Greek identification of existence with ideas. Plato, for example, ascribed true reality to ideas alone. Since abstract

---

5. Frankfort, "Myth and Reality," in *The Intellectual Adventure of Ancient Man*; Jacobsen, *The Treasures of Darkness*, chapter 1.

concepts are intangible and universal, under Greece we still perceived ourselves as part of something larger than ourselves and our immediate environment. But concepts are intelligible – at least potentially. So despite their elevation above material reality, they are still part of our comprehensible universe. Relative to Near Eastern engagement with the unknowable, Greek idealism presented a critically shrunken reality.

But even the consolation of Greek idealism was short-lived. Rome's ascent to power and to the role of arbiter of civilization marked a further shift of our center, this time beyond our thoughts to full identification with our awareness of our individuality. Under Rome, ideas ceased to be considered true existence and instead became tools for control; science and metaphysics gave way to engineering and ethics. Since isolation within our experience of individual self is rooted in our distinct physical bodies, matter came to be perceived as the basis of reality. In such a context concepts of values and morality slowly lose their compelling force, as any sense of reality for things that are not tangible ebbs away. The Sages view Rome as the cultural progenitor of our Western society. These changes established the foundations for the perspectival awareness that defines our modern experience with its loss of the sacred.

**THE AGE OF REASON**

The cultural conquest of the Jews by the Greeks, the point when the Jews were swallowed up by this man-centered reality, is identified with the writing of the Septuagint when Ptolemy II forced the Sages to translate the Torah into Greek. The rabbis considered this a disaster.[6] The Greek language was a honed instrument for describing a man-centered reality. Greek words, with their nuances of meaning, could not contain the Torah on its most essential level, which relates to reality as existing in God.

The rabbis compare this translation to the worship of the Golden Calf;[7] the Calf was a rerun of Adam's original sin, which resulted in man's ejection from the Garden of Eden. So this is rabbinic code for something that so profoundly alters our experience of reality that it is comparable to changing worlds. The translation of the Torah marked our entry into

---

6. *Massekhet Soferim* (within Avoda Zara), 1:7.
7. Ibid.

## Appendix

a much more barren spiritual landscape. Appropriately, Rav Shapiro's *levaya* was on the 10th of Tevet, the day identified with this translation.

Rav Shapiro explained this transition with the observation that the same rabbis who recognized the tragic inadequacy of the translation declared this translated version of the Torah a legitimate Torah scroll – it could be used to fulfill obligations to read Torah![8] The only way to understand this paradox is to realize that we were no longer able to read the Torah in genuine Hebrew even when we read it in the original. We had come to understand reality in a Greek way, so that even if we would read the Torah in Hebrew, our Hebrew would be a translation of Greek; all the nuances of meaning that were part of a God-centered world had been lost. Our problem was not that we were stuck in a Greek world; rather, we were stuck in a Greek worldview. We, as well as the Torah, were translated.

Rav Moshe's genius was evident in the example he returned to frequently to illustrate this point, as simple as it was compelling. The word "*davar*" is today translated as "thing." "Thing" is a completely neutral designation leaving the understanding of the object completely open. But the Hebrew term "*davar*" is related to the word "*dibur*" which means "speech." The implication is that what *we* relate to as a world composed of arbitrary "things" which are empty of intrinsic meaning and which may be defined according to our perspective and appropriated as we see fit, is actually a world of words – elements in a conversation with the Creator spoken with intention. We do have to interpret the meaning of the words, but they must be understood in the context of the divine conversation. Imagine how profoundly altered our view of reality would be if we experienced it in this way! But today, when we think "*davar*" we think "thing," regardless of what language we speak.

This conveys something of the radical nature of the shift that occurred in the time of Greece when civilization moved from East to West. It also speaks to the complications introduced to the project of achieving genuine religious conviction: a relationship with God was no longer integrated into the structure of our perception of reality.

---

8. Megilla 9b.

With the passing of this intuitive connection, a much more conscious approach to spirituality was required. At this time the Jews developed the Oral Torah, which dissects our relationship with God down to its minutest detail, understands the function of each part, and then consciously reconstructs it.

This, however, leaves us like a musician with great technique and no passion. The body of the relationship can be recovered in this way, but its soul is shockingly diminished.[9] Rav Moshe was acutely aware of how profoundly compromised our religious experience has become. On more than one occasion he voiced his embarrassment at being fated to live out his life in a time when human experience is so shallow. It was precisely this clarity and honesty about our situation together with his ability to communicate it to us with such lucidity that made his Torah fresh, powerful, and unique.

**CHOOSING DEPTH**

These changed circumstances are not all darkness. With faith no longer intuitive, with its fit so unnatural to our form of awareness, any genuine belief achieved is an accomplishment rather than a gift. The scope of meaningful choice has expanded dramatically.

But if it is so unnatural and counterintuitive, how can we be true to ourselves and yet choose faith? To clarify the question: we instinctively consider real that which echoes our experience of self. This instinct is well grounded, because self offers the only possibility of experiencing being as opposed to appearance. It is who we are. For this reason, Rav Moshe taught us, the word *ani* ("I") is a name of God.[10] In the ineffable experience of self, as we shift our awareness from observation of structured reality to purely private and personal awareness, we taste being and existence, becoming transparent to our Source. In other words – and this shows how broken our language is for this discussion – subjective experience is our only access to objective reality.

Whether or not we are fully cognizant of what constitutes our self in any given age, its nature colors our assumptions about reality.

---

9. See the Vilna Gaon's commentary on Song of Songs 1:5.
10. Mishna Sukka 4:5 with Rashi; Sukka 45a, 53a.

## Appendix

Today we accept perspectival awareness with its rejection of any objective truth or legitimate faith – any sacred ground – because it reflects the hollowness of our inner world. But if this is so, what are we to make of this emptiness?

Even though self can be our window on existence, the emptiness we experience today does not penetrate to the full depths of reality because it does not penetrate to the full depths of self. Our rabbinic tradition, stretching beyond Greece to the earlier civilizations of the Near East, makes us aware of the dramatic changes over time in our subjective experience. Subjectivity cannot reflect objective reality *in any simple manner,* for it is historically and culturally determined. In other words, our subjectivity is not "objective subjectivity."

There are many facets to human personality. Some are linked to our true self and some are based in more superficial aspects of or foreign attachments to our personality. In this generation the default center of consciousness is so distant from true self that we even have difficulty engaging subjectivity – we are lost to ourselves and must exert effort to escape relating to ourselves as objects, which is the underlying origin of perspectival awareness.

We need not, however, remain so shallow. We can grow, integrating and identifying with increasingly essential aspects of self. But if not every form of subjective experience reaches the authentic and essential self, what is our basis for identifying which aspects of self are true? We must return to that difficult word with which we began this piece: honesty. Someone who is honest with himself can discern when he is becoming more himself and when he is losing himself, or when he is becoming more integrated as opposed to being co-opted by selfish inclinations.

Genuine honesty in this regard is extremely challenging. This leads us back to Rav Moshe, who was painstakingly honest. He also had a powerful resource to assist him: Torah, that three and a half thousand year old document that has been guiding us to uncover our humanity from the earliest stages of civilization.

Rav Moshe was a master of this document – a guide to the guide. For him every event, experience, joy, and tragedy – and there was no shortage of these in his life – was a springboard for honest growth, an opportunity to explore under the direction of Torah ever deeper aspects of the self. After decades of this dedicated focus, he achieved a different kind of humanity. Though remarkably normal and possessing a very sharp sense of humor, he projected the solidity and strength of a person drawing from the wellsprings of being. When he spoke, his words rang with an unseen depth and seemed to bear the momentum of history. He embodied the greatness that a human being can attain and was a living rebuttal to the shallowness of our age.

Rav Moshe carried the pain of seeing that shallowness, yet this did not stop him from appreciating the profound depths that a human being is capable of reaching. He struck a delicate balance between accepting the reality of our present and expecting meaningful personal achievement from himself and his students. His mission was to share wisdom, but he was careful to ensure that his Torah deepened our reality rather than leading us into what was for us fantasy. His success is measured in the extraordinary number of his students who are now prominent and influential educators.

People of this caliber are very rare. And if their example is important for our age, the present generation is absolutely desperate for them as we watch what little humanity we have left leak away through the holes created by our many devices. We can all appreciate that with Rav Moshe Shapiro's passing something remarkable and precious has been lost – one of the rarest of individuals, a man who was honest. His passing is an occasion for us all to reflect upon where we stand in relation to true existential honesty.

*The fonts used in this book are from the Arno family*